Run for the Wall

RUN FOR THE WALL

Remembering Vietnam on a Motorcycle Pilgrimage

RAYMOND
MICHALOWSKI   &   JILL
DUBISCH

RUTGERS UNIVERSITY PRESS
New Brunswick, New Jersey, and London

Library of Congress Cataloging-in-Publication Data

Michalowski, Raymond, 1946–
    Run for the Wall : remembering Vietnam on a motorcycle pilgrimage /
Raymond Michalowski, Jill Dubisch.
        p. cm
    Includes bibliographical references and index.
    ISBN 0–8135–2927-1 (cloth : alk. paper) — ISBN 0–8135–2928-X
(pbk. : alk. paper)
    1. Run for the Wall (Organization) 2. Vietnam Veterans Memorial
(Washington, D.C.) 3. Motorcycling—United States. 4. Social interaction—
United States.
    I. Dubisch, Jill, 1943– II. Title.

DS559.83.W18 M53 2001
303.6'6—dc21
                                                        00–046871

British Cataloging-in-Publication data for this book is available from the British
Library

Manufactured in the United States of America

*To those everywhere who bear witness to the effects
of the Vietnam conflict in the hope that future
generations will be spared the sufferings of war*

Contents

Preface and Acknowledgments

This is not a book about the Vietnam War. Nor is it a book about veterans or bikers. Rather, it is a book about the ways in which the war, veterans, and motorcycles combine with key elements of American culture—particularly cherished beliefs about freedom, individuality, and community—to produce a remarkable ritual, the healing pilgrimage called the Run for the Wall. It is also a book about our own participation in this pilgrimage, as a sociologist and an anthropologist, and as two individuals, male and female, who came of age in a time when the Vietnam War and the events surrounding it were tearing apart the society in which we were trying to make our way toward adulthood. It is about other individuals as well, particularly the veterans and those who love them who continue to struggle with the memory of the combat years, those who still wait to know the fate of their loved ones, and all those Americans who did not fight in the war but still search for some meaning in all the loss it caused, both at home and in Vietnam. And finally, it is about a journey that is both a physical passage through the nation and a spiritual and emotional journey toward healing and understanding.

Our motivation to tell the Run for the Wall story has two sources, one professional and intellectual, the other personal and emotional. As social analysts we hope to contribute to the understanding of how narrative and ritual interact with political controversy and culture to produce memory—in this case memories about the Vietnam War and those who fought it. As Vietnam-era Americans in midlife, we hope to contribute in some small way to the healing we know has yet to happen before the many Americans whose lives were touched by the war, either as soldiers or civilians (ourselves included), will be able to lay to rest their troubled memories of a war whose meaning still remains in doubt. By telling the story of how some people search for peace, understanding, and personal healing through a motorcycle pilgrimage dedicated to the POW/MIA cause, we hope to make it clearer, particularly to those who are not part of the Vietnam generation, why so many Americans are still searching for a way to understand the Vietnam War and their roles in it.

An undertaking such as this book is always a risky one. We have not written about research subjects, about people we have observed from a distance. This book is about friends with whom we have shared camaraderie, risk, and most importantly, powerful emotional experiences. Yet, it is not written as a straightforward story about a motorcycle journey we shared with our friends. It is written as a social analysis of the Run for the Wall and those who participate in it. Writing social analysis involves giving meaning to and interpreting events and actions in ways that are often different from the way those being written about would describe them. The greatest value and the greatest curse of social analysis is that it relocates the story being told to a place that is always somewhat distant from the immediacy of personal experiences. The advantage of an analytic approach is, we hope, that it can allow us to see the larger patterns and meanings involved in the Run for the Wall, patterns and meanings that are not always immediately evident when one is in the midst of the experience.

The difficulty posed by taking an analytic approach is that talking about general patterns and broader meanings can seem to dissolve the highly personal experiences of our friends (and ourselves) into impersonal generalities. As analysis searches for patterns and meanings, it mutes the poignancy and power of the individual human experiences involved. Herein lies the personal risk in writing such a book. Our friends appear in this book, but not necessarily as they would present themselves. Their stories are told in our writing, but not always as they would tell them. We can only hope that what we have seen by looking at the Run for the Wall with analytic eyes, as well as by listening to it with open hearts, is informative, not just for the public who may read this book, but also for the people whose stories we have told.

No book is ever written by its authors alone, and this is particularly true for ethnographies. Ethnographies are stories about how people live their lives, and ethnographers owe their first and greatest debt to those they have written about. For this reason we want to acknowledge all the Run for the Wall riders who have created the pilgrimage about which we have written. Beyond that, however, we want to specifically thank those who in big and small ways have shared themselves with us as we rode together to the Wall. First of all, we thank the 1996 national coordinators, John and Linda, who made us feel so welcome on our first Run, as well as Deekin, Skipper and Redlite, and Iron Mike for getting us safely down the road in the years that followed. For their candor, friendship, and the particularly important roles they have come to play in our lives we owe a special thanks to Deekin, Dave, Fyreckr, Linda, Mountain Man, Phil, Puma, Som'r, R.C., and Tigger. For sharing the road and their stories we also want to specifically acknowledge the contributions that Barbara, Big Dave, Cap, Centerpunch, Christina, Cookie Monster, Crumbs, Cufs, Doc, Dick Darnell and all the kitchen crew, Dragon and Miok, Fireman George, Fishman, Gunny, Hal and Maddy, Iron Mike, Kay and Fidel and the kids, Linda and George P., Lonewolf, Mudflap, Rich, Two Lane, Pup, Redlite, Rock, Sarge, Skipper, Slick, Smoke, Strangelove, Suzanne, Tammy, Wiley, and Woody have made to our ability to tell the Run for the Wall story. Finally, we want to thank all the other Run for the Wall riders and supporters we talked with at gas stops and lunch breaks, in bathroom lines and motel parking lots, during community-sponsored breakfasts and dinners—people whose names we never learned, but whose stories have made both our lives and this book richer.

There is another group of Vietnam veterans who, though not associated with the Run for the Wall, have been critical to our understanding. By sharing their stories and their lives with us before we ever rode the Run, they set us on the path that eventually led to this book. Our thanks go out: to Fracture, Bones, and Tailpipe, wherever you may be—though you were the patients, you spoke with more clarity and understanding than most of the staff; to Dennis, for long hours of Vietnam talk in a small boat on a wide river; to Terry, who bore witness to the damage that war can do but continued to face life with courage and determination; to John, for talking about his jungle nightmares; to Larry, who, by sharing his past and his present, added to our appreciation of what it means to claim the identity of Vietnam veteran in a world that doesn't want to know; to Doug, the cousin that Jill never knew; and to Pete—may he always ride in freedom.

We also owe a debt of gratitude to our university colleagues whose insights helped us in writing this story. In particular we would like to thank Alex Alvarez, Larry Gould, Ron Kramer, James Livingston, Fred Solop, Jim Wilce, and Nancy Wonders for sharing ideas and perspectives that found their way into these pages. We also want to thank Bill and Pernila Chambliss for giving us shelter and support at a critical moment in this project. There is nothing that moves a book project forward like reviewers who are simultaneously supportive and insightful. We were fortunate to have two such reviewers, Joel Best and Andrew Maxwell, and we thank them for making this a better book. We also want to thank our editor, David Myers, who had more faith in this project than we did at the outset. Finally, our thanks go to Sylvia Brealy for her attention to bibliographic details, Christina Getrich for searching the library, and Ingrid Davis and Kathy Spitzer for helping manage all the paper we produced along the way, and for making it possible to be both a writer and a department chair at the same time.

Run for the Wall

1

"I THOUGHT I WAS JUST GOING FOR A RIDE"
Introduction

> When heroes die, when their relics heal, that is when you find pilgrimage.
>> Tony Walter, "War Grave Pilgrimage"

> Welcome home brother,
> And let the wind dry your tears,
> For the healing begins at the Wall,
> your pain of all the years
>> Posted on the Run for the Wall message board

They began assembling at the Queen Mary, the luxury-liner-turned-hotel, in Long Beach, California, shortly after dawn on the morning of May 13, 1998. Under scudding gray clouds that enveloped the scene in a thin watery light, groups of denim- and leather-clad bikers drifted out to the hotel parking lot. Grabbing coffee and doughnuts from a table set up by the hotel entrance, they greeted one another and then moved off to their motorcycles to stow their gear in preparation for the long trip ahead. Soon the morning air was filled with the rumble of motorcycle engines and the acrid smell of exhaust as riders began maneuvering their bikes into a double column that stretched along the curb in front of the hotel. Leaving the bikes in formation, the riders assembled in front of the platform where Skipper, the national coordinator for the 1998 Run for the Wall, waited to greet the group. As a news helicopter circled overhead, Skipper outlined the rules of the road for the upcoming journey and spoke to the assembled bikers about the purposes of the Run: to ride in memory of Americans killed in Vietnam and America's other foreign wars, to increase public awareness about those who remain either prisoners of war or missing in action (POWs/MIAs) in Southeast Asia, and to seek personal healing for the psychic wounds left by the Vietnam War. Phil Wright, one of the group's several chaplains, then offered up a prayer for "traveling mercies" on the long road ahead. When he was done, Skipper announced, "Ten minutes," and the riders hurried back to their bikes. Precisely at 8:00 A.M., the Queen Mary sounded her horn, and the riders responded with a thunderous roar from their machines. Led by a vanguard of police cars and fire engines, and accompanied by a salute from the water cannons of a fireboat in the harbor and the thumping of the news helicopter, the long line of bikes and chase vehicles surged forward. As the 140–bike caravan rolled out of the parking lot, the riders—many of them Vietnam veterans—were touched by the excitement of the moment, the gravity of their mission, and the challenge of the three-thousand-mile journey that lay ahead. Their pilgrimage toward the Wall and the 58,183 names memorialized there had begun.

We were riding together on one of those motorcycles that left Long Beach that day on the Run for the Wall, often simply called "the Run" by its participants. This book is the story of that journey, an annual pilgrimage through a land where many people have not yet healed the wounds or resolved the problems left by the war in Vietnam. It is a story of how people still struggle over the personal and collective meaning of America's longest and most divisive war, even though more than a quarter of a century has passed since U.S. troops were withdrawn from Vietnam. Most importantly, it is a story about how these Americans use the tools of their culture, particularly ritual, pilgrimage, and the social construction of memory, to make meaning, find healing, and communicate political messages on a cross-country motorcycle journey.

As the 1998 Run for the Wall participants assembled that day in May, contradictions seemed to abound. It was raining in Southern California, the land of sunshine. Many of the veterans wore beards, long hair, denim clothing, bracelets, and necklaces more reminiscent of 1960s antiwar protesters than of the clean-cut looks of their own military past. A number of these former warriors had beaten swords into plowshares by embracing the role of minister or preacher. The entire endeavor, planned and led largely by Vietnam veterans, was organized more along the lines of consensus-building, do-it-yourself anarchy than on the hierarchical command structure of the military. And men with all the appearance of super-male warriors publicly cried together and embraced one another without shame.

Much of this is contradictory only at the level of surface appearances, however. Beneath that surface is a cultural framework that ren-

FIGURE 1. A typical Run for the Wall vest with the Run's insignia and memorial patches.

ders these seeming contradictions meaningful—and even compelling. At the heart of the story we have to tell are the ways that people on the Run for the Wall, including ourselves, use this cultural framework to construct meanings around broad themes—war and peace, suffering and healing, honor and dishonor, and manhood and womanhood—as well as to address less abstract matters such as the practicalities of bringing a motorcycle caravan safely across the country

Our own story began in 1996 when we were given a flyer for the Run for the Wall by a close friend and Vietnam veteran who knew of our tentative plans for riding to Rolling Thunder, an annual

Memorial Day motorcycle parade and rally in Washington, D.C. When we read that the route for the Run for the Wall would pass through our hometown of Flagstaff, Arizona, we each felt an inexplicable yet immediate and strong desire to join the Run. It was not the simple romance of a transcontinental motorcycle trip that drew us. We had been a motorcycling couple for a number of years and had made other long trips, including a cross-country journey. The pull was deeper, something to do with the Vietnam War, perhaps. Yet our biographies seemed to make us unlikely prospects for joining the Run for the Wall. We were not Vietnam veterans. We were not veterans at all. Nor had we been supporters of U.S. military involvement in Vietnam. In addition, we were not properly mounted. We knew that for many bikers, particularly Vietnam veterans, the only *real* motorcycle is a made-in-America Harley Davidson, a machine whose link to memories of America's glory years rendered it a cultural icon in the post-Vietnam era. By contrast, we knew that many hard-core bikers considered our Honda Gold Wing to be "Jap-crap," even though it was manufactured in the United States.[1] Thus, as nonveterans riding a "non-American" motorcycle, we felt some apprehension about whether we would be welcomed on the Run.

Yet we knew that joining the Run for the Wall was something we felt compelled to do. Our own lives had been touched by the war in many ways. Ray had lost high school and college friends on the battlefields of Vietnam. His Catholic-school-bred belief in the inherent morality of U.S. foreign policy was forever altered by Vietnam veterans who returned from Southeast Asia opposed to the war, and he himself eventually became a target of hostility at the religious college he attended for endorsing early U.S. withdrawal from Vietnam. In the late 1960s, while working as a psychiatric social worker at a mental hospital near New York City, Ray learned firsthand about the psychic wounds left behind by the Vietnam War from the hospitalized veterans he met there. Jill had been abroad at the height of the war and had experienced the anguish of having to watch from a distance while her country was torn apart by internal dissension. At the same time, she had feared for her then fiancé, her brothers, and other male friends and relatives who might be called to fight. She lost one cousin she never knew in Vietnam and has another cousin whose life was forever changed by his experiences there. Over the years we have also had a number of close friends and acquaintances who are Vietnam veterans, many of whom remained troubled by their wartime experiences. With these as our personal legacies of the Vietnam War, we decided to join the Run. When Ray called John Anderson, the national coordinator for the 1996 Run for the Wall, John assured us that everyone was welcome on the Run as long as they supported the other participants and came with "no attitudes."

Despite these assurances, however, it was not without considerable anxiety that we waited outside Flagstaff on the morning of May 12, 1996, to meet the riders as they prepared to enter town. As they roared off the I-40 exit, a motley crew of leather-clad, long-haired bikers, most of them mounted on Harleys, we scrambled to pull our bike in behind them, tailing at the rear of the parade with its police escort as it headed down Route 66 to the American Legion Hall in Flagstaff. We drew our Gold Wing behind the other bikes in the Legion parking lot, and while the riders took a break to refresh themselves with coffee, orange juice, and doughnuts, we introduced ourselves to John Anderson and signed in. There was a small ceremony at the Vietnam memorial in the town park across the street from the Legion hall, where the mayor of Flagstaff addressed the group. When the ceremony was over, we fell into line behind the other riders as they followed a police escort out of Flagstaff onto Interstate 40 toward Gallup, New Mexico, still unsure of what we were doing.

In Gallup, the Run for the Wall contingent was treated to lunch in the downtown community center. While we were waiting for the group to get on the road again, we hung around the parking lot, taking pictures of the bikes and the riders, still feeling out of place. We didn't know anyone in a group in which it seemed that everyone else was well acquainted. It was not until later that we learned that many of those we observed were making the journey for the first time themselves, and the closeness we saw was the camaraderie of the road forged after only a day or two of traveling together.

Just before the group left Gallup, we were approached by an attractive older woman who asked us if we were going all the way to the Wall. When we said yes, she handed us a small bouquet of dried yellow flowers and a twenty-dollar bill. She asked if we would please place the flowers at the Wall beneath the name of a man who had been her student when he was in junior high school in Gallup, and who later became the first New Mexican to die in Vietnam. She had been exceptionally fond of him, she said, even though he "wasn't the best of students," and she had been greatly saddened by his death. Knowing that it was unlikely that she herself would ever make it to D.C., she had come to find someone on the Run to take her remembrance to the Wall. We tried to return her twenty dollars, saying she did not have to pay us to fulfill her request, but she insisted. We talked for a while about her own cross-country motorcycle trip with her husband just after World War II, and then she departed. We never learned her name, and yet once she had left, we knew that any doubts we had about whether or not we would go all the way to D.C. had been replaced by our obligation to this woman. We had accepted—from a total stranger—the responsibility of memorializing her student, and in doing so we had the first of many experiences of the power of a memorial pilgrimage. We secured the flowers on the bike, and the following day we donated her twenty-dollar bill to the Vietnam Veterans Memorial at Angel Fire, New Mexico. Eight days later, at the Wall, we would place the flowers under her student's name.

Our journey was an unforgettable, and ultimately life-altering, experience. We shared the physical and emotional highs and lows that are an intrinsic part of this cross-country motorcycle pilgrimage. We repeatedly heard Vietnam veterans speak about the pain of returning to a country that they felt never really welcomed them home from the battlefield. We heard about struggles with addictions, unsupportive parents, failed marriages, difficult work lives, physical and emotional ailments, and fear of seeing the Wall for the first time. We also heard tales of how the war, even though it was the worst of times in the lives of many of these veterans, was simultaneously the best of times when it came to camaraderie, friendship, and a sense of mission. We rode in memory of a man we never knew—Vincent Trujillo, who had died of AIDS from a blood transfusion during treatment for Agent Orange–induced cancer—to whom that year's Run had been dedicated. For us he came to stand for all the others we never knew who had died in Vietnam. Rather than mass-media stereotypes of maladjusted Vietnam combat veterans, we met many strong caring people who shouldered their burdens, got on with their lives, and reached out with supportive hands to those who needed them. We saw towns turn out to welcome Vietnam veterans in ways they had not in the 1960s and 1970s. We shared tears and embraces, observed ceremonies that both moved and disturbed us. We rode, we ate, we laughed, we hugged, we sweltered, we froze. And all the time we kept moving, moving toward the Wall as the goal and reason for our journey.

By the time we reached Washington on that 1996 trip, we knew we had been touched by the Run, and that we would go again. And we did. In 1997 we rode from the Run's starting point in Ontario, California, to its annual visit at the Vietnam Veterans Memorial in Angel Fire, New Mexico. In 1998, the tenth anniversary of the Run, we rode "all the way"—from Long Beach, California, to Washington, D.C. In 1999 we again went all the way to D.C., and in 2000 we rode once more with the Run as far as Angel Fire.

No two Runs are exactly alike, yet they all share common themes. As an anthropologist (Jill) and a sociologist (Ray), we could not avoid seeing the Run, not just as a personal experience, but also as a distinctive social phenomenon. The more we talked about what we were experiencing, the more we began to appreciate the Run as a collective endeavor that combines the political history of the Vietnam War, the emotional power of the Wall, and homemade rituals and secular pilgrimage into a strategy for constructing new meanings about the Vietnam War and its aftermath, for healing the troubled, and for creating new identities as veterans.

Social analysts, particularly sociologists, often ignore the routine activities of daily life that occur outside the large-scale structures of economy, education, religion, and politics. Yet as anthropologists point out, it is often through these smaller, less institutionalized activities that people create central meanings for their lives and construct their understanding of both the present and the past. The Run for the Wall provides a compelling story of how politics, ritual, personal biography, and history intersect to create a powerful public performance—in this case a cross-country motorcycle pilgrimage to memorialize the dead and heal the living. Because our participation in the Run was personal as well as intellectual, our goal is to write about the Run with deep respect for those who have ridden across the country in one another's company with the purpose of remembering—in many different ways—what the Vietnam War did to us and for us, as individuals and as a nation. This is the story we have to tell.

REMEMBERING VIETNAM

U.S. involvement in the Vietnam War was, and remains, a contested part of America's past. This has left many Americans still struggling to transform their uneasy memories of the Vietnam War into new narratives that can provide some degree of closure or peace with the pain caused by that war. Our national memory of the Vietnam War remains shadowed by its failure to achieve political or military goals that would seem to justify the destruction, suffering, and loss it entailed, for both the United States and Vietnam. Unlike America's other foreign wars, the war in Vietnam did not end with a satisfying victory that healed internal conflict and reaffirmed our national purpose. Instead, the war's unsatisfactory end left a deep political divide that is, perhaps, its most significant legacy.

The conflicts that emerged over the Vietnam War were about much more than the war itself. The war became the political and ideological terrain on which a battle between Cold War anti-communism and liberal anti-imperialism was fought. In the United States this ideological conflict shaped the lives of those who fought, either willingly or reluctantly, in Vietnam; those who never fought but were part of the Vietnam-era military; civilians who sought to support the troops with increased military build-ups in Vietnam as well as those who sought to support the troops through movements to "bring 'em home"; and finally, all those, regardless of their political standpoint, whose lives were somehow disrupted by the war—in other words, the majority of Americans. As one woman who had spent eight years as a volunteer at the Vietnam Veterans Memorial in Washington, D.C., and who was with us on our first Run, put it, "Sometimes I see people [at the Wall] who look a little lost. When I ask them if they need any help finding a name, they tell me, 'Oh, I'm all right. I didn't lose anyone in the war.' Sometimes I want to tell them, 'If you think you didn't lose anyone, you haven't been paying attention.'"

From the perspective of the Run for the Wall, one of the most significant consequences of the conflict over the Vietnam War was the lack of domestic support many Vietnam veterans feel they experienced after returning home from Southeast Asia. The lack of a warm and *public* "welcome home" is one of the most enduring themes within the culture of today's Vietnam veterans.[2] It is an ongoing source of sadness for many veterans, and a common element in literature written by them. One of the poems left at the Wall captures this sense of confusion and anger we heard from many veterans on the Run for the Wall.

> I returned to the world I left, but things were out of place.
> People treated me like scum and spit insults in my face.
> All their ignorant abuse confused me and my mind became quite hazy
> Soon the protected and ungrateful people convinced me I was crazy.[3]

In contrast to this image of a uniformly hostile society, others contend that there is little evidence that returning Vietnam veterans were publicly abused. For instance, Jerry Lembke, author of *The Spitting Image*, argues that the absence of any news stories about Vietnam veterans being spit upon suggests that these events are part of post-Vietnam mythology rather than descriptions of real events. Lembke dismisses the stories of veterans themselves as anecdotal, and therefore unreliable, evidence.[4] On the other hand, Lawrence Tritle, author of *From Melos to My Lai,* argues that Lembke's dismissal of soldiers' stories is "a convenient way around an inconvenient piece of evidence," and that we need to see these stories as evidence of real hostility directed toward Vietnam veterans.[5] The current debate over whether or not Vietnam veterans were spit upon or otherwise publicly abused is just one example of the continuing struggle over the nation's memory of the Vietnam War and its aftermath. From our perspective, however, what matters is that nearly all the Vietnam veterans we have encountered carry in their hearts a deep conviction that they were rejected by their country for having done what they saw as their duty to that country. Arguing the specifics of how they came to feel that way is far less important in understanding the Run for the Wall than recognizing that they *do* feel that way, and that this feeling has had very real consequences for their lives, for the lives of those around them, and for the country as a whole.

Another common theme of homecoming accounts is that of a country that is not hostile, but simply indifferent, of friends who do not reject, but who also have no interest in hearing about the war. Among the many letters sent to *Chicago Tribune* columnist Bob Greene in response to his request for stories about homecoming experiences was one that read: "I can remember several times either at work or social occasions when people would ask where I had been, and when I would tell them they would immediately want to talk about something else. Before I went in the service, it seemed as though everyone was going; when I returned it seemed that no one had gone. The people who had not gone didn't want to hear what was happening or even talk about the war."[6]

Similar stories of civilian disinterest are common among Vietnam veterans on the Run. They typically involve not so much the disinterest of parents, teachers, or adult relatives, but the disinterest of eighteen- and twenty-year-old peers. As one person said, "I went to a party the day after I got back. A friend of mine asked, 'Where have you been?' When I said, 'Vietnam,' he just said, 'Oh,' and passed me a joint. He never mentioned it again." This sense of disinterest—especially from the returning veteran's peers—is an important contributor to the alienation that many of those on the Run report experiencing after returning to "the world."

The conflict over the Vietnam War also claimed a cultural casualty as well: the national memory of the war. Vietnam was America's first foreign war to end badly. The United States devoted fifteen years to the war, sent more than three million military personnel to serve in Vietnam, suffered 58,183 combat deaths and 303,713 wounded, dropped three times the total bomb tonnage that was dropped in all of World War II, and drove the U.S. economy into hyperinflation.[7] Despite all of this sacrifice, the United States failed to achieve its expressed goal: "to maintain a friendly, non-Communist South Vietnam."[8]

After other foreign wars, the United States was able to forge a broadly shared memory about their meaning, purpose, and ultimate national benefits, despite the internal conflicts each of them generated in their time. The loss in Vietnam allowed no such ready construction of a unifying national history. Instead we are left with uneasy memories in search of meanings that can help explain, or at least help ease the pain, of the sufferings and losses caused by that war. The Run for the Wall is one example of how, long after the withdrawal of U.S. troops from Vietnam, Americans continue their struggle to construct an acceptable national memory out of the Vietnam War, and to reconstitute a national self-image in which they can take patriotic pride.

THE RUN FOR THE WALL

The first Run for the Wall took place in 1989. It was conceived as a one-time event, a memorial ride to the place where the names of dead

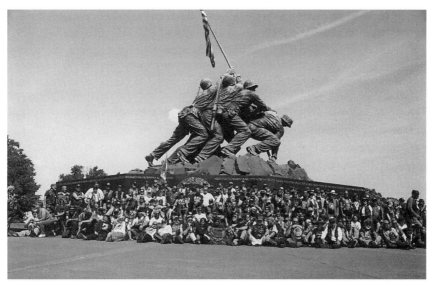

FIGURE 2. All-the-way riders gather in front of the Marine Corps Memorial for a photo op before heading to the Wall.

comrades were inscribed. As one of the original organizers put it, "We were just going to say goodbye." The route had been scouted in advance, and various communities along the way knew the bikers would be stopping there. What the riders had not anticipated, however, was the welcome they would receive in these communities and the rituals that would be performed on their behalf along the route. "About halfway through the ride," this same person said, "we realized that we would have to do it again." And so every year since 1989 a group of riders has departed from Southern California in mid-May on a schedule that will bring them to Washington, D.C., on the Friday of Memorial Day weekend.

Although some riders traverse the entire country, earning the All the Way patches that signify they completed the transcontinental journey, the Run includes many more participants during its ten-day course. All along the route, at gas stops, lunch breaks, and overnight stays, riders join the Run to travel some or all of the remaining distance to the Wall. In 1998, for instance, while about one hundred people went all the way, the total number of people who traveled some distance as part of the Run was closer to one thousand.[9]

As a public event the Run encompasses more than just the riders, drivers, and passengers who make all or part of the journey. In cities and towns along the route, individuals and groups demonstrate support for the Run and its causes and make their own political statements about POW/MIA or other veteran issues. At VFW halls, community centers, and rest stops, local organizations feed the riders and perform ceremonies in their honor, while area veterans' groups and motorcycle clubs arrange for free fill-ups for the several hundred bikes and other vehicles on the Run. Thus, the Run provides an important focal point for the sentiments and concerns of people in the small towns that have disproportionally borne the losses of war and links these communities to the bikers' pilgrimage, and to the Wall itself.

The Run's schedule brings it to Washington, D.C., in time to join Rolling Thunder, the largest motorcycle parade in the country, and one of the few with stated political themes. The first Rolling Thunder was held on Memorial Day weekend of 1987, fourteen years after the main U.S. forces had been withdrawn from Vietnam. According to Rolling Thunder, Inc.'s promotional material, the event began as "a protest ride to our nation's Capitol to focus attention on those we left behind and to honor those that served and died." As the organizers note, the name was chosen to evoke memories of the war: "Rolling Thunder. The name itself reminds us of the Vietnam conflict. . . . The name arose from B52 bombers carpet bombing vast stretches of jungle during the conflict."[10] Today, this "rolling thunder" is replicated by the roar of several hundred thousand motorcycles parading through the streets of Washington, D.C.

Rolling Thunder, Inc., lists its primary objective as pressuring the U.S. government to obtain a full accounting of Vietnam-era POWs and MIAs.[11] In recent years, however, organizers have increasingly framed the ride as a more broad-based veterans' support event. Both promotional materials and statements made during news coverage of the event typically now refer to MIAs from *all* of America's twentieth-century foreign conflicts, from World War I to the Gulf War, as well as to issues such as veterans' benefits and veterans' health. In May 2000, for instance, the Rolling Thunder rally on the steps of the Lincoln Memorial showcased the current Miss America, Heather French, who dedicated her reign to helping disabled and homeless veterans and who urged the assembled vets to be tested for hepatitis C, the liver-destroying disease that has infected a disproportionate number of veterans.[12]

On the morning of Rolling Thunder, thousands of motorcycles

pour into the Pentagon parking lot, most bearing license plates from nearby states. By contrast, many of the plates on the Run for the Wall motorcycles bear witness to the long cross-country journey that the participants have made. In recognition of this journey, in past years the Run for the Wall contingent was given a place of honor near the head of the Rolling Thunder parade as it threaded its way through downtown Washington, D.C., on its way to the Wall (although this was not the case in 1999 and 2000).[13]

The Run for the Wall, however, is not just a ride to Rolling Thunder. Rather, as its name implies, it is a journey to the Wall, our nation's saddest and most visited memorial. It is here that the Run completes its mission. For ten days riders flow toward the Wall's embrace. For most of them the Wall is a continual presence in their consciousness during the Run. As each day passes and Washington comes closer, the pull of the Wall increases, becoming more visceral with each mile. On the Friday before Rolling Thunder, the Run reaches Washington, D.C. Here, at journey's end, the riders park their motorcycles on a grassy field near the Vietnam Veterans Memorial and walk the last few yards to the Wall. It is here that, like pilgrims everywhere, they lay the offerings they have brought with them. It is here that they touch the name of someone remembered from long ago. It is here that those who are encountering the Wall for the first time are supported by their friends and companions from the Run as they search for dead comrades among the thousands of names inscribed in the black granite. And it is here that they face their own reflections, and their memories, in the Wall's polished surface.

There are other Run for the Wall events that follow during the weekend: a celebratory "family dinner" on Friday evening, a night patrol for those who wish to spend time alone at the Wall without the intrusive presence of tourists, a wreath-laying at the Tomb of the Unknown on Saturday, and finally the Rolling Thunder parade on Sunday. Each of these events has its own importance for those who participate. But it is arriving at the Wall that makes sense of the journey that brought them there.

Although the Wall is the goal of the journey, it is the journey itself that is the primary site for making meaning and constructing memories about the Vietnam War and Vietnam veterans. The Run for the Wall takes the *run*—a key component of biker culture, and one we will explore in greater detail further on—and transforms it

FIGURE 3. The belief that live POWs remain in Vietnam plays an important role on the Run.

into a *pilgrimage*, creating a framework for addressing our uneasy memories of the Vietnam War.

THE RUN FOR THE WALL AS PILGRIMAGE

As a collective event, the Run serves many purposes. Its initial and most expressed purpose has been to keep the issue of U.S. soldiers still missing in Vietnam on the American public agenda. The Run's literature, web site, pins, patches, and bumper stickers, as well as public pronouncements by its leaders, all emphasize the need to obtain a full accounting of American MIAs. The back patch worn by many Run for the Wall riders includes the words "You Are Not Forgotten," the same words found on the POW-MIA flag, and most bikes on the Run fly the POW flag.

Another, and in recent years an equally important, purpose of the Run is to be a healing pilgrimage for those seeking to ease the pains and unresolved emotional wounds of war. This is not just our interpretation; it is how participants themselves frame their own involvement in the Run. They speak of "healing" and call themselves "pilgrims" and refer to their ride as "a pilgrimage." The Run for the Wall Mission Statement emphasizes that the philosophy of the Run is "to maintain a safe, supportive and private atmosphere in which all participants can reflect and heal on their journey to the Vietnam Memorial in Washington, D.C., in the hope that they can return home to a new beginning." Many who come on the Run in search of this kind of healing are Vietnam veterans. However, the Run's attraction as a healing journey is inclusive: veterans suffering the effects of pre- or post-Vietnam military conflicts, people with friends or family members named on the Wall, people who love and perhaps live with those who bear the physical or psychic scars of the Vietnam War, and people like ourselves, neither Vietnam veterans nor family of a Vietnam veteran, who knew they needed something the Run had to offer as soon they heard about it, without knowing exactly why.[14]

Around the world, individuals and groups undertake pilgrimage for a variety of reasons: to acquire spiritual benefits, to seek healing for physical or psychological problems, to honor the holy places of their religious traditions, to establish or affirm their own religious, cultural, or personal identity, and to express political or social protest. Therefore, participants in the Run for the Wall are quite right to term their journey a "pilgrimage." Like the pilgrimages associated with the major world religions, the Run combines a ritual journey with seriousness of purpose, ending in the arrival at a sacred goal. And like other pilgrimages, it can have a powerful, even transformative, effect on its participants.[15]

Making the journey by motorcycle also plays an important symbolic role in this particular pilgrimage (a theme we will explore further in chapters 4 and 5). Riding together across the country joins the participants in the Run in a common brotherhood of the road, while simultaneously setting them apart from people making cross-country journeys by more ordinary (and more comfortable) means.[16] For veterans, the hazards and discomforts of the Run also serve as a remembrance of the hardships—and the camaraderie—of the Vietnam experience itself, and in doing so connect them to their comrades who did not return. The Run rides not only in memory of the dead—"We ride for those who died" is a slogan found on a number of pins and patches on the Run—but also in 1998 literally *with* the dead, as the ashes of a recently deceased veteran were carried with us to the Wall.

The Wall as a Pilgrimage Destination

While the journey is what gives pilgrimage its shape, it is the destination that gives it its purpose. When the Vietnam Veterans Memorial was dedicated in 1982, no one expected that it would become an important American shrine. To date, however, nearly 10 percent of the population—more than twenty-four million people—have visited the Wall.[17] According to the growing literature about the Wall, the vast majority of those who visit there find it a deeply moving experience, one that calls forth powerful feelings about personal losses and about the collective loss of so much youth in so many wars.[18]

Beyond calling forth sorrow for the dead, the Wall also plays a critical role in the nation's struggle to confront its uneasy memories of the Vietnam War. Many Americans, particularly Vietnam veterans, have a desire to understand the Vietnam War as something other than a military and moral disgrace. What does it mean to have fought, to have been a prisoner, to have lost comrades or loved ones, in a war that brought neither victory nor public honor? What does it mean to continue to suffer as a veteran, or as someone close to a veteran, when it is unclear if anyone actually benefited from the war that led to this suffering? How can Americans reconstruct memories of the Vietnam War that are colored with national pride when, by the war's end, the majority of U.S. citizens felt that the political underpinnings of the war were at best erroneous, and at worst shameful?[19]

In recent years the search for new memories about the Vietnam War has come to focus not on the war itself, but on those who fought it, that is, on the Vietnam veteran. Increasingly the answer to troubling questions about the Vietnam War has been to submerge the contested politics of the war beneath the image of the U.S. soldiers who fought it. Wars are political enterprises pursued by military means, and failed wars are not equivalent to dishonored warriors. As a result, the fallen soldier, the missing soldier, the returned veteran suffering from wartime experiences or a spoiled "Welcome home," have become key images in the struggle to construct a new, more acceptable national memory out of the Vietnam experience. Focusing on the veteran enables us to turn away from the memory of the public conflict over what many felt was a "bad" war, and instead remember the "good" Americans who fought in Vietnam.

The very creation of the Vietnam Veterans Memorial reflected a desire to establish a focus for memory of the Vietnam War that did not revive the public conflict over the war. There were only four de-sign criteria for the juried competition for the memorial's design. One of them was that it make no political statement about the war.[20] Thus, the most politically controversial war in U.S. history is remembered with a monument that deliberately avoids explicit political comment. This is not to say that the Wall is devoid of political meaning. It is the deliberate political ambiguity of the Wall that has enabled visi-tors to assign it their own meaning, from a memorial to brave sol-diers who fought in a good and noble war, to a testament to the everlasting shame of politicians who sent so many to die in pursuit of policies they knew could not succeed, to a testimony to the wrong-ness of all war.

Within the community of biker-veterans there is a popular t-shirt that captures this desire to separate the memory of Vietnam veter-ans from the memory of the Vietnam War: A rider stands next to his customized Harley Davidson in front of the Wall, where he touches the reflection of soldiers behind the names. Above this image the shirt reads "Forget the War," while below it says "Remember the Warrior." This t-shirt not only captures the need to construct a memory that will enable Americans to render the Vietnam War a less troubling part of the past but also demonstrates the importance of the Wall as a site for forging just such a memory. The Wall has become a focal point for negotiating the meaning of a war that disrupted our national con-sensus of what it means to wage war and to be a veteran. At the Wall many different voices seek, in both private and public ways, to re-construct these meanings. As Kristen Hass writes in her analysis of objects left at the Wall: "The Vietnam War has a restless memory. More than twenty years after its official end it continues to haunt the American imagination. . . . Americans deeply crave a memory, or a thousand memories together, that speaks to the ways in which this war disrupted their sense of American culture and their place in it."[21]

Considerable attention has been given to the ways people, alone or in small groups, use the Wall to negotiate new meanings of the war and the warriors.[22] Much less has been said about larger-scale, collective uses of the Wall, such as the Run for the Wall.[23] The Run differs from many other efforts at Vietnam-related memorialization because it is an extended collective performance, a ten-day pilgrimage rather than a momentary or solitary act of homage or protest at the Wall. For a week and a half, the Run exists as a mobile community of memory, a rolling support network where individuals address a diverse array of personal issues, a patriotic cross-country parade that helps communities along its route deal with their own Vietnam War wounds, and an extended protest of the government's failure to care for its veterans, both those who are still missing and those who returned.

A *Community of* Healing, Protest, *and* Aid

A journey made in the company of others to the Wall as a shrine, as a sacred place at the end of a pilgrimage, provides a healing community that is not readily available to solitary visitors to the Wall. Indeed, one of the indicators of the Run's healing power is that after several days in the company of others making their way to the Wall, veterans who had joined the Run because they saw it only as an interesting opportunity for a motorcycle ride across the country often find themselves confronting long-buried memories. This unanticipated power of the journey was demonstrated by one Vietnam veteran on the third night of the 1996 Run at a ceremony in Limon, Colorado, honoring POWs and MIAs. Rocked by unexpected emotions, he kept repeating, "I thought I was just going for a ride," as tears rolled down his cheeks.

The troubles that participants bring to the Run, and eventually to the Wall, are often chronic. Coming to terms with the psychological and emotional wounds of war, as with other chronic ills, often involves not so much a "cure" that eliminates the source of the pain, as learning to live with it in dignity and acceptance rather than with anger and depression. In this sense many people come to the wall to be *healed* rather than to be cured. Achieving and maintaining this healing, however, is not a once-and-for-all event. It often requires continuing support. For this reason, many participants, like pilgrims to other sacred places, return to the Run year after year, seeking the emotional reinforcement that comes from participation in a collective journey of healing that has now become an important part of their identities and of their search for wholeness and peace.

Beyond the political agenda of keeping the POW-MIA issue alive and searching for personal healing, the Run encompasses several other important, though somewhat less prominent, goals. One is to serve as a political vehicle for concerns, complaints, and action regarding veterans' issues, particularly government failure or slowness to address the postwar consequences of such things as exposure to Agent Orange, the Gulf War Syndrome, and post-traumatic stress disorder (PTSD), and what many participants see as a continual, general erosion of veterans' benefits.[24] In public ceremonies and media contacts along the route, spokespeople for the Run frequently call attention to one or more of these issues, as well as reiterate the Run's POW-MIA theme. In addition, the Run seeks to help those who are "lost" in another sense. A commonly cited image is that of the "bush veteran" who is "living in the wilderness," and the hope is often expressed that the Run will bring such individuals "out of the woods" and into the company of fellow veterans and other supporters who can bring him back into "the world."

A subtheme of "riding for those who can't" is played out through the Run's visit to disabled vets in VA hospitals along its route. One of the main purposes of these visits is to remind the disabled veterans that they have not been forgotten. Bringing comfort to the hospital bound helps compensate for the inability to significantly reduce the number of Americans who will never come home from Vietnam, alive or dead. In some cases these hospital visits also serve as a beacon of hope or a future goal for hospitalized veterans. In 1996 a nurse at the VA hospital in St. Louis told us, "After Veterans Day, your visit here is the most important day of the year for many of these guys. It gives them a dream of what they would do if they could." After the 1997 Run visited one VA facility, two men who had been hospitalized there managed to join the following year's Run.

The Run is also about personal satisfaction, about experiencing the comradeship of the road, exchanging jokes and wisecracks, recounting beautiful or terrifying moments of the day's journey, in short, enjoying the pleasures that come from sharing incidents of travel with co-voyagers. Deep and sustaining bonds of friendship are forged on the Run and, in some cases, even marriages. For a number of participants, the Run has become not only a vehicle for political expression and personal healing, but also an important social network that continues throughout the year. In recent years this has been facilitated by a Run for the Wall web site that enables participants to stay in touch and to disseminate information about the journey and its purposes.

ETHNOGRAPHY OF A CYCLIC RITUAL

As we stated earlier, our participation in the Run for the Wall was motivated by strong feelings that we *had* to go, feelings whose sources are even today not entirely clear to us. At the same time, once we became involved, we could not help thinking about the Run in terms of our own academic training. We were not drawn to the Run as an academic exercise or a scholarly project, nor did the idea of this book begin to take shape in our minds until the third year of our participation. Nevertheless, as people whose professional responsibilities for the last twenty-five years have required us to take an analytic perspective on social life, we could not separate our personal identities from our professional selves, particularly because part of what motivates us as social scientists is our personal commitment to social issues. In our view, the personal nature of our participation in the Run, rather than being separate from or at odds with our roles as social analysts, is essential to those roles.

The method of living and sharing with those one writes about has been termed *participant observation* by anthropologists and others engaging in ethnographic research. In most cases of participant observation, the researcher shares in some activity *in order to* observe and analyze it. Our approach here, however, is more that of *observant participants*. Although this book takes an analytic perspective, we began our involvement with the Run for the Wall not as researchers, but just as riders. Over the last five years we have shared all the discomforts, hazards, and pleasures of riding with other bikers on the Run.[25] We laughed with them, cried with them, conversed with them, shared food and endless cups of coffee, grew sad, angry, happy, and thoughtful by turns. We bought raffle tickets, listened to complaints (and made some ourselves), offered opinions and suggestions, and in 1997, 1998, 1999, and 2000 participated in planning for the Run. In many ways these experiences bound us to the other riders and enabled us to understand their cause more than any simple verbal statement of purpose or ideology from them could ever have done.

As participants first, and observers second, we can never be as personally and emotionally distant from the Run as are researchers who participate in some activity primarily to observe it. At the same time, the personal nature of our participation in the Run has given us the opportunity to *feel* how it affects those who join it, and to make those feelings part of the story we tell. Of particular interest to us has been the ways in which we ourselves are part of what we are writing about.[26] What do *we* feel when we arrive at Angel Fire or take that final walk of our journey to the Wall? What do we think of various ceremonies that are performed along the way? What is our own understanding of how the Vietnam War is presented and interpreted by individuals and groups in the course of the journey? Thus, while the book is not *only* about us and our reactions—in fact our primary goal is to present as clearly as we can what the Run means to its other participants—it is *also* about us, as bikers, as children of the '60s, as people whose early adult years were deeply touched by the Vietnam War, and as Americans.

The Run, however much participants may think about it between events, occupies less than a two-week period, once a year. But that brief time is exceptionally intense, filled with ceremonies, speeches, stories, conversations, and emotions. Interspersed with these activities are long periods of riding, in which one is with, and yet isolated from, the hundred or so other bikers who travel side by side in their long column across the country. While we knew from the very beginning that we wanted to keep journals of our experiences, at the end of long days of riding we were often too tired to do more than make a few notes, and at times it was difficult to capture in words the many emotions we had experienced in the course of the day. Moreover, some things that we heard from other participants were told in confidence, and we have respected that confidence in putting together this book. For all of these reasons, it was only after participating in several Runs that we felt we could even consider writing about what we and others experienced as participants in the Run for the Wall.

While many of those we met on the Run seemed at first to lead very different lives from our own, it also gave us an opportunity to meet and become close to many people we would not otherwise have had the chance to know. We also came to realize that whatever individual experiences people may have had during the Vietnam War, and however different those may have been from our own, we had all lived through that time, and it had deeply marked the course of all of our lives.

This is a book about the Run for the Wall. At the same time, it is about many other things as well, for like any popular phenomenon, the Run cannot be understood outside its historical and cultural context. For that reason, we will be addressing a number of different topics in the chapters that lie ahead: not only the history and aftermath of the Vietnam War, but also biker culture in American society, the nature of community in America, pilgrimage and ritual therapy, gender, and through it all, the social construction of memory and history. In all our discussions we take what has been termed a performance or practice approach to our analysis of American culture.[27] That is, we see culture, not as a fixed set of values and rules that determine behavior, but rather as a creative, ongoing process in which individuals and groups shape cultural materials to structure and give meaning to their lives. In this approach, rituals are not a simple expression of beliefs and values but rather "the very form in which culture as a system actually exists and is reproduced" and one of the means by which "people . . . appropriate, modify, or reshape cultural values and ideals."[28] This creativity on the part of all those involved in the Run for the Wall is a central theme of the book.

Above all, however, we seek to create a "feel" for the Run, for what it is like to participate in a cross-country motorcycle pilgrimage with a hundred or more other bikers, for what it means to ride on a journey that is both a political protest and a healing ritual, and for the grief, anger, and joy of the veterans and their supporters who make this pilgrimage together through what the riders call "the heartland of America." So before we approach other topics, we begin with a day-by-day account of the 1998 Run for the Wall. We have chosen the 1998 Run as our starting point for three reasons: It was the Run's tenth anniversary; it was the first time that we rode "all the way" from Los Angeles to Washington, D.C., with the group; and it represented the first year of a new level of national organization for the Run. We invite you to ride with us.

2

THE PARADE THEY NEVER HAD
Chronicle of a Cross-Country Pilgrimage

MAY 11, 1998: DAY 1, FLAGSTAFF TO EHRENBERG, ARIZONA

A beautiful spring day in Flagstaff—blue skies, clear mountain air, and morning sunshine warm enough for us to strip down to t-shirts as we gassed up the bike at the Giant station just off I-40 in Flagstaff for the first leg of our journey. As we stood around enjoying the sunshine and waiting for the other riders who would accompany us to the Run for the Wall starting point in Long Beach, California, we thought back to our first experience with the Run. Two years ago, we had been anxious and uncertain about joining a group of Vietnam vet bikers we had never met. Now, we felt like Run for the Wall old-timers. We could visualize the route the Run would take across the country, and we were (we hoped) better prepared to handle the difficulties and hazards posed by a cross-country journey in the company of a hundred or more other motorcycles. We had packed more efficiently than for our first Run, pared down to the bare essentials—a change or two of clothes, some toiletries, and the all-essential rain gear. And we now wore the symbols of our participation in previous Runs—vests with Run for the Wall patches, RFTW t-shirts from earlier years, and pins from various stops along the way.

What *was* new this year—in addition to the fact that we were planning to make the entire Run from California to Washington,

D.C., for the first time—was that we were waiting to join one of the Runs *to* the Run—groups of riders traveling together from various regions around the country to the Run's 1998 starting point. This year, the newly established RFTW web site had helped link these groups together as they made their way to Long Beach, which was how we came to be waiting for a Run to the Run that had originated in Oklahoma. When we read on the web site that the group would pass through Flagstaff, we contacted Dave, its organizer. We suggested a route from Flagstaff to California that would avoid the traffic congestion of Phoenix, and we arranged to meet Dave and his fellow riders when they came through town.

We were expecting a large group of Run to the Run bikers to pull off the highway in Flagstaff that morning, but there were only two, Dave and his friend Rich from Colorado. Both were riding Harley-Davidson "baggers" (motorcycles with permanently mounted hard luggage and a fairing to protect the rider from the wind) and had the look of serious riders—sunburned, windblown, and comfortable with their machines. As they gassed up, we exchanged introductions. This was the second Run for both of them, they told us, and they spoke movingly about their experience with the 1997 Run. (We had not met them the previous year because they both joined the Run after we had left the group in Cimarron, New Mexico.) This year they planned to earn the All the Way patches that riders who travel the entire distance from California to the Wall are entitled to wear.[1] As we basked in the clear mountain sunshine, Dave said that after the bad weather he had encountered thus far—hail, wind, tornadoes— he was looking forward to a day of good riding.

We mounted up—off to our third Run for the Wall. The ride southbound off the Mogollon Rim and through the Verde Valley on Interstate 17 treated us to the spectacular vistas and distinctive smells of the Arizona upland. Just north of Phoenix we stopped for lunch at the Rock Springs Café, a restaurant favored by bikers from the valley and travelers in general. As usual the café was crowded. While we sat and surveyed the other diners, we discussed the difference between ourselves and tourists around us. Unlike them, we were not on a pleasure jaunt. In Rich's words, we were "pilgrims on a mission." We all agreed.

A short distance south of Rock Springs we pulled our Gold Wing into the lead, guiding our companions onto the winding two-lane roads that would take us roughly northwest through saguaro-covered hillsides into the town of Wickenberg. From there we led our little band southwest, descending into Mojave Desert country as we headed toward I-10 and California. The weather was perfect for riding, sunny but not too warm. The rainy El Niño winter and late spring had brought a profusion of cacti—saguaro, cholla, prickly pear, ocotillo— all into bloom at the same time. There was color everywhere we looked. As we rode, the smells of the desert, the pavement, and the bike combined into the kind of distinctive aroma that can evoke memories years later. With warm sun overhead, desert around us, dry sharp mountains in the distance, a nearly deserted road, and companions to ride with, it felt good to be on the motorcycle and on the road.

When we stopped for gas, Dave commented he could imagine "everything heading west." In his mind's eye he envisioned bikers from around the country flowing toward California for the beginning of the Run. He was excited by the thought of all these people converging on Long Beach, and his excitement touched the rest of us.

By late afternoon when we reached the town of Ehrenberg, Arizona, our stop for the night, it had grown quite warm. We checked into our motel and waited for the arrival of another group of riders who were coming from southern Arizona. This time there were three people on three bikes—our friends Mountain Man and his wife, Som'r, and their neighbor Tammy, a rancher from Dragoon, Arizona. We had a joyful reunion and over supper caught up on the news and exchanged reminiscences of past Runs. Then it was to bed for an early start for Long Beach the next morning.

MAY 12: DAY 2 OF THE RUN TO THE RUN, EHRENBERG, ARIZONA, TO LONG BEACH, CALIFORNIA

The weather this morning was not so nice—cool and windy. We rolled onto the highway later than we originally planned because of a tire problem on Tammy's bike. As the morning progressed, the weather began to deteriorate, with increasing clouds and rising wind.

Midmorning, as we crossed the Mojave Desert, we stopped for gas and restrooms. As we were getting ready to mount up again, the strains of Peter, Paul, and Mary's version of Woody Guthrie's "If I Had a Hammer" reached out to us from the tape player on Tammy's bike. As our companions began swaying to the music and humming the tune, our thoughts flashed back to the 1960s, when that tune had been one of the hymns of the civil rights movement and other manifestations of social protest. Back then, it would have been hard to imagine that thirty-five years later we would find ourselves riding with a group of Vietnam veterans and their supporters, listening to a song that had once been so closely associated with our longing for a more just and peaceful world. It was a reminder that all of us—male and female, vets and nonvets, war sympathizers and war resisters—belong to the same generation, a generation that had been divided and confused by the Vietnam War. It was also a reminder that healing the divisions created by that war is one of the reasons we ride with the Run for the Wall.

As we continued west, the wind became stronger. By the time we stopped in Banning for lunch, it had also begun to rain. From Banning we climbed westward toward the forest of madly spinning windmills that dot the eastern side of the coastal foothills—not that we needed the windmills to tell us we were dealing with a strong wind. The fact that all the bikes were leaning sharply to the left like sailboats in a strong breeze was indication enough.

Before the Run we had been anxious about having to deal with Los Angeles traffic on a motorcycle. Our worst fear was having to manage it in the rain. And that is just what the Fates decided we should do. The rain that had been intermittent since we left Banning turned steady as we approached Long Beach with Dave leading the way. Although he had never been to Long Beach, Dave rode calmly and steadily, as if he knew the route by heart. We followed trustingly, and our trust was rewarded as he led us through freeway traffic, on and off the various entrance and exit ramps, and into the parking lot of the Queen Mary Hotel. Later we learned that we had witnessed a fine display of seat-of-the-pants bravado. Although Dave had carefully placed a note card with directions for the route to the hotel on his bike's dashboard, the rain had quickly turned his handiwork into an unreadable mess. From then on it had been guesswork, instinct, and luck.

As we parked our bikes next to those that had already arrived, the rain intensified. We hurriedly unpacked our gear and made our way to the hotel lobby to register. Dripping and squishing across the lobby of this elegant ocean-liner-turned-hotel, we greeted the few warm, dry bikers who had already checked in. Once in our room, we wasted no time getting into dry clothes ourselves. Then we set off to explore the Queen Mary and enjoy an early dinner in one of the ship's dining rooms.

When we arrived, about thirty-five bikes had been parked in front of the hotel. As the afternoon wore on, riders continued to pull in. In the parking lot and the lobby, old friends greeted one another, commiserated about the weather, and caught up on the news. By early evening, bikers were still lined up at the registration desk with their rain gear dripping water on the lobby floor, and their hands stained after hours of riding in wet black-leather gloves.

After dinner, we wandered back to the lobby, where the Run had provided pizza and soft drinks for the riders. People munched pizza, socialized, and bought RFTW pins, patches, and t-shirts. Conversations centered on the weather, or on whether or not this or that person was planning to join the Run farther down the road, and who was and who wasn't going all the way this year. We mingled with the group, greeting friends and acquaintances from previous Runs as they came in, and meeting new people—some new to the Run, some new to us. This year it was easy to spot those joining the Run for the first time. Most were wearing stickers with FNG in bold black letters against a yellow background. These were the "fuckin' new guys"—a designation once given to soldiers newly arrived in Vietnam, who, for their own well-being and that of the group, needed help in learning the ropes.[2]

While we were in the lobby, our friend and Run for the Wall veteran R.C. asked if we would ride with him as part of the missing-man formation. This formation consists of a pair of riders side by side, followed by a lone rider in the left-hand portion of the lane with no companion rider to the right, the empty space symbolizing fallen comrades. (Different individuals ride missing man on various segments of the journey.) Another pair of side-by-side motorcycles follows behind, creating a box formation around the missing-man slot. This year, Skipper, the Run's national coordinator, and his wife, Redlite, would ride side by side at the front of the pack, followed by the lone rider. R.C., who had taken charge of the missing-man formation, wanted a reliable rider on his right-hand side to create a pair of riders that could close the gap behind the missing-man rider as the road guards moved in and out of the pack to perform traffic

FIGURE 4. A rider sports his FNG button, announcing he is new to the Run.

control. Flattered by his regard for Ray's ability as a rider, and wanting to help our friend, we agreed to take up this position.

MAY 13: DAY 1 OF THE RUN FOR THE WALL

We awoke to the ominous sound of rain on water. Through the porthole we could see a steady downpour pockmarking the surface of the bay. This was not an auspicious start. Riding in bulky rain gear is never pleasant, but on the Run rain gear poses an additional problem, as it covers up the Run for the Wall "colors"—back patches and other insignia worn by riders on jackets and vests—making it more difficult to draw public attention to the Run's POW/MIA mission.[3] Fortunately, by the time we hauled our luggage and gear from our room and out to the parking lot, the rain had slackened to a drizzle, and the sky looked as if it might even clear.

Once our gear was stowed on the bike, we signed the register of participants and then wandered around the parking lot, taking pictures, greeting people, and availing ourselves of the free coffee and doughnuts set up on tables near the entrance to the hotel. As the bikes began to form up, Ray maneuvered our blue Gold Wing, Desert Dolphin, into the right-hand position next to R.C.'s Harley.

A little before 8:00 A.M., Skipper called the riders over to the front of the hotel-ship with a bullhorn. He welcomed everyone to the Run, reminded people of the Run's purposes—increasing awareness of the POW/MIA issue and "healing ourselves"—and gave road instructions. Then Phil, a minister who with his wife, Linda, regularly makes the Run, offered a prayer, which we had some difficulty hearing because of the news helicopter circling overhead. Once the prayer was over, Skipper gave the order to mount up, and the riders headed for their bikes. As 168 motorcycles and eight chase vehicles rolled out of the parking lot, a fireboat in the harbor sprayed its hoses, and the hotel-ship sounded its horn. With this send-off, the tenth-anniversary Run for the Wall was on its way.

The going was slow at first. Behind a police escort, the group crept through Long Beach, and then finally onto the freeway. For awhile the pack was traveling in the opposite direction from the morning rush-hour traffic, so it was not particularly difficult to maintain formation. Once we entered the 110 loop, however, things changed dramatically. The rain started up again, and now we were in the middle of a solid stream of commuters. Riding became more stressful and more hazardous as drivers entering and exiting the freeway cut through the long line of motorcycles. Earlier concerns that some riders might miss exits after becoming separated from the column in heavy traffic proved correct, as several clusters of bikes exited prematurely. (In one instance a group of riders followed a biker off the highway and onto local streets only to find out he was not part of the Run for the Wall.) The organizers had arranged a California Highway Patrol escort for this portion of the journey. Unfortunately, as we later learned, they were overwhelmed with rainy-morning accidents and could not spare vehicles for escort duty.

Finally we escaped the heavy commuter traffic and headed out of Long Beach, only to have the rain turn into a blinding downpour as we made our way through the pass that would take us across the coastal mountain range and into the desert beyond. Heavy rain creates a tense situation for motorcyclists anytime, but especially on crowded highways, where trucks and other vehicles continually toss clouds of spray that obliterate the view of the road ahead. For a long line of motorcycles riding side by side in tight formation, the risks—

and the anxiety—are even greater. All around us riders were struggling, as we were, to keep their eyeglasses or face shields clear enough
to see. As we followed the taillights of the bikes ahead, we could only
hope that *they* could see the road. It was not until we began descending into Moreno Valley and the rain began to ease that Ray's grip on
the handlebars returned to normal.

After the rain, the lunch stop at Chiriaco Summit was especially
welcome. Although the air was still chilly, the sun had come out. Bikers took advantage of the sunshine by spreading out wet clothing,
in an effort to dry off and warm up a little before the next leg of the
trip. The small restaurant at Chiriaco Summit served the riders a pre-
arranged one-price lunch of tasty Mexican food. After lunch the group
walked next door to the General Patton Museum, where the Run organizers presented the museum's curator with a POW/MIA flag. Then
it was back on the road.

The sky grew sunny and the weather a little warmer as we continued east, into the California desert. It was hard to imagine that
the previous year our desert crossing had been so hot that several riders had suffered dehydration. At Blythe we crossed the Colorado River
into Arizona. Just over the border, the group paused for the ritual
removing of helmets, because, unlike California, Arizona does not require motorcyclists to wear helmets. This year, however, a number
of the riders who would normally have elected to go bareheaded
opted to keep their "lids" on for warmth. Once the riders had, in
Skipper's words, "exercised their freedom of choice," we headed toward Parker, Arizona, where the local VFW served us watermelon, soft
drinks, and coffee. From Parker, the column followed a two-lane road
alongside the Colorado River into Lake Havasu City. This proved to
be one of the most beautiful stretches of that day's ride. Red rocks
and the river colors dominated the foreground, while dramatic cloud
formations rose in the distance, and for awhile the weather was mild
and sunny. Shortly after we rejoined Interstate 40 outside Lake Havasu
City, however, the fickle weather gods turned against us once more.
Clouds covered the sun, and a cold wind began buffeting the bikes
as we rode toward Kingman. At one point the leaders directed the
group onto an off-ramp where riders could once again don rain gear,
which proved to be a spectacularly difficult task in the strong wind.
Up and down the line, riders struggled with orange, yellow, and blue
slickers that inflated like balloons and in several cases escaped into

the open field next to the road. As we got underway again, the rain turned to sleet. Our final exit of the day, just east of Kingman, was welcome indeed.

It was dusk as the Run pulled into the Kingman KOA campground, where the Arizona chapter of the Vietnam Veterans of America had prepared dinner for the riders. Those of us who were not camping at the KOA ate quickly and headed for our motels, too cold to linger. We were sorry that the weather and our late arrival made it hard to stay, because our hosts not only had served up a hearty steak-and-potatoes meal but also had planned entertainment. We did get to see an unusual sight at dinner, however. Many bikers who typically wore helmets only when the law forced them to, stood around eating dinner with their helmets on to protect themselves from the rain and cold.

When the Run had reached Kingman the previous year, it had been so warm we spent several hours that evening standing on the balcony of our motel, watching and chatting with bikers and other travelers coming and going while we sipped scotch. This night, however, we simply shut ourselves in our room and turned on the heat.

MAY 14: DAY 2, KINGMAN, ARIZONA, TO GALLUP, NEW MEXICO

The morning was sunny but still chilly. We bundled up, knowing it would get colder as the Run headed east on I-40, toward the Colorado Plateau. By the time we pulled into Ash Fork, Arizona, for gas, the sky had turned gray and heavy. Truckers reported rain ahead, and so once again riders struggled into rain gear. As we climbed the plateau toward Flagstaff, it began to rain. And then suddenly we were in snow. Thick white flakes plastered the bikes and, even worse, began collecting on the road. Soon all we could see was the white world around us and the taillights of the two motorcycles immediately ahead.

We were probably more anxious about the snow than many of the other riders. As Flagstaff residents, we knew just how quickly sudden squalls—even in May—could turn this particular stretch of highway from passable, to treacherous, to fatal. We breathed a sigh of relief as the Run exited Interstate 40 just west of Flagstaff to meet up with our escort into town. It was a small miracle that not a single bike had gone down, avoiding what surely would have been a serious

FIGURE 5. Skipper addresses the group before departure in Kingman, Arizona.

pileup given the low visibility and the slippery road. Off the highway, the local roads were wet but not snow covered, and the snowfall itself seemed to be lessening. Unlike previous years, this year only a few members of the local chapter of the American Brotherhood Aimed Toward Education (ABATE) were waiting to meet us, and this year our police escort showed up in patrol cars rather than on motorcycles. Who could blame them? It was the kind of day that made us wonder why *we* were riding a motorcycle.

Our escort led us down Route 66, America's "Mother Road," and into the parking lot of the American Legion Hall in downtown Flagstaff. Bikes with snow-crusted windshields and mud-splattered engines nearly filled the parking lot. The previous two years, when the Run came to Flagstaff the lot had been only half full. Whether it was because of the new RFTW web site that gave the event more publicity, or because it was the Run's tenth anniversary, it was clear that participation had grown substantially.

We hurried into the American Legion Hall, seeking food and warmth. Few riders bothered to remove their outer garments as they consumed the sandwiches, chips, and coffee prepared by Flagstaff ABATE. It would be a long time before we would shake the chill of this day's ride. Because the weather had put us behind schedule, once again it was eat and run. We felt bad for all the people who had worked to provide us with a meal. We hoped they would understand. With that thought in mind, we mounted up, maneuvered into place, and prepared to follow our police escort out of Flagstaff.

It was a damp and chilly group of bikers that continued east on I-40 that afternoon. We encountered no more snow, but the weather remained cloudy, cold, and windy. At gas stops, we all huddled inside the convenience stores, gulping down coffee or hot chocolate, trying to suck in a little warmth before resuming our frigid journey. We ourselves marveled at how sparingly we had packed for this trip—there was so much space in our tail trunk and rack bag. Then we realized this was because we were wearing most of the clothes we had brought. Even so, we were chilled to the bone. And on a Gold Wing, as on many touring motorcycles, the cold is much worse for the passenger, who sits higher and more exposed than the driver, who can at least hunker down behind a windshield. When we rolled into Window Rock on the Navajo reservation later that afternoon, a bank thermometer read forty degrees. Forty degrees is merely cool when you are standing still. At highway speeds of sixty-five to seventy miles an hour, however, wind chill transforms forty degrees into the equivalent of zero degrees Fahrenheit.

Shortly before crossing into New Mexico, we left the highway and entered the Navajo reservation near Lupton, where we were met by an escort of Navajo police. We thought we were heading directly to Window Rock for ceremonies there, but to our surprise, our escort turned off at the Lupton schoolyard, where a welcoming crowd of Navajo awaited us. When the bikes rode into the schoolyard, the crowd burst into applause. As the riders circled, parked, and dismounted, Navajo moved forward, shaking hands, hugging us, and thanking us for coming. It was an incredible surprise—not just the unscheduled stop, about which the Run organizers had known nothing—but also the warmth and enthusiasm of the reception. We were ushered toward the schoolhouse and a receiving line of Navajo elders that waited for us on the porch. We shook the fragile wrinkled hands of aged Navajo, their fingers and wrists laden with silver-and-turquoise jewelry, and smiled into sparkling dark eyes set into lined and weathered faces. They greeted and hugged us and again thanked us for coming. It was incredible. Why were they so glad to see us? Why were they thanking *us*?

Inside the schoolhouse we were served coffee and fry bread, a welcome offering to people on the edge of hypothermia. Back outside, Navajo children ran back and forth among the parked motorcycles, bikers snapped their pictures, and Skipper exchanged formal greetings and gifts with Navajo community leaders. Before we departed, an elderly Navajo woman who was introduced to the group as "a very spiritual person" blessed us with a long prayer in her native tongue. Thinking about the difficulties behind and ahead, the riders echoed her concluding "Amen" with sincerity.

Then we mounted up and, behind our police escort, sped deeper into the reservation. All along the route, groups of Navajo were standing next to cars and pick-up trucks waving and applauding as we rode by. We were now several hours behind schedule. This meant that the Navajo who had come from their widely dispersed settlements and "outfits" to line the road on our behalf must have been waiting there much of the afternoon. Had they come out of simple curiosity, or did this parade of bikers with its military theme mean something more to them? Whatever the reason, we were moved by the effort they made on our behalf.

As we pulled into the parking lot of the Navajo Nation administrative center, beneath the dramatic formation that gives the town of Window Rock its name, we saw crowds of Navajo gathered around the lot and on the rocks above. We had been told that this was the first time the Navajo Nation had formally invited outsiders to participate in its Memorial Day ceremonies. What's more, they were holding these ceremonies a week earlier than planned in order to coordinate with our arrival. As we rolled to a stop, the crowd burst into enthusiastic applause. In response the bikers revved their engines in

FIGURE 6. Snow hits the Run in Flagstaff, Arizona.

a collective roar. By now the sun was sinking low, the day growing colder still. But we felt warmed and honored by the welcome we had just received.

From the podium at one end of the parking lot, a Navajo leader said, "Look around you, white men—you're surrounded by Indians. We'll take your bikes. You can have our horses." With that comment he set the tone for the evening, acknowledging both the differences that separated his people from this predominately Anglo group of bikers, and the shared history, particularly military history, that bound them together.

There are many vivid images from the ceremonies that followed: Navajo leaders giving the Run a Navajo Nation flag to carry to the Wall, a Navajo folksinger performing a song he wrote in memory of a brother who died in Vietnam, Navajo children taking our pictures while balancing precariously on the rocks above as elderly Navajo watched with curiosity and approval, the demonstration by World War II Code Talkers;[4] Navajo and American warriors saluting while a bugler played taps as the afternoon light dimmed around the mystical formation of Window Rock.

As during any Memorial Day ceremony, there were also speeches. Many of these touched on the complex status of a sovereign Navajo

Nation *inside* the United States, and the disproportionate contribution made by the Navajo people to the ranks of U.S. warriors. Navajo speakers affirmed that defending the United States was also defending "our own nation," that the well-being of the United States affected the well-being of the Navajo Nation, and that all warriors, regardless of race, are "brothers in the foxhole." Their calls for all warriors to be strong and to practice their craft underscored the value of the warrior in Navajo culture and helped explain the enthusiastic welcome that the "Rez" had extended to the Run for the Wall.

After the ceremonies, we wandered over to a picnic area, where we were served mutton stew, fry bread, salad, and fruit. The mutton stew was hot and welcome, but our hands were shaking so badly from cold that we had difficulty spooning it into our mouths. As we sat with the Run coordinators, a Navajo leader approached with a large glass jar filled with money. This jar had been sitting near the speaker's stand, and people were asked for contributions. We had all assumed the money was to help defray some of the expenses of hosting us, and we had been glad to contribute. But now the man was offering the money to Skipper. There was a moment of confusion. At first Skipper tried to refuse, clearly feeling it was not right for us to take money from our hosts, but then he quickly realized the moment called for gracious acceptance of a gift kindly offered. We sat there staring at the jar on the table, marveling at the incredible generosity of people so willing to give from what little they had.

We would have liked to stay to tour the Navajo Veterans Memorial, but it was getting dark, and Jill was in danger of serious hypothermia. So instead we rode into Gallup, gassed the bike for the next day's ride, and checked into our motel. Before Ray had even finished unloading the luggage, Jill was in the room, soaking in a tub of hot water. Later we agreed that, as grueling as the day had been, we would not have missed it for anything. The power of the ceremonies at Window Rock, and the warmth of our welcome, were experiences we would never forget.

MAY 15: DAY 3, GALLUP TO CIMARRON, NEW MEXICO

Chilly but clear this morning, with the welcome promise of warmer weather to come. Everyone seemed more cheerful when we arrived at the Gallup KOA, our departure point for the day. The owners of the KOA, who last year had decided to provide free camping when they realized the Run's purpose, served breakfast burritos and coffee while the riders gathered for announcements, a rundown of the day's itinerary, and the daily statement of the order of flight—"bikes first, then bikes with trailers, trikes, trikes with trailers, then trucks and cars." As he did every day, Skipper reminded us that we ride to create awareness of the POW/MIA issue and for our own healing. He also informed the group that effective today, U.S. post offices would be required to fly the POW/MIA flag on six national holidays.[5] This news brought an enthusiastic cheer from the group. Skipper choked up as he further informed us that the body of the Vietnam Unknown Soldier was being exhumed that day for DNA testing to satisfy the claims of two families who each thought these might be the remains of a family member lost in Vietnam.[6] While on the one hand it could bring closure to some man's family, he said, it also meant the loss of an important symbol for the POW/MIA cause. Next came the daily 50/50 drawing, which the Run uses to raise money by selling raffle tickets and then splitting the pot with the winner.[7] The meeting concluded with a prayer. Skipper told us he had been informed that he had neglected the morning prayer yesterday, and that this might account for the miserable weather we had experienced. After the prayer, we mounted up and prepared to depart for our next ceremonial stop, the Vietnam Veterans Memorial at Angel Fire, New Mexico.

It was a smooth ride to the pull-over just west of Albuquerque where we met our police escort. Fifteen motorcycle police led us into Albuquerque and onto northbound I-25. On the northern edge of town we stopped for gas, and then for lunch provided by Chick's Harley Davidson. After lunch, it was north toward Santa Fe, where we were met by another police escort. Despite the police presence, winding through Santa Fe traffic proved to be as tense as in previous years. Once again we were amazed by how many Santa Fe drivers ignored the flashing lights of the police escorts bearing down on them. At least one motorist was pulled over and ticketed for his inattention. We felt relieved when we finally cleared Santa Fe and headed toward Taos and the mountains. As the road narrowed and began its twisting journey through the Rio Grande River canyon, the group switched from riding side by side to staggered formation. Without a motorcycle just a few feet to the left of us, we could relax and enjoy the beautiful climb through the canyon. The river rushing behind

FIGURE 7. The Sacred Window Rock of the Navajo looks down on the Run.

us, the steep cliffs on either side, the sharp scent of the pines in the warm afternoon sun, and the dancelike pace as we leaned into one curve after another made this one of the nicest stretches of riding so far.

Just south of Taos, we turned east on the road that would take us to Angel Fire. This steep, winding mountain road, with its hair-pin turns and gravel-strewn corners, can be a challenge for experienced riders, and a white-knuckle ride for inexperienced ones. This was our third year riding this road with the Run, and the previous two years someone had gone down, fortunately both times with only minor damage to rider and bike. This year a rider from California went down in a curve. (The damage was slight, and the rider went the rest of the way to D.C.) Everyone else made it safely to the bottom of the last twisting stretch of road and into the wide green valley where the next stop of our journey awaited.

For many, Angel Fire is known only as the site of a ski resort, but for us it is forever a sacred place indelibly associated with the Run for the Wall. Nor are we the only ones for whom it holds a special meaning. Over and over we have heard stories from Vietnam veterans who felt their own journey toward healing, their opening up to the memories and the wounds of war, began at Angel Fire. Although we ourselves are not Vietnam veterans, Angel Fire is also the place where our own emotional connection to the Run and our memories of the war years had begun two years earlier.

The setting alone is breathtaking. Approaching from the west, the rider drops into a wild valley surrounded by snow-capped mountain peaks. Settlements are scattered around the valley, but mostly the impression is of space—of mountains and forest, meadows and sky. At the center of the valley, on a high knoll, the Angel Fire Vietnam Veterans Memorial appears in the distance only as a sweeping white wing reaching toward the sky. As the rider climbs the long drive toward the memorial, the white wing resolves into a pristine chapel standing silent against a hard blue sky dotted by soaring eagles.

As we approached the memorial's parking lot this year we were welcomed by contingents of bikers that had ridden from Colorado and Oregon to meet the Run at Angel Fire. As riders dismounted, old friends exchanged greetings, hugged, slapped each other on the back, and shared the joy of being together again. We greeted friends from previous Runs and exchanged news before making our way to the memorial itself.

The memorial's main building and museum overlooks the valley and the distant mountains. One of the museum's more striking features is the large map of Vietnam that dominates the entryway. The map's long, thin form underscores how much pain and turmoil, both in the United States and Vietnam, resulted from the struggle over such a small slice of Southeast Asia. Inside the building is an emotionally hard-hitting museum that features photographs from the Vietnam War along with the text of letters home by U.S. soldiers. The memorial's chapel, the white wing so visible from the road below,

FIGURE 8. The chapel at Vietnam Veterans Memorial in Angel Fire, New Mexico.

stands down a short path from the museum. Inside the chapel a tier of benchlike seats descends to a large cross planted in the prowlike front of the building. At the base of the cross lie offerings of flowers and other remembrances left by visitors.

Inside the memorial building this year, cake, coffee, soft drinks, and snacks were provided for the riders. We spent a few moments looking once again at the war photos and accompanying excerpts from battlefield letters that comprise the exhibit. Viewing the photos of the war, we were again struck by the youthfulness of these U.S. soldiers; many of them looked to be barely out of their teens. We also had a chance—sometimes rare on this hectic journey—to chat with our friends. Although riders on the Run travel together, much of their time is spent alone on their bikes. It is only at stops for lunch, gas, or ceremonies, and in the evening, that people have much chance to talk. Here at Angel Fire, as some people circulated through the building, wandered outside, or visited the chapel, others took the opportunity to talk with some of their fellow pilgrims.

As we stood talking with Mountain Man, the conversation turned to whether the Run had grown too big. We said we missed some of the intimacy of our first Run in 1996. Mountain Man replied that some of the participants in the earliest Runs think that because the

Run has changed, newcomers can't get the same thing out of it that the original riders did, but that's not true. "If the Run hadn't changed, it would have died," he went on. "Everyone's first time is different, and no time is quite like the first time." Is that why, as beautiful and haunting as Angel Fire is, we nonetheless felt some disappointment at our stop there this time? we wondered. Or is it because, unlike the first time, this year there was no collective ritual here? Or could anything ever come close to the emotional power of that first visit in any case?

The 1996 Run for the Wall—the first time we rode with the Run—was dedicated to the memory of Vincent Trujillo, a Vietnam veteran and Run for the Wall rider who had died the previous year. The cause of death was AIDS, the result of a blood transfusion while he was being treated, in the years before routine HIV screening of the blood supply, for cancer caused by exposure to Agent Orange. Although we had never met Vincent Trujillo, we came to know him through the memorial service in the chapel at Angel Fire. As part of the service, Trujillo's wife and numerous friends from the Run spoke eloquently of the man, and of the concern for others that many felt had been the hallmark of his life. His wife thanked us for allowing her to remember and to mourn, particularly because, in other parts of her world, friends counseled that she should put mourning behind her and get on with her life. But these veterans, of all people, knew that this was not so easy. They understood that space must be created for grieving, and that, contrary to America's "get over it" approach to death, grief can last for years, decades, even a lifetime. At the end of the memorial, a young woman with a clear, strong voice sang "Amazing Grace." When she had finished, even the roughest-looking biker was in tears. And so were we, for it is not only Vietnam veterans who find their restless memories of the war years stirred by Angel Fire Memorial. Here, in this simple chapel, we too found ourselves revisiting long-buried memories of the years of struggle and turmoil surrounding America's war in Vietnam.

The power of Angel Fire to evoke memory was underscored that day in 1996 by a conversation Ray had after the memorial service with Firedog, a rider who was also making his first Run for the Wall. At fifty-three, he was one of the older Vietnam veterans on the Run, and he had long believed that the war had not shaped his life. "I went in '65 and was home by '66. I always figured I was lucky. I'm not like some of the guys here. I was long gone before things started to get really bad in '68. I didn't see what the guys who went later saw. When I came home the war was over for me."

After returning from Vietnam he had become a firefighter and "got on" with his life. Now he was coming to understand that he had chosen a high-risk career partly because his wartime experience had made him an "adrenaline junkie."

After our emotional introduction to Angel Fire in 1996, we were disappointed at the lack of any ceremonial event when the 1998 Run reached that point in its journey. Needing something more than just snacking, chatting, and strolling around the memorial's grounds, we went to the chapel for a private moment of meditation before departing. We were alone there except for a man circling the cross, performing his own private ritual—a not uncommon scene on the Run, where riders recognize and respect the need for individual as well as collective acts of memory and commemoration. As we left the chapel, we were silent, each gripped by the painful emotions and memories of the Vietnam War years that the chapel evoked.

It was a lovely late afternoon as the group left Angel Fire and headed toward Cimarron, our stop for the night. While the road was not as steep or sharp as the road into Angel Fire, fresh tar strips on the pavement kept the riders alert, since two-wheelers are prone to wiggling and sliding on these mushy surfaces, especially on curves. It was also deer-grazing time, and as every biker knows, hitting a deer at any speed is serious trouble for both the rider and the deer. At one point, brake lights flashed in sequence down the line of bikes as the leaders slowed for deer crossing the road. Fortunately, there were no further encounters with Bambi's relatives, and we arrived safely in Cimarron, where we checked into our motel and proceeded to the dinner being held for us at the Church of the Assumption parish hall.

Dinner at Cimarron was typical of the many community-hall dinners we would eat along the way: particleboard tables with fold-down legs, gray folding metal chairs, paper plates and plastic utensils, and groaning boards of food prepared and served free by citizen-volunteers to hungry riders. Tonight it was spaghetti, a choice of several salads, iced tea, coffee, and cake.

After dinner we wandered back to our hotel. There in the parking lot Ray found himself in another post–Angel Fire conversation, this time with a veteran who had spent two years in Vietnam as a door gunner on a medevac chopper. The man spoke of how PTSD had ended his twenty-year career as a medical technician, and of how riding his motorcycle and coming to Angel Fire were important parts of trying to cope with his problems. When Ray left him, the former door gunner was sitting on the sidewalk contemplating his bike, as the smoke from his cigarette vanished into the cool night air, much like his medical career.

MAY 16: DAY 4, CIMARRON, NEW MEXICO, TO LIMON, COLORADO

At the morning meeting before our departure from Cimarron, Skipper told the assembled riders, "We trained together, we served together, we came home together, now we ride together," a theme he would repeat a number of times during our journey. He went on to say that we also ride for the missing and added, "Whether you ride with us for an hour, a day, all the way, you are part of the family," another recurrent theme on the Run. Then he gave the order to mount up. We pulled onto New Mexico 64, heading east toward I-25 and Colorado. The year before, we had ridden this stretch of New Mexico alone, having left Cimarron ahead of the group, in order to photograph the Run from a highway overpass as it headed north on the interstate. It had been a lovely morning, the sun barely up, the road deserted. Every few miles, antelope had stared at us across the barbed wire fences that separated road from ranch land. There were no antelope this morning, however, as last year's quiet hum of a single Gold Wing was replaced by the roar of more than a hundred bikes, many of them equipped with only token mufflers. Even without the antelope, though, it was still a beautiful ride all the way to the interstate. Once we reached I-25, we headed north, the snow-capped peaks of the Colorado Rockies gradually appearing to our left.

We stopped for gas in Trinidad, about eighty miles south of Pueblo, Colorado. Planning gas stops for the Run is no simple matter. In addition to the stops being spaced no more than a hundred miles apart to accommodate bikes whose range is limited by small tanks, the stations chosen for gas stops need to have multiple pump islands and, ideally, multiple bathrooms. The latter requirement is the most difficult to meet, and along the way more than one male rider has availed himself of nature's facilities after discovering he was the twentieth or so biker in line for the single lavatory.

With the addition of the Colorado and Oregon contingents that had joined up at Angel Fire, the pack that pulled into the Trinidad truck stop was a large one. Here, following the Run's established fill-up procedure, the bikes pulled up to the gas pumps and riders filled their tanks while still astride their machines, then passed the hose to the next person in line, after which they took their places at the staging area for the next departure. Paying for the gas is another matter. In some states local organizers will raise enough money to pay for the Run's gas, as was the case in New Mexico and Kansas in 1998. At stations where riders must pay for their own fuel, they pass not only the hose, but also whatever it cost to fill their tank, to the next person in line. This growing wad of money moves from rider to rider on down the line. In theory, the last rider to gas up should have enough cash in hand to pay for all of the gas pumped. Any extra money goes into the Run kitty.

Up to that point we had been riding near the front with R.C., but the day before, he had gone ahead of the group to have a clutch problem repaired in Colorado Springs. He asked us to take his space in the left-hand portion of the lane behind the road guards, and to take over his task of closing the gap behind the missing man when the road guards left, signaling them when it was clear for them to pull in as they returned.

The road guards are an important feature of the Run. They stand guard at exits and intersections, blocking traffic so that the long line of bikes can leave the highway or make turns onto city streets without the traffic congestion that would ensue if a line of a hundred or more motorcycles came to a halt. They also police the line, urging riders to pull up more tightly, and sometimes place themselves ahead of sixteen-wheelers as the Run passes, so that riders do not cut too closely in front of the trucks as they pull back into the lane. Sometimes there are not enough road guards to deal with situations that arise, and other experienced riders are drafted on the spot to help out.

As we came into Pueblo, the traffic increased, and the freeway exits and entrances grew more numerous. By then the group was more than two hundred bikes long, stretching in a line that taxed the road guards' ability to return to their position at the front of the group. A two-hundred-bike line stretches for more than a mile and a half at road speeds, and it took road guards ten to fifteen minutes, riding at nearly a hundred miles an hour, to overtake the pack once it had passed the interstate on-ramps they were guarding. At one point going through Pueblo the group ran out of road guards before it ran out of on-ramps. Although those riding two up (rider plus passenger) were not supposed to serve as road guards, the captain of the road guards pointed to us as we approached an exit, indicating that we were to stop traffic there. We quickly discovered that blocking a busy urban highway entrance ramp with a motorcycle is scary business—as well as only quasi-legal.[8] We could only hope that the cars bearing down on us would stop when they saw the long line of bikes and chase vehicles roaring by. Once the pack had passed, we found ourselves having to race to the Pueblo Vietnam Veterans Memorial where ceremonies were to be held. By the time we arrived, we had to weave through a pack of several hundred parked motorcycles to reach our place behind the road guards. As Ray maneuvered the bike at walking speed, his foot slipped off a steep repaved section of the street, and like a tall tree falling, the bike tipped in seeming slow motion into the high curb above a storm drain—not a serious accident, but an embarrassing one. By the time the bike was righted and moved into place, and the gouged and cracked plastic assessed, we had missed most of the ceremonies.

A few miles from Pueblo, the Run pulled into the Pinon Track Stop, where we were treated to free gas, as well as lunch provided by the Postal Workers of Pueblo, Colorado. After our small mishap in Pueblo, we decided to treat ourselves to a meal in the air-conditioned restaurant rather than wait in line outside for the free meal. After we left Pinon, the column headed north on I-25, turning off at Colorado Springs. Our first trip through Colorado Springs, during the 1996 Run, had not been a happy one. We were short of road guards that year too, and there were no local police to take us through the busy urban intersections. At one intersection a single road guard had managed to stop traffic coming from our right. The bikes ahead of us crossed with no difficulty, but as we started to enter the intersection, so did several cars from our unprotected left. The rider behind us, whose eyes were fixed on the traffic ahead, realized too late that we were making a full-on panic stop. His bike rear-ended ours, and we went down. We were not injured, and the damage was mostly to plastic and a nonessential rear light, and so we were able to continue. (Later we would find that the "minor damage" involved a bent subframe and a $1,000 repair bill.) As we heard (and felt) the collision, we both had the same thought: "Oh, no, we won't be able to finish the Run." Later, when Jill told this to Linda Anderson, wife of that year's national coordinator, John Anderson, Linda said, "We would have gotten you there." The motto of that year's Run was "We will leave no one behind," and as we learned about the extraordinary efforts made by chase vehicles that hauled disabled bikes to repair shops and back to the Run, we realized this motto didn't apply only to POW/MIAs.

Fortunately our ride through Colorado Springs in 1998 was entirely different. The route skirted the central part of town, we had an escort from the county sheriff's department, and members of a local Harley Owners Group (HOG) chapter not only stopped traffic for us but directed us through the intersections. We were also escorted by a chapter of the Blue Knights, the national motorcycle club for law enforcement officers. As we rode through Colorado Springs, people stood on corners waving flags, holding banners, and cheering as we passed. Then we were out of town heading toward the town of Limon, our stop for that night.

After we had settled into our motel room in Limon and unpacked our gear, we rode to the KOA, where we assembled for the ride to the little town of Hugo for dinner. This was the first time we had attended dinner in Hugo, which has become an annual and much appreciated part of the Run's itinerary. The first year we made the Run, the year of our accident in Colorado Springs, we stayed in Limon to tend to the bike and make what repairs we could on the damaged taillight. Remaining behind that year, however, had its benefits. After we saw to the bike, we headed for the swimming pool and hot tub to unwind. Here we met Suzanne. Suzanne had been a volunteer at the Wall, where, she said, she had found her life's work. As we sat in the motel pool and talked with her about the war years, more memories of that time returned. We had remembered the public events of those troubled times, but we had forgotten the impact on our daily lives. Who would enlist, who would be drafted, who would not come back, and who would return wounded in body or spirit? We had forgotten the way our lives had been on hold during those years. Suzanne said she and her husband had not even bought furniture after they married, not knowing if they would be living together or if he would be going to Vietnam. We reflected on how in these and countless other ways, the war dominated the lives of so many people, even those who did not go to Vietnam.

In 1998, however, we were looking forward to participating in events that had come to characterize the Run's stop in Limon. In Hugo, the Brothers Vietnam had arranged a dinner of roast beef, fried chicken, mashed potatoes, green beans, rolls, tea, coffee, and homemade pies. Little food was left by the time some two hundred hungry bikers had helped themselves from the laden buffet tables. Then we rode back to Limon for a ceremony by the Colorado chapter of Task Force Omega.

The ceremony was held at the KOA campground, where, as the sun grew low, a small group formed a semicircle around a man locked inside a bamboo cage (an image that would reappear at various points along the trip). Those performing the ceremony each read a portion of a poem about the plight of those left behind and those who waited for them. This was followed by a recitation of the Fourteenth Psalm, alternating with the voice of the symbolic POW in his bamboo cage speaking of his years of imprisonment. Then, as the names of Colorado's MIAs were read, a woman sprinkled salt from a stone jar to symbolize the years of separation and the tears of loved ones. After each name, the group intoned, "Missing but not forgotten." To complete the ceremony, everyone joined hands in a "healing circle." The Task Force Omega program was a clear example of the power of ritual. Whether or not someone believed there were live POWs still remaining in Southeast Asia, they would find it hard not to be moved by the ceremony's dramatization of the anguish of those, whether home or abroad, for whom the Vietnam War has yet to reach closure.

MAY 17: DAY 5, LIMON, COLORADO, TO SALINA, KANSAS

In comparison to the previous four days, today was less eventful—mostly riding. We started across the Great Plains, spending the entire day on I-70, droning eastward. The only difficulty we encountered was the strong wind that sprang up in the afternoon. The entire pack traveled for hours with the bikes at pronounced angles of lean as riders balanced against the north wind. The wind also took its toll on gas mileage, and well before our scheduled stop at Salina, we could see riders reaching beneath their tanks to switch on their reserve gas supply. Even this was not enough for some of the riders, whose bikes ran dry before they reached Salina, a fate we barely escaped ourselves. We pulled into the first filling station we could find after exiting in Salina, with the needle on the gas gauge lower than we had ever seen it in our forty-five thousand miles on this bike. Putting 5.8 gallons of gasoline into the Gold Wing's six-gallon tank underscored just how close we had come to running dry ourselves.

Food and entertainment were waiting for us when we reached Thomas Park in Salina. Since we are accustomed to the drier air of the West, we found it a little difficult to adjust to the warm and humid midwestern evening. But after our earlier days of rain, snow, and cold we were not about to complain. By the time we arrived, riders and local supporters had lined up for smoked ham, turkey, hot dogs, salads, soda, and beer. Off to one side a band on a flatbed trailer played country western music. Salina has been a regular stop since the beginning of the Run, as we later learned from a video of the first Run. As a testament to changing styles and tastes, the video showed the same band on the same flatbed in 1988, playing rock tunes of the '60s and '70s instead of the '80s and '90s country music it offered tonight.

At Salina, Mountain Man introduced us to a veteran who had tried several times to join the Run when it came through Kansas but had found it more than he could handle emotionally. He felt like a "a wimp," he told us, because he still could not deal with his Vietnam experience. Even if he just *thought* about the Wall he would start to break down. Although he had tried several times to join the Run, he had just "chickened out." With deep compassion Mountain Man told him, "You didn't 'chicken out.' The time wasn't right. When it is, it will happen." We felt saddened that someone already so troubled should feel even more inadequate because he couldn't do what he saw others doing—riding to the Wall. And yet he was hardly the only one on the Run who has had trouble completing the journey. We knew other riders who had tried several times before they could bring themselves to face their dead comrades on the Wall. And they *do* face them—the idea of contacting the dead at the Wall is more than metaphor. Many of those we have ridden with believe that they touch the spirits of their dead comrades in a literal, rather than just a symbolic, way when they are at the Wall.

Riding down the road, the Run can easily be mistaken for a biker gang. In actuality, however, the Run is a gathering of people struggling individually and collectively to construct tolerable memories of the Vietnam War. A number of those on the Run are also struggling against physical or emotional difficulties, or both, resulting from the war. Some take a variety of medications for medical or emotional problems. At least a third of the Vietnam veterans we have known on the Run are recovering from drug and alcohol problems. In this sense, the Run for the Wall is not a representative sample of Vietnam veterans, or even of motorcycle-riding Vietnam veterans, many of whom made less troubled adjustments to ordinary life once they returned from the war. Rather, the Run is often attractive to veterans with particularly pressing needs for healing. Part of the healing that the Run offers is to allow veterans like the man we met in Salina to know they are not the only ones with these fears and they are not wimps or chickens, and to find understanding and support from others who have "been there."

After everyone had eaten, the band asked people to form a large circle. Then, as the band played the anthem of a particular service branch, veterans from that branch were asked to come to the center and meet their comrades. Men came forward, hugged one another, and made their own circle in the center of the larger group. (This commemoration of the different service branches struck us as something new—at least we didn't remember encountering it on the other Runs in which we had participated.) Once the ritual recognition of service branches was over, the band asked the entire group to join hands and form "the largest friendship circle we have ever had." Then, with everyone holding hands, the band led the group in singing "Amazing Grace" while the circle contracted toward its center and moved back to its widest perimeter several times. Once again, the ritual worked its emotional power as we felt the human bond pass from hand to hand. As we sang the words, "I once was lost, but now I'm found," they seemed to appropriately sum up the impact that many felt the Run had made on their lives.

MAY 18: DAY 6, SALINA, KANSAS, TO WENTZVILLE, MISSOURI

Cloudy, overcast, humid. The group gathered at the park in Salina for departure. After the usual morning orientation, 50/50 drawing, and morning prayer, we were off across Kansas, heading east again on I-70. According to the "sitrep" for that day on the RFTW web site, we pulled out with 138 motorcycles and twelve chase vehicles, many of the riders from western states having turned back after Colorado. We followed a police escort through Topeka, Kansas, the first of the major cities that we would hit as we crossed the Midwest and eastern states. As we rolled through Kansas, gas, turnpike tolls, and lunch at a rest stop were provided courtesy of several chapters of Kansas ABATE. Entering the turnpike in Kansas with the toll prepaid is always a thrill, since an official Department of Transportation road sign saying "RFTW THIS WAY" directs the pack through its very own private toll booth. In addition to the sign this year, the RFTW lane was lined with American flags.

This year there were porta-johns at the stop where ABATE provided lunch. When we made this same stop in 1996, there had been none. The men simply took a few steps from the road, turned their backs, and unzipped. The women had to climb the hill above the stop and squat down in the grass—to the great interest of the man who was operating a mowing machine nearby. The following year R.C. had brought a cloth screen he had made to give the women some privacy. This year full bathroom justice prevailed.

With lunch over, the Run made a brief stop at the Kansas City, Missouri, Veterans Administration Medical Center, where we were served cookies, soda, and coffee. At the Missouri border the Run stopped so that those who ride without helmets could put theirs on, as Missouri law mandates helmets for motorcycle riders. Helmets in place, the Run then proceeded to Wentzville, where most of the group headed to the VFW for dinner and camping. At this point we broke off and went straight to our motel, done in by the heat and humidity. While we appreciated all the food that had been prepared for us along the way, we decided that a meal on our own—and one that included fresh vegetables—was in order.

MAY 19: DAY 7, WENTZVILLE, MISSOURI, TO CORYDON, INDIANA

We pulled out on our own this morning. We needed to stop somewhere along the way to replenish our dwindling film supply, since it is difficult to find the place or time to buy anything more than snacks and gas when we are with the group. We also wanted to get ahead of the pack in order to photograph their arrival into Mt. Vernon. In addition, we felt we needed a little break from riding with all the other bikes. On our first Run in 1996, we went everywhere and did almost everything with the group, but with more experience, we felt freer to ride our own ride now and then.

The main body of the Run was served breakfast at the VFW and then rode through Wentzville to visit the first Vietnam veterans memorial in the United States, dedicated in 1967. After that, they proceeded to the Jefferson Barracks VA Medical Center in St. Louis to visit with the patients and staff. As Skipper put it later, "We reminded them all that they are not forgotten and we are riding for them." While the group was doing this, we rode on to Hade's Truck Stop at Mt. Vernon, Illinois, where a number of riders were awaiting the Run's arrival along with a police escort to bring the group into the truck stop.

Once again, we were served lunch, along with soft drinks and little packets of sundries for the road (toothpaste, shampoo, sanitary products for the women)—a nice touch. While some people sat on the grassy slope next to the parking lot, a small group of us, seeking some respite from the midday sun, huddled in the thin strip of shade offered by a parked semi, hoping the driver would not come out before we finished eating. Before we left, Christina, supporter of Vietnam veterans, led a ritual remembrance of the missing. One by one, as the anthem of each branch of service played, she called a soldier symbolizing the missing from that branch to stand by a chair tilted forward against a Remembrance Table. The table was set with white china symbolizing the "purity" of the hearts of those who had served, and a red rose for "the blood they shed." After the ceremony, the Run, which had now grown back to 180 bikes, rode through the town of Mt. Vernon, past the high school where the students were lined up along the street, waving and cheering, and around the town square full of American flags and white crosses set up in memory of veterans who had died this past year. Then it was back to the highway, and across Illinois to Indiana and that night's stop at Corydon.

Pulling into Corydon was a little tricky, since there was some confusion on the part of the leaders as to exactly where we were turning once we exited the highway, but eventually we made it safely to the fairgrounds. Here we were greeted by our local hosts and were read a poem written by a local twelve-year-old girl about her uncle, a Vietnam vet who had never spoken about the war. Again we were struck by the remarkable do-it-yourself creativity shown by so many of our hosts along the way—the poetry and artwork of children, the rituals and speeches devised by the members of local communities who greeted us.

The tradition in Corydon is a fried-fish dinner provided by supporters for the Run. We were so sticky that night that we had no appetite, so we decided that we would head for the motel and a shower before we even tried to think about eating. We maneuvered the bike out of the line and headed off.

MAY 20: DAY 8, CORYDON, INDIANA, TO HUNTINGTON, WEST VIRGINIA

It rained and thundered last night, rousing those camped at the fairgrounds but not disturbing us and the other riders sleeping soundly in the motel. The day, however, was fair, although still warm and very humid. We did not have to backtrack to the fairgrounds this morning, since the group assembled in a parking lot next to the motel. At the morning address Skipper said that as we approached the Wall, our emotions were running high, but we should remember that we are there for each other. R.C.'s prayer that morning also stressed that we were feeling more emotional as we get closer to the Wall, but he added that we also needed to maintain our concentration, since we would be encountering more and more traffic as we began traveling into densely populated urban areas.

The Wall always looms ahead on the journey, but its presence is felt more keenly as the Run draws closer to D.C. Like our companions, we began to anticipate our arrival at the Run's ritual destination. This anticipation can fill many veterans with dread, especially those who have not been to the Wall before. "I'm terrified of getting to the Wall," one vet had confided on our first Run, there at that same stop in Corydon. Some vets, like the one we spoke to at Salina, simply can't make it or have to try many times before they can. Later that day a disabled vet being interviewed at the Kentucky memorial in Frankfort by a local television reporter echoed this theme, saying that he had tried five times to go to the Wall before he was able to do it.

Our first stop today was in Louisville, Kentucky, at the Veterans Medical Center, where we were served refreshments and stayed for almost two hours. One of the riders from New Mexico, who had injured his foot when his bike went down earlier in the trip, took the opportunity to be x-rayed while we were there. Then it was on to the Vietnam memorial in Frankfort.

The Vietnam memorial at Frankfort, Kentucky, is a remarkable place. Unlike the Wall or Angel Fire, it does not have an immediate emotional impact. As the design of the memorial becomes clear, however, its meaning can be devastating. The memorial consists of a large plaza in the shape of a sundial. The names of all those from Kentucky who were killed in Vietnam are scattered, seemingly at random, across the granite stones that serve as the base of the sundial. On the month and day of the year that someone died, the shadow cast by the upright arm of the sundial falls over that person's name, transforming the random distribution of names into a celestial memory of the war. The course of the war is easily read from the way the names are distributed, some densely clustered, some more alone. The density of names located at January and February 1968, for instance, marks the U.S. casualties of the Tet offensive. The biblical verses that remind us that everything has its own season are inscribed around the base of the upright arm. Here and there a flower or a small note has been inserted in the crack between the granite bricks, a testimony to the ongoing need to remember, even after so many years.

After leaving the memorial, we stopped for lunch near a highway off-ramp that offered a number of chain restaurants. When we returned to the parking lot of the restaurant where we were to regroup, we saw one of the road guards standing there, looking distressed. People were lined up in front of him, passing something into his hands and hugging him. When we asked what was going on, we learned that in the scramble that had ensued when the group got underway at the last gas stop, he had gone down while trying to get back to his place near the front of the pack. He was bruised and shaken, and his bike was barely rideable due to suspension damage. The people in the line were giving him money and comfort, and we joined them to do the same. This strategy of passing the hat is a common way to help individuals who suffer accidents or breakdowns on the Run. It is particularly important because each year there are some riders living on slim financial margins who have had to sacrifice even to begin the trip.

By midafternoon we were in Huntington, West Virginia, our stop for that night. This early stop was a welcome change; most days we

FIGURE 9. The shadow cast by the Kentucky Vietnam Veterans Memorial falls on the names of those who died in the current month.

did not pull off the highway until late afternoon or early evening. Huntington demonstrates a particularly impressive community solidarity with the Run for the Wall. Here the local Harley dealer reserves hotel rooms for all the riders and keeps his shop open all night for bikes that need repairs, oil changes, or new tires, charging only for parts. The local HOG chapter does its part by providing food, beer, and a free bike wash.

Finally, after eight and a half days on the road, we had time for leisurely socializing. Up to this point there had been few opportunities to just sit around and talk with old friends and new acquaintances, so the early stop in Huntington was very welcome. Relaxed, well fed, and with a clean bike in the bargain, we spent the evening talking with our friends about how the Run was going. Much of the conversation was dominated by problems arising from the size of the Run. These included problems posed by some of the day riders, who saw the Run as merely a good time rather than a serious pilgrimage, and the very long days between the morning pull-out and the evening pull-in. Other topics included the people who had mooned the Run at an overpass earlier in the trip, and the two women who had flashed bare breasts at the group from an overpass in Colorado—a sight that several of the male riders in the group could not believe they had missed. Everyone agreed that this kind of behavior was inappropriate for the Run, and that it detracted from the public image the Run was trying to create. "This isn't Sturgis," one person observed.[9]

As this group of "old-timers" with two or three years of Runs behind them talked in the hotel parking lot that still, humid evening, the subject turned to why most of us felt that the Run was not as emotionally gripping as it had been on earlier occasions, and why we were feeling a little less connected to it this year. Perhaps it was just because the Run was so much bigger this year, we speculated. The combination of the new web site and the Run's tenth anniversary had drawn almost twice the number of participants as in 1996, our first year on the Run. Or maybe, we thought, it is just not possible to repeat the emotional intensity of the first time, when everything is new, and unanticipated waves of emotion follow one after the other. Nevertheless, we all agreed that the Run had become part of our lives, and that we would continue to be involved with it, even if we didn't go all the way every year.

MAY 21: DAY 9, HUNTINGTON TO RAINELLE, WEST VIRGINIA

Another short day. Rainelle is one of the highlights of the trip for those who have made the journey before, and a surprise for first-timers. (Skipper wouldn't tell the FNGs what awaited them in Rainelle; he wanted it to be a surprise.)

Today, instead of droning along the interstates as we had been doing since Colorado, we rode on local roads through the beautiful hills of West Virginia. Because the group was so large, we divided into two packs for the ride along the winding two-lane road that would take us to Rainelle. At the Glen Ferris Inn on the New River, the pack stopped for the group photo that is taken every year from the fire

FIGURE 10. Bikes surround the athletic field in Rainelle, West Virginia.

escape of the inn. The inn's owner is the mother of a Vietnam veteran, and she has welcomed the group for this picture every year since the beginning of the Run. Then it was mount up and off to Rainelle.

While the twisty road descending toward Rainelle reminded us of some of the canyon and mountain roads we ride regularly in Arizona, some riders found the sharp downhill curves intimidating. One hairpin turn in particular is a guaranteed gut wrencher for the uninitiated. The road curves sharply to the right, almost doubling back on itself while dropping steeply. The bikes ahead seem to simply drop off and disappear. It takes a pure act of faith to follow them for the first time. Reports of gravel on the road, washed down from heavy rain the night before, did nothing to make this portion of the ride less anxiety provoking. But then suddenly we were out of the hills and heading into the little coal-mining town of Rainelle.

In previous years the Run had stopped just at the edge of town to regroup, but this year we rode straight through the town and into the schoolyard where the welcoming ceremonies would be held. The town's schoolchildren were lined up along the main street. As we rode in, they began to jump up and down, screaming and waving yellow pompoms. It was an amazing sight, one that can bring tears to the eyes of even those who have seen it before. What effect it had on those experiencing this welcome for the first time we could only imagine. The bikes circled into the schoolyard, and as we parked and dismounted, we could hear the cheers and shouts from the main street as the second contingent of bikers rode into town.

Rainelle has been a stop ever since the beginning of the Run, and the children had celebrated this tenth anniversary with a poster contest. "Ten Years of Friendship," the posters proclaimed. Both the children *and* their parents look forward to the event all year, we were told. And every year the children collect autographs from the bikers—on pieces of paper, in scrapbooks, on t-shirts. It is an amazing sight to see the bikers in their leathers and vests, many with beards, long hair, earrings, and weathered faces, kneeling down next to fresh-faced school kids, signing autographs.

In 1996, the first year we visited Rainelle with the Run, the ceremonies there had a strong military flavor, with a representative from the local reserve base lecturing on the need for soldiers to go wherever their president sends them, without question. When he had finished, it was clear his message had not resonated with all of the assembled Vietnam veterans, some of whom stood scowling, their arms crossed, while others applauded politely. This year the ceremonies were different. There was a repetition of the Remembrance Table ritual that had been performed in Mount Vernon, Illinois. Christina, the mistress of ceremonies, emphasized that the government should not send its children to war and then leave some of them behind, and she spoke of the importance of bringing remains home to rest on American soil.[10] A bamboo cage with a man inside was again brought out to symbolize the plight of POWs. One vet standing at the edge of the crowd broke down at the sight of the cage, while those on either side supported him, tears running down their faces as well. This year, the children of Rainelle were also honored. Prizes were awarded for posters, and an honor guard of Boy Scouts, the closest thing to a military contingent this year, was presented with RFTW t-shirts.

Most of those who stayed in Rainelle that night camped at the school grounds, as Rainelle's only motel has a total of ten rooms. The lucky few who had booked these rooms had made their reservations on February 1, the first day that the motel would accept reservations for the coming May. So like many of the others who were not camping, we were staying in Lewisberg, sixteen miles east of Rainelle. The

FIGURE 11. Bikers give autographs to children in
Rainelle, West Virginia.

Rainelle Moose Lodge served a meal to several hundred people that
night, but we left early for Lewisberg in order to arrive before dark.

That evening as we were sitting in our motel room, Dave knocked
on the door to tell us that someone was showing a video in the motel lounge of the first Run for the Wall. We hurried over and found
a small knot of other riders there, including Al, who had participated
on the first Run. Al showed us both an edited and an unedited version of the video. It was interesting to see what had changed since
the first Run and what hadn't. It was clear that many of the procedures and rituals that have come to characterize the Run for the Wall
were created on that first ride. Although the first Run had taken a
more northerly route, both Salina and Rainelle were part of the origi-

nal itinerary. On that first Run the riders were younger and their bikes older. But overall, the first Run and the tenth were clearly much the same.

MAY 22: DAY 10, RAINELLE, WEST VIRGINIA, TO WASHINGTON, D.C.

We left Lewisberg on our own, planning to join up with the Run at their first gas stop. With the exception of our short ride from Corydon to Mt. Vernon, we had been riding just behind the road guards for the entire trip, and it was becoming a stressful position for us. We were not official, as the road guards were, and there was some resentment at those of us who regularly rode at the front of the pack, some seeing it as a privileged position. We were caught between not wanting to create ill will and fulfilling our promise to R.C. When we reached the gas stop, however, we found that R.C. and several other of our closest friends on the Run were also planning to ride to the Iwo Jima memorial separately from the main body of the Run. We decided to join them, although we still felt a little torn. It seemed wrong not to ride into D.C. with the whole pack, and yet the people we felt closest to on the Run were themselves not riding in with the group. They were also dedicated to the Run, and we respected their decision to ride separately. Why had they decided to separate? There were various reasons. One of the veterans said he needed some "quiet time" away from the stress of riding in the pack. Others said that the inexperience of some of the riders and the "hotdogging" of others made pack riding uncomfortable. Everyone agreed that the longer pack had increased the rubber-band effect that forces riders farther back to constantly speed up and slow down, making the riding that much more stressful.

Our little band enjoyed an easy ride through D.C. to the Iwo Jima memorial in Arlington, Virginia, where the Run would stop before heading to the Wall. Some other riders from the Run who had come on their own were already there ahead of us. It was exciting to see the main pack ride in, as we waved the riders on and experienced the full impact of several hundred motorcycles roaring past.

At the Iwo Jima memorial, a variety of group photos were taken. Everyone who had arrived at this point was photographed. Photos were taken of those who had come all the way from California.

FIGURE 12. Not all bikers are two-legged.

Another photo was taken of the "all-the-way women." This year there were also photos of those representing different branches of the service, photos of those who were firemen, and photos of the children who had traveled with the Run. The firemen's group was sizeable, indicating the propensity for high-risk work among this group of veterans. (There should also have been a photo of the dogs, as several canines had made the journey with us, including one who rode all the way on her master's motorcycle, equipped with her own goggles and scarf.) Once all the photos were taken, it was time to head to the Run's true destination—the Wall.

The departure from the Iwo Jima memorial was a mad scramble, the lines spread out and disorganized. We fell in near the back, and by the time we neared the Wall, the pack had settled into a more orderly pattern. We were disappointed, however, that once the bikes were parked on the grassy field at the Mall, everyone immediately dismounted and headed for the Wall on their own, rather than gathering together one last time before we confronted our destination. This disappointment came in part from our first experience with the Run, when John and Linda Anderson, the 1996 leaders, gathered the group together, offered thanks for arriving at our destination safely, and asked everyone who had not ever been to the Wall to raise their hands. Those of us who had been to the Wall before were asked to take note of those who hadn't so that we could be close by to offer support if they needed it when they got to the Wall.[11]

In 1998, as in previous years, once at the Wall the riders proceeded at their own pace along the expanse of black marble, many of them performing private rituals. At several places along the Wall people had left the little woven hearts that had been a souvenir from the dinner at Hugo, and we did too. We visited the name of the first New Mexican killed in Vietnam, to whom we had delivered flowers from his seventh-grade teacher in Gallup on our first Run. Jill took the set of miniature moccasins she was given by a Navaho girl at Window Rock, and because she did not know any specific Navaho warrior who died in Vietnam, she looked up a Begaye from New Mexico. The name and place of origin almost guaranteed that he was Navaho, and she left the offering there. Ray approached a name he had not had the courage to face on five previous trips to the Wall. As we stood facing that name, one of the riders, a young man from New Mexico who had been censing the Wall with burning sweetgrass stopped and passed the cleansing smoke over the names where we stood. Our own rituals completed, we got ready to leave for our motel.

The Wall may be a healing place, but it is not an easy cure, nor is it necessarily a permanent one. Rather, it opens wounds anew. To us it speaks of the human waste of wars in general, and of this one in particular. And it reveals how the pains of one generation are visited on the next. Perhaps one day we will become reconciled to the memory of the Vietnam War, or at least feel some lasting peace when we visit the Wall. But most likely we never will. Instead, like so many others, we return periodically to its black granite reflections to remember, rather than to forget.

That night the riders gathered for a family dinner at the Black Eyed Pea restaurant in Fairfax, Virginia. The meal was paid for with money the Run had made from selling t-shirts and other items along the way. Here people celebrated the successful end of our pilgrimage and relaxed and chatted with the other riders. Thanks and recognition were given to various individuals and groups who had served the Run along the way. The gathering, however, was not purely festive, as some people still felt the effects of that afternoon's visit to the Wall and needed the help and support of their friends.

Late that night, long after the dinner, some riders joined the Night Patrol, a visit to the Wall after the crowds of tourists are gone. This is the time, one veteran told us, when his real healing takes place. We did not join the Night Patrol, leaving it to the in-country veterans for whom it has a particular meaning. Alone at their shrine, it is a sacred time for them, and one on which we do not want to intrude.

MAY 23: DAY 11, WASHINGTON, D.C.

This is a day when a group from the Run goes to Arlington Cemetery. In 1998 representatives of the Run placed a wreath on the Tomb of the Unknown, an event we witnessed later on video, as we did not attend the ceremony. For us, the Run was essentially over, having culminated in the visit to the Wall and the dinner that followed. We spent that Saturday doing laundry and buying food supplies at the shopping center across the street from the motel for the next leg of our journey. As we walked across the busy street next to the motel that morning, we felt strange being in a city after almost two weeks of riding through open country and visiting so many small towns. No longer absorbed in the all-encompassing world of the Run, where we were a center of attention in the small towns we passed through, we were now in an alien world where we made no impression at all.

MAY 24, SUNDAY: ROLLING THUNDER

The Run met at a Fairfax restaurant for breakfast, a final gathering, and a prayer before we rode as a group to the Pentagon parking lot for Rolling Thunder. Once we arrived at the Pentagon, we faced a four-hour wait. The parade was not scheduled to leave until noon, but we were there by eight o'clock in order to take our place near the front of the procession. There was some confusion about exactly where we should line up, and we relocated several times before we finally settled in. Several people from the Run passed the time by donning armbands and directing the incoming stream of motorcycles that continued to pour in until the parade got under way. Bikers passed the time exploring the vendors located at one end of the massive parking lot, buying t-shirts, patches, pins, and refreshments, while the roar of bikes and the smell of exhaust filled the air.

Finally the word came to mount up, and we were underway. According to official estimates, *260,000 motorcycles* rode across the

Potomac, into the District, and around the Mall that day.[12] Crowds lined the streets, cheering and waving, raising clenched fists and reaching out to touch our hands. Here and there women stood and watched us silently, tears running down their cheeks. Who were these women, we wondered, and why did their tears flow as our parade went by? We will probably never know, and yet we were moved by the fact that our ride had some powerful meaning for them.

As we were at the head of the parade, we were able to park and watch the stream of bikers riding in. Then we wandered around the mall, perused the Gettysburg Address at the Lincoln Memorial—especially the part about needing to "bind up the nation's wounds"—listened to the band playing by the Reflecting Pool, and treated ourselves to ice cream bars. By the time we left, nearly three hours after Rolling Thunder began, motorcycles were still roaring into the Mall. But it was over for us. Really, it had been over for us after the dinner on Friday night. We returned to our hotel in Fairfax, began saying goodbye to friends, and prepared for an early departure for the next day's ride to upstate New York, where we would visit Ray's parents.

In years past, the Rolling Thunder parade brought the events of the Run for the Wall to a close. For many people, ourselves included, this was still the case. This year, however, a small contingent left D.C. on Sunday bound for the North Wall—the Canadian Vietnam Veterans Memorial in Windsor, Ontario. Some members of the Run had added this additional leg to the annual pilgrimage as an act of solidarity with the Canadians who volunteered for service in Vietnam—war veterans who now fail to qualify for veteran benefits in either country.

MAY 23: DAY 12, WASHINGTON, D.C., TO SCHENECTADY, NEW YORK

By seven o'clock on a cool, sunny morning we were carrying our gear through the hotel lobby and out to the parking lot. We said last goodbyes as we hugged old and new friends, most of whom we would not see for another year. Then we left. The Run is so vivid, so emotional, so encompassing when we are in the midst of it. Now we were just another couple on a motorcycle heading west on I-66 through the green hillsides of eastern Virginia. Or were we? Pilgrimages are more than trips. Motorcycle pilgrimages are more than rides. They are journeys that change the traveler in small, and sometimes big, ways. After three years of participating in the Run, we found that much had changed for us. Our understanding of how Americans, both soldiers and civilians, struggle to address the emotional aftermath of the Vietnam War a quarter century after the withdrawal of U.S. troops was both more complicated and more contradictory than before. Now we had a network of riding friends that spread around the country, friends who would welcome us to their homes should we ever pass through their towns. And we found we had a growing need to better understand how the legacy of the Vietnam War and the desire to create new ways of remembering that war combined to produce a unique and yet very American event—the annual motorcycle pilgrimage called the Run for the Wall.

3

"WE WILL LEAVE NO ONE BEHIND"
The Politics of Remembering an Uneasy War

The Run for the Wall is both a protest ride and a healing pilgrimage. As a protest ride, the Run has the public, political goal of pressuring the U.S. government into using diplomatic, economic, or even military measures to compel the government of Vietnam to release any U.S. prisoners of war (POWs) still captive in Southeast Asia, and to provide a full accounting of all Americans who remain missing in action (MIAs). As a healing pilgrimage, it is a journey in which participants create collective and private rituals to pay homage to fallen brothers and sisters, and to ease the psychological and emotional wounds left by the Vietnam War. These two purposes interact and reinforce one another in ways that give the Run for the Wall its distinct character.

As a form of political action, the Run for the Wall is part of a larger POW/MIA social movement in the United States, which itself is an expression of a broader climate of conflict and uncertainty over the meaning of U.S. involvement in Vietnam. Although the Vietnam War has always been a controversial subject for Americans, several pivotal events during the early 1990s have intensified efforts to reconstruct the memory of the Vietnam War as more than a political and military failure. One of these was the fall of the Soviet Union, which is now being interpreted by some as partly a consequence of U.S. willingness to hold the line against communism in Vietnam.[1]

Another key event was the Gulf War, which reestablished a degree of national pride in the U.S. military and, in doing so, created a receptive climate for new theories that suggest that the Vietnam War was also a military success, even if it might have been a political failure.[2] A third factor, and one central to the theme of this book, is the increased attention that has been given to Vietnam veterans as men and women who suffer from the consequences of the Vietnam War rather than as perpetrators of that war. In order to place the Run for the Wall in the context of the ongoing controversy over the meaning of the war, this chapter explores three political themes: how conflicts over the Vietnam War reflect deeper debates over the meaning of post–World War II America, how unresolved questions about the Vietnam War led to a social movement centered around POW/MIA issues, and how this movement gave rise to the Run for the Wall as a cross-country motorcycle pilgrimage in memory of the fallen and the missing.

REMEMBERING THE VIETNAM WAR

For Americans, Vietnam has been a cultural battleground longer than it was a military one. Although the Vietnam War was America's longest war, with direct military involvement that lasted fifteen years, the cultural battle over the meaning of the Vietnam War has now lasted more than forty years, and it still goes on.[3] For those on the Run for the Wall, just as for many other Americans, not only is it the meaning of the Vietnam War that is at issue in these debates, but also, and very importantly, what it means to have fought in that war. As Vietnam veteran Michael Norman observed, for him the memory and reality of that war are so blurred that he has "no truth." He is, instead, an "empty man" who will spend his life trying to find what he lost when he went to war.[4] For many of the veterans on the Run for the Wall, this is also their goal—to build a coherent sense of themselves, no longer shadowed by the Vietnam War.

From Vietnam-era draft resistance, to characterizations of President Bill Clinton as a draft dodger, to the attention given during the 2000 primary season to the Vietnam War records of presidential hopefuls George W. Bush, Al Gore, and John McCain, the appropriateness of fighting or not fighting in the Vietnam War has been part of a wider debate that began in the 1960s over what America should be.[5]

FIGURE 13. The POW/MIA flag, symbol of a social movement.

The Vietnam War is not the only, nor even the most visible, element of this debate. Since the 1960s, conflicts over equality between men and women, abortion, racial discrimination, affirmative action, homosexuality, the death penalty, gun control, and the appropriate separation of church and state have occupied center stage in the ongoing struggle over America's values. But whenever the meaning of manhood, nationalism, patriotism, or the U.S. role in world affairs is at issue, unresolved conflicts about the Vietnam War are present, either as an explicit part of the controversy, or as the unrecognized backdrop against which the debate takes place.

Unresolved conflicts over the meaning of the Vietnam War have created what Kristen Hass characterizes as "a restless memory that continues to haunt the American imagination."[6] Was U.S. involvement in Vietnam a noble attempt to save brave allies from being overrun by godless communists that was thwarted by liberals and cowardly draft dodgers at home? Was it a cynical effort to use the overwhelming military power of the United States to protect a corrupt South Vietnamese government in order to guarantee that American corporations would continue to benefit from the resources, labor, and markets of Southeast Asia? Or was it something more banal, a long series of foreign policy and military blunders by presidents unwilling to be the first to lose a war, even though its continuation would ultimately leave more than fifty-eight thousand Americans and more than a million Vietnamese dead and seriously damage the economies of both nations, all to no good end? There are no final answers to these questions. All that Americans have, and all that they may ever have, are conflicting interpretations of the past.

Americans share no story about the Vietnam War the way they share a common story about the American Revolution, World War I, or World War II. Aside from the occasional revisionist history, most Americans view these wars as "good wars," fought for noble purposes by selfless and dedicated people.[7] There is no comparable dominant narrative, no national consensus, about the Vietnam War. The Vietnam War ended badly and, as a result, is a poor foundation for a unifying narrative.[8] Instead, disagreements that began in the 1950s over the U.S. role in Vietnam continue today across a broad spectrum of American society.

There are several reasons that the Vietnam War failed to produce a unifying national memory. First, from the U.S. government's earliest entanglements in Vietnam in the 1950s, it was never able to establish a solid national consensus that creating and protecting a noncommunist South Vietnam was either necessary for U.S. national security or even simply the morally correct thing to do.[9] This failure eventually generated the widest and most politically disruptive antiwar movement in U.S. history. Wars are large-scale national efforts requiring substantial national solidarity. Wars carried out in the face of strong political opposition are unlikely to produce military victory, and they are even less likely to result in postwar national unity, particularly if the war is lost.[10]

Second, many American soldiers and civilians could not make strategic sense out of U.S. military policy in Vietnam. The Vietnam War was a four-way conflict involving the forces of North and South

Vietnam, communist insurgents in South Vietnam, and the U.S. military. American troops frequently felt they were fighting a war that had no battle lines, and often against citizens of the very country they had presumably come to protect. The contradiction of destroying villages in order to save them, and the futility of capturing and retreating from the same ground many times over, was not lost on U.S. soldiers. A recurring theme in written firsthand accounts by Americans who served in Vietnam, regardless of what the writer felt about the overall purpose of the war, is the incomprehensibility, and sometimes seeming lunacy, of U.S. military strategy there.[11] A war whose strategic outlines were never clear to either those who fought it or the nation that watched it is not likely to produce a unifying national memory once the war is over.

Finally, Vietnam was the first war that America could be said to have lost. The failure of U.S. military efforts in Vietnam threatened a core American belief—the conviction that the United States was invincible—and in doing so, it created a crisis of meaning for many Americans. If the United States had been defeated by a Third World opponent, its claim to being the most powerful nation on earth—a claim with which many Americans identified—would seem to be meaningless. One way around this problem that leaves the belief in American invincibility intact is to conclude that the United States was not defeated in Vietnam but simply withdrew because of lack of national purpose and unity. But this view leads down another dark alley of confusion. If the United States withdrew from Vietnam just because the nation was tired of fighting the war, the deaths, injuries, and personal and social disruption that resulted from our war in Southeast Asia are stripped of meaning. This is why questions about the Vietnam War continue to haunt America's national consciousness, and why as a nation we have been unable to construct a common narrative about the Vietnam War. This search for answers, for a new narrative about the Vietnam War, is also part of the motivation that leads veterans and others to join the Run for the Wall. Through political action and healing rituals, the Run provides an opportunity for its participants to find answers and to fashion new meanings about the Vietnam War, about the Americans who never returned from Southeast Asia, and about those who returned but never heard someone outside their own families say "Welcome home."

SOCIAL MEANINGS AND SOCIAL MOVEMENTS

For the men and women who fought it, past and present conflicts over the Vietnam War are more than academic debates. They are struggles over the meaning of a significant, and often a defining, period of their lives. For many Vietnam veterans, including those on the Run, conflicts over the meaning of the Vietnam War have been reconstituted as struggles over their understanding of themselves. Was I a willing (or unwilling) accomplice in a war that was as shameful as it was unsuccessful? Or am I a heroic patriot, or at least a dutiful citizen, who answered the call of my country in a time of need? And if I am a heroic or dutiful American, how do I reconcile this identity with the rejection I felt when I returned home from Vietnam? How do I create a sense of pride and respect for having been a soldier when I sense that my nation would prefer to forget the war I fought? And for many combat veterans, perhaps the worst question of all: Why did I survive when many of my comrades were killed? Questions such as these link the larger political conflicts over the meaning of the Vietnam War with the private needs of Vietnam veterans, particularly those who are still struggling to create a contemporary understanding of themselves that is more at peace with having once fought in an unpopular war.

It is difficult for either individual veterans or a nation to address these questions in the abstract. For some time, however, the issue of whether POWs might still be held captive in Southeast Asia and the goal of identifying and repatriating the remains of every American MIA have provided a concrete way for some Vietnam veterans to begin constructing new, more acceptable memories about the Vietnam War and their role in it. By devoting energy to a movement on behalf of POWs and MIAs, veterans can find what Robert Jay Lifton terms a "survivor mission," a task that gives purpose to having escaped death while friends and comrades died.[12] Within the wider culture, focusing attention on POWs and MIAs as *victims* of the Vietnam War also helps construct an image of all those who fought as heroes rather than as villains or failed warriors. By extension, this gives Americans a way to remember the Vietnam War as an honorable, rather than a humiliating, episode in American history.[13]

As long as social action groups publicize the belief that Americans continue to be held against their will in Southeast Asia, or that the governments of Vietnam, Laos, Cambodia, Russia, and China are willfully withholding information that could answer unresolved questions about MIAs, or that the U.S. government has not made every effort to obtain a full accounting of MIAs, the debate over the meaning of the Vietnam War is not over. If the war remains a current issue, not just something to be analyzed by historians, there is still time to redeem the experience. As Edward Hagan observed, "When we have lost a war we have an even greater need than usual to find some justification to keep the issue open so that perhaps some day we can 'win.'"[14]

Many years ago the sociologist Herbert Blumer observed that social problems are defined by social movements.[15] That is, a situation only becomes a social problem when people who see it as such organize to demand some social or political remedy. Today, harms caused by secondhand smoke, sexual harassment, child abuse, or global warming are recognized as problems by many Americans only because social activists, people whom Howard Becker termed "moral entrepreneurs," created social movements dedicated to developing general awareness that these conditions are *public* problems, not just private troubles, and that they can be resolved by public action.[16] In a similar fashion, all of the individuals and organizations involved in lobbying the government on behalf of those missing in Southeast Asia, when taken together, constitute a national POW/MIA social movement. This movement has worked to establish the belief that the failure to account for every American who fought in Vietnam (or in any war) is a national problem that can, and should, be resolved by government action.

While the need to account for missing soldiers may seem like common sense to many people today, it is a relatively new idea. Before the end of the Vietnam War, missing soldiers were typically accepted as an inevitable consequence of war, much like dead and wounded ones. At the end of World War II, even after the United States was able to search every battlefield, 78,750 soldiers, representing 19 percent of all U.S. service personnel lost in World War II, remained missing in action. The Korean War left 8,000 Americans, 15 percent of all U.S. casualties there, listed as MIA. By contrast, the 2,069 Americans listed as MIA by the Library of Congress Missing in Action Database in 1999 constitute just 3.5 percent of all Americans lost during the Vietnam War. Yet, the numbers of MIAs resulting from

World War II and the Korean War sparked no national social movement comparable to the one that arose to demand that the government do something to account for the much smaller number of Americans missing in Southeast Asia. While many American families after World War II had to bear the sorrow of having loved ones leave for war never to return, either alive or dead, this was generally viewed as a *personal* problem. In most cases, they did not hold the government responsible for the fact that they had no body to bury. They mourned and memorialized their missing, but they did not protest. One of Ray's childhood memories, for instance, was of throwing flowers into the water on Memorial Day from a bridge spanning the Mohawk River in upstate New York in remembrance of an uncle whose bomber was lost over the English Channel. There was never a sense that this missing man had been betrayed by his country because he remained missing. He was just another honorable man who had disappeared in the chaos of war while serving his country.

The Vietnam War was different. Its meaning and purpose had never been clear to many Americans, and in the end there was no victory to celebrate. It is difficult to let Americans missing in Southeast Asia rest in peace because, as a nation, *we* are not at peace with the Vietnam War and its aftermath in the way that the World War II generation could be at peace with that earlier war. It is out of this uneasiness that the POW/MIA social movement arose.

The various organizations involved in the POW/MIA movement do not speak with one voice, no more than the antiwar movement or the civil rights movement spoke with one voice. If we take one step back from the specific POW/MIA organizations, however, we see that they have a number of basic propositions in common: (1) The U.S. government *knowingly* left some Americans in captivity in Southeast Asia when it withdrew from the Vietnam War; (2) after the war the U.S. government hid information about POWs remaining in Southeast Asia rather than demanding their release; (3) it is *possible* to obtain a complete, or nearly complete, accounting of all Americans missing in Vietnam; (4) the U.S. government failed to pursue aggressive strategies that would have forced Vietnam to provide this accounting; and (5) nothing will be done on behalf of POWs and MIAs unless those outside the government demand action. The Run for the Wall, as a motorcycle pilgrimage in protest against the U.S.

IN AN ERA OF ADVERSITY AND PROTEST
THEY PROUDLY SERVED THEIR COUNTRY

VIETNAM VETERAN'S MEMORIAL - ANTIGO, WISCONSIN

WE RIDE IN MEMORY
OF OUR FALLEN BROTHERS
AND FOR THOSE WHOSE
FATES ARE STILL UNKNOWN

Ride Along With Us @
www.rftw.org

FIGURE 14. Promoting a new image of Vietnam veterans.

government's failure to account for its POWs and MIAs, is one manifestation of this wider POW/MIA movement.

Before we explore the political and cultural origins of the POW/MIA movement in greater detail, we want to emphasize again that our goal is not to defend one side or the other in the ongoing debates about the Vietnam War, the existence of live POWs, the possibility of ever obtaining a full accounting of American MIAs in Southeast Asia, or the rejection or nonrejection of returning Vietnam veterans by the wider society.[17] For us, the important question is not whether the U.S. military could have won the shooting war in Vietnam if it had been allowed to invade North Vietnam or to bomb Vietnam "back into the Stone Age," as Air Force general Curtis E. LeMay once suggested.[18] Our concern is to understand how and why so many veterans we have met on the Run, like so many other Vietnam veterans, *believe* that the U.S. military could have triumphed had it not been for a lack of political will on the home front.[19] Nor is it our goal to proclaim whether or not there are live American POWs remaining in Southeast Asia, or whether or not the current government of the Socialist Republic of Vietnam is deliberately withholding information about American MIAs. A modest library could be filled with books supporting one or the other of these positions.[20] Rather, what interests us is why, more than a quarter century after the withdrawal of U.S. troops from Vietnam, there is a growing social movement based on the propositions that live POWs remain in Southeast Asia and that it is *possible* to obtain an accounting of every American MIA. In the final analysis, we are interested in understanding why some Americans believe so passionately in the POW/MIA cause that they will ride across the country—some wearing t-shirts that declare "Bring them home or send us back"—to demand that the U.S. government do whatever is necessary to secure the release of possible POWs and obtain a full accounting of MIAs.

THE CULTURAL ROAD TO A CONTROVERSIAL WAR

America's role in Southeast Asia has been the source of troubling questions for almost fifty years. U.S. political and military involvement in Vietnam began with the use of Central Intelligence Agency (CIA) personnel in the late 1940s to support France's efforts to reestablish control over its former Southeast Asian colony.[21] At about the same time that the U.S. government began covertly assuming leadership in the struggle against the communist-led Vietnamese liberation movement, two widely read works of fiction, Graham Greene's *The Quiet American* (1955) and William T. Lederer and Eugene Burdick's *The Ugly American* (1956), framed an emerging cultural divide, not only over U.S. policy in Southeast Asia, but also over our understanding of post–World War II America—a divide that continues into the present.[22]

Using Southeast Asia as their backdrop, the authors of *The Ugly American* characterized U.S. State Department operatives living overseas as self-promoting career bureaucrats more concerned with leading comfortable lives and currying favor with local leaders than with promoting U.S. policy. Lederer and Burdick used their story of these comfort-loving bureaucrats to symbolize what they saw as a more general lack of moral resolve on the part of U.S. politicians and the American public. For many political and moral leaders in 1950s America, the consumption-oriented aftermath of the U.S. victory in World War II was a clear sign that the nation was going soft. For them, *The Ugly American* was a call to rekindle the kind of willingness to sacrifice that Americans demonstrated during World War II, this time to help the nation fulfill its destiny of bringing American-style free markets and democracy to the rest of the world. Soon after its publication, *The Ugly American* became a lightning rod for public debate about the conduct of U.S. foreign policy, particularly in the face of what was seen as a growing communist threat to the American way of life. Its message influenced a number of political leaders, including then president Dwight D. Eisenhower and soon-to-be president John F. Kennedy. As cultural historian John Helman notes, "*The Ugly American* helped create the atmosphere in which President John F. Kennedy would call for a national fitness program, declare America's willingness to 'bear any burden,' found the Peace Corps, build up the American Special Forces, and emphasize new tactics of counterinsurgency to combat the communist 'people's war' in South Vietnam."[23] This kind of call to purification through sacrifice was consistent with America's long history of revitalization movements. It tapped that part of American culture that has long viewed the country as having a special obligation to fight evil.[24] In post–World War II America the struggle against "godless communism" fit well with a culture that saw such moral battles as fulfilling the nation's destiny.[25]

By contrast, in his novel *The Quiet American*, British author Graham Greene portrayed U.S. policy in Vietnam as an explosive mix of neocolonialism and national egocentrism. For Greene, the real motive behind U.S. foreign policy in Vietnam was an old neocolonial one, the desire to ensure that once Vietnam ceased to be a French client-state, it would become an American one. In *The Quiet American*, Greene portrays U.S. State Department officials and intelligence operatives, not as pleasure-seeking career bureaucrats, but as foreign policy zealots so convinced of the moral superiority of the American way of life that they accept the killing of innocent civilians as a lamentable but necessary means of achieving America's noble goals. For Greene, Americans are dangerous innocents who believe that whatever they can do to promote the American way of life is justifiable. At one point in the book, as a U.S. operative confronts the deaths caused by an American-instigated bomb plot against communist sympathizers in Saigon, Greene's fictional narrator says, "He looked white and beaten and ready to faint, and I thought, What's the good? He'll always be innocent, you can't blame the innocent, they are always guiltless. All you can do is control them or eliminate them. Innocence is a kind of insanity. . . . He was impregnably armored by his good intentions and his ignorance."[26] Although fiction, *The Quiet American* proved to be an accurate portrayal of how the United States initially responded to the possibility that Vietnam might become united under a communist government.[27]

In April 1954 the Geneva Conference ended the war between France and the Communist-led Viet Minh army of national liberation with two accords. The first accord called for a separation of the warring forces on opposite sides of a demilitarized zone set at the Seventeenth Parallel and an exchange of prisoners. Based on this agreement, the Communist Viet Minh forces would keep to the north, while the French would temporarily retreat south of the Seventeenth Parallel as the first step toward an orderly withdrawal from the country. The second accord specified that the division along the Seventeenth Parallel was a *temporary* military demarcation, not a new political boundary. The second accord also specified that, after a period of truce, Vietnam would be politically unified under a government chosen through nationwide election.[28]

The Paris Peace Accords of 1954 offered little comfort to U.S. leaders at the time. The Viet Minh and their Communist leader, Ho Chi Minh, had just defeated Vietnam's French colonizers. As a result, many Vietnamese both above and below the Seventeenth Parallel saw them as national liberators, not as a foreign Communist threat. To make matters worse, the more populous, northern part of Vietnam was a stronghold of pro-Communist sentiment. The result of any election would likely be a unification of Vietnam under a Communist government led by Ho Chi Minh. As part of a covert plan to forestall a Communist electoral victory, the U.S. government deployed Colonel Edward G. Lansdale to Vietnam with instructions to use his "expertise in black propaganda and every other form of unconventional warfare"—including sabotage—to intensify anticommunist sentiment in South Vietnam and weaken support for reunification under Ho Chi Minh. In words reminiscent of those used by Greene to characterize his fictional operative, historian Frances Fitzgerald describes Lansdale as someone who "had faith in his own good motives, and believed that Communism in Asia would crumble before men of goodwill with some concern for 'the little guy' and the proper insurgency skills."[29] The problem was that a U.S. policy based on a belief in the natural superiority of the American way of doing things failed to adequately comprehend the complexities of Vietnamese history and culture. Or in the words of Le Ly Haslip, a former Viet Cong operative who became a U.S. sympathizer and eventually an American citizen:

> Most of you did not know, or fully understand, the different wars my people were fighting when you got here. For you, it was a simple thing: democracy against communism. For us, that was not our fight at all. How could it be? We knew little of democracy and even less about communism. For most of us it was a fight for independence—like the American Revolution. Many of us also fought for religious ideals, the way the Buddhists fought the Catholics. Behind the religious war came the battle between city people and country people—the rich against the poor—a war fought by those who wanted to change Vietnam and those who wanted to leave it as it had been for a thousand years. Beneath all that, too, we had vendettas: between native Vietnamese and immigrants (mostly Chinese and Khmer) who had fought for centuries over the land. . . . How could you hope to end them by fighting a battle so different from our own?[30]

As a consequence, Americans found themselves taking sides in a debate over a war being fought in a place that was poorly understood by both those who supported the war and those who opposed it.

It is commonplace to characterize Vietnam as America's most divisive war, and in many ways it was. But Americans were divided over Vietnam not because a small former French colony in Southeast Asia was critical to America's future, but because it crystallized the larger debate over what post–World War II America should be. World War II had been a unifying experience for the American public and the U.S. government. Once the war ended, however, that unity began to evaporate. The United States was too diverse geographically and ethnically, too troubled by its own racial and class divisions, and too confused by its contradictory beliefs in free markets on the one hand, and in equality and popular democracy on the other, to remain unified. While many Americans saw the nation's victory in World War II as a sign that the United States had both the right and the obligation to fight the spread of Communism, others saw the nation's next important battle as the struggle for social justice at home. Consequently, many post–World War II social activists in the United States looked sympathetically upon socialist and anticolonial movements in the Third World, rather than seeing them as evils that needed to be eradicated.[31] Thus the stage for domestic conflict over the Vietnam

War was set well before the United States sent troops into Southeast Asia.

As soon as the U.S. military became fully engaged in the Vietnam conflict in the early 1960s, there was public opposition to this widening of U.S. involvement. This early opposition came not from antiwar college students but from religious groups, particularly American Quakers, as well as from political and public leaders who were wary of growing overseas entanglements.[32] The first large-scale public demonstration against U.S. military involvement in Vietnam was held in New York City in May of 1964, months *before* the Gulf of Tonkin Resolution authorized a full-scale escalation of U.S. involvement in the Vietnam War.[33] By 1966, America's expanding military role in Vietnam, and particularly the increasing sacrifice in terms of lives lost and men missing or wounded, had focused the once larger debate over the goals of post–World War II America on the much narrower issue of the Vietnam War.

Students for a Democratic Society (SDS) provides a good example of how the Vietnam War narrowed the domestic political horizon. Today, SDS is remembered as an organization of vocal antiwar activists. SDS, however, had been founded in the early 1960s as a political movement to unite white college students and white and black blue-collar workers into a new political party devoted to economic justice and racial equality.[34] Rather than being an antiwar party, it was modeled on the leftist student-worker parties of Europe.[35] Nevertheless, by 1968, the domestic programs and broad political goals of SDS had been almost entirely overwhelmed by its involvement in the growing antiwar movement.[36] In a similar fashion, for many white Americans, Martin Luther King's public opposition to the Vietnam War overshadowed his calls for a nonviolent path to racial equality and social justice in the United States. By the end of the 1960s the Vietnam War had become the focus, or in Edelman's terms, the "condensation symbol," of the struggle over what the country should become.[37]

Once joined, the debates over the Vietnam War could not end when the war was over, for two reasons. First, the debate was always over something larger than the war itself. It was about the legitimate boundaries of the U.S. role in the world, and about the relative priorities that should be given to foreign versus domestic policy problems. As a result, the Vietnam War continues to be read either as a story about why America should avoid interfering in the domestic struggles of other nations—what some have called the "Vietnam syndrome"—or as a cautionary tale about why America must be ready to commit itself *fully* whenever it finds a need to use military power to achieve its foreign policy goals.[38] Second, the Vietnam War lends itself poorly to the creation of a satisfactory national memory because it does not easily allow for a way to remember those who fought it. As Peter Ehrenhaus notes: "Only when the soldiers who come home are celebrated, when the dead are property memorialized, and when those held prisoner are returned, is there a sense that closure has been accomplished." This is not always easy, however, because "narratives of closure must always provide a focused and deliberative reaffirmation of the legitimacy of purpose for which those calls for sacrifice were issued."[39] The problem is that without national agreement on the legitimacy of U.S. intervention in Vietnam, it becomes hard to make collective moral sense out of the death and suffering that resulted from that war.

On the Run for the Wall, one way of resolving the problem of how to create an acceptable collective memory of the Vietnam War is, in the words of the t-shirt previously mentioned, to "forget the war" but "remember the warrior." Thus, nearly all of the rituals and much of the conversation on the Run focus on those, living and dead, who fought the war, rather than on the reasons for which it was fought. This is in large part why the politics of the Vietnam War are not a significant part of the public rhetoric of the Run for the Wall. During our five years on the Run there have been some group events at which speakers praised America's mission in Vietnam or condemned those who opposed the war or "dodged" the draft. These instances, however, are outnumbered by public presentations we witnessed that focused only on the dead and the missing, the need to heal the wounds of war, or the honor due Vietnam veterans because they served their country when asked. Similarly, while Vietnam veterans on the Run will often discuss their combat experiences with one another, the politics behind that combat are rarely topics of conversation. Yet for most of these Vietnam veterans, remembering the warrior inevitably means revisiting the horrors of war as well, facing the damage done to youthful optimism in a conflict where friends were killed in battles that seemed to make no sense, and experiencing again their return to a divided society that could not welcome

FIGURE 15. A symbolic POW looks out from a "tiger cage."

them home the way it had welcomed their fathers after World War II.

Thus, remembering the war and the political conflict it created is part of the Run. It cannot be avoided. But it operates in the background, more a dark presence to be disturbed very carefully rather than a constant focus. Instead, riders and Run leaders prefer to remember the dead, the missing, or the damaged, and to struggle to create a new focus and a more noble memory of the Vietnam veteran than the one they feel dominated earlier postwar years. The Run's approach to remembering the warrior while forgetting the war is perhaps best captured on a trailer that served as one of the Run's chase vehicles in 1998 and 1999.

> In an era of adversity and protest they proudly served their country. We ride in memory of our fallen brothers and for those whose fates are still unknown.

The war itself is not named, and the nature of the adversity and protest are undefined. The conflicts surrounding the Vietnam War are registered without appearing to take any stand on them, except to honor those who fought. Such conflicts are removed to a distance, while those who fought are brought into the foreground. In this way, the trailer—along with many similar messages on the Run—provides a framework for remembering the Vietnam War. The favored memory is that of soldiers doing their duty, not that of a nation at war with itself. "Forget the war, remember the warrior" messages have the positive potential of demanding that the nation accept the full human consequences of sending men and women to fight wars, including losing wars. It also has the danger of muting whatever lessons the Vietnam War has to teach Americans about foreign policy by shifting attention away from the politics of the war and onto those who "proudly served their country."

Another political contradiction on the Run is that many veterans who felt the war was wrong or futile at the time they were fighting it also feel betrayed by those at home who opposed the war. When they speak about the antiwar movement, veterans on the Run do not talk about those who fought in Vietnam who became part of the opposition movement when they returned to the United States. Antiwar efforts of groups such as Veterans for Peace and the Vietnam Veterans Against the War, the support networks that developed between antiwar groups and GIs, particularly through near-base coffee houses, as well as the increasing levels of AWOLs, desertions, and disciplinary charges against soldiers as the war progressed, all point to a fighting force that included many who were disaffected with the war, the way the government was running it, or both.[40] Nevertheless, in conversation about domestic opposition to the Vietnam War, veterans on the Run often characterize those who protested as "chickenshit college boys," "cowards," or "good-for-nothing hippies," or in similar disparaging terms. As one rider said, "The war was bullshit. But I did my duty . . . I wasn't one of those gutless scumbags who protested." For him, as for many others, there is no irony in the fact that the antiwar protesters they revile typically wanted nothing more than to bring Americans home from a war that they too thought was "bullshit." Whether or not they agreed with the goals or the conduct of the war, veterans on the Run often make it clear that they cannot forgive civilians who publicly spoke out against a war these veterans had chosen to or had been required to fight. On the matter of Vietnam veterans who protested the war, they are largely silent, although there is some sentiment that only those who served in Vietnam have any right to comment on the war. As one patch worn by several riders says: "If you weren't there, shut your mouth."

Alongside the general rhetoric about antiwar protesters on the Run, there is another theme that sometimes emerges in conversations. A few of the veterans on the Run have told us that while they do not support those who opposed the war, they feel those who took a *public* stand against the war at least demonstrated more "guts" than those who, in the words of one vet, "just took a deferment and ran." Veterans who take this position find themselves trying to balance two important elements of American culture. One is the value of patriotism expressed in the slogan "My country, right or wrong." The other is the value American culture places on "standing up for what you believe in," even if your beliefs are unpopular or if they directly challenge mainstream sentiment. From westerns in which courageous sheriffs back down the angry lynch mobs to stories about good cops fighting corrupt or cowardly police hierarchies, American popular culture is filled with heroes who defy law, cultural convention, or the social majority because they answer to a higher set of values— their beliefs about right and wrong. Indeed, pop culture figures such as Rambo and Dirty Harry are archetypes of the American male hero. As one combat veteran on the Run said in explaining his own acceptance of those who protested the war, "What can I say? We all did what we believed was right."

While veterans on the Run will sometimes admit a grudging respect for sincere antiwar activists, the same cannot be said of their attitude toward "draft dodgers." For many veterans on the Run, any draft-age man who was not in service during the Vietnam era is a "draft dodger" unless proven otherwise, even though the demographic reality of the Vietnam era suggests a different interpretation. A little more than three million Americans served in Vietnam. This represents approximately 11 percent of the twenty-seven million men who were draft eligible during the war years. An additional eight million Americans served in the armed forces sometime during the Vietnam War but were never in Vietnam, accounting for another 29 percent of the draft-age male population during the war years. In all, sixteen million American men—almost 60 percent of those who were eligible for service during the Vietnam War—never served in uniform, let alone in combat.[41] Vietnam veterans on the Run typically refer to this anonymous body of nonveterans as "draft dodgers," even though most of these men were simply not called to serve by a Selective Service System that ultimately had all the men it needed. As

FIGURE 16. Sympathy toward veterans' issues is not limited to Vietnam veterans.

one nonvet on the Run said, "I was number seven on the lottery. When I didn't hear from my draft board for some time, I got worried and called them. I thought maybe I'd missed something. But they said, 'We'll call you if we need you.' I never got called."

The hostility many Vietnam veterans feel toward "draft dodgers" reflects a wider set of issues about who did and did not serve in the Vietnam War, and about how having served in Vietnam made the lives of many veterans more difficult than those of their counterparts who did not fight in the war. Unlike veterans from World War II, a war in which military service, and even combat duty, were the norm for many men, Vietnam veterans, particularly combat veterans, inhabit a much smaller slice of their cohort. As we noted, only 11 percent of all draft-age men during the Vietnam era fought in Vietnam.

Those who did end up serving in Vietnam typically either enlisted or were unable to obtain the draft deferments or the military assignments to somewhere other than Southeast Asia that seemed to be available to nearly everyone else. For a number of Vietnam veterans on the Run, disdain for those who avoided the draft through college deferments has a social-class edge. As one veteran said, "I wasn't brought up to go to college. I was brought up to go to work, and so I got drafted." While coming from a middle- or upper-middle-class background may have insulated some draft-age men from having to fight in Vietnam, it did little to protect men from advantaged backgrounds who did serve in Vietnam from the negative effects of that experience in later life. In a study of men who had graduated from an Ivy League college and subsequently served in Vietnam, Bookwala, Frieze, and Grote found that these men were more likely to have experienced depression, engaged in frequent alcohol use, changed jobs, been dissatisfied with their career and finances, and questioned their values than men from equally advantaged backgrounds who did not fight in Vietnam.[42] Thus, regardless of social-class origins, many of those who served in Vietnam have a sense that their wartime experience has exacted a continuing price on their subsequent lives. This is why veterans we have met on the Run who came from working-class backgrounds, but who eventually returned to school on the GI Bill after the war and subsequently came to enjoy middle-class lives, still express resentment toward those who did not have to fight a war in order to obtain a college degree.

A number of the veterans on the Run who served in the military during the Vietnam War were not there by choice. They either had been drafted or had enlisted in service branches such as the Navy or the Air Force specifically to avoid being drafted and sent to Vietnam as Army foot soldiers. This latter strategy did not always work, however. As one navy enlistee said, "Shit, I enlisted in the navy to stay *out* of Vietnam, and what happens? I end up as a fuckin' navy corpsman [a medic] for the Marines." There are others, particularly former Marine combat veterans, who volunteered both for military service and for duty in Vietnam. Yet, whether they were volunteers or draftees, the smallness of their number has left many of these Vietnam veterans feeling that they belong to an isolated minority. As a result, most of the Vietnam veterans on the Run seem to harbor at least some resentment toward the vast majority of draft-age men whose lives were seemingly unaffected by the war, who did not see their closest friends killed by armed enemies, and who were able to move ahead with education, careers, and families while they themselves were fighting an unpopular war. In this sense, the general characterization of men who did not serve in uniform as "draft dodgers" is not simply an issue of whether people dodged the draft, but the result of a broader resentment these veterans feel about having been called to a duty that so many others were not asked to fulfill.

A third contradiction resides in the belief expressed by many Vietnam veterans on the Run that the United States could have won in Vietnam if the government had only committed itself fully to the war. There are two sources for this view. The first is the cultural belief in American invincibility. It simply makes no sense to these veterans that the "strongest nation in the world," equipped with a world-destroying nuclear arsenal, could have been defeated by a modestly armed Third World insurgency. From a purely military standpoint they are probably correct. What is often not added into this equation, however, is that war is only a means to political gain. Throughout the Vietnam War, U.S. political leaders remained sensitive to just how much military force the United States could apply to Vietnam without losing the support of its allies. In a secret 1967 memo to President Lyndon Johnson, Secretary of Defense Robert McNamara stated: "The picture of the world's largest superpower killing or seriously injuring 1,000 noncombatants a week, while trying to pound a tiny backward nation into submission on an issue whose merits are hotly disputed, is not a pretty one."[43]

The result of these concerns was that the United States found itself fighting a "limited" war using conventional weapons against an enemy who was far more politically capable of withstanding a long war of attrition. As early as 1966, the commanding general of the Fleet Marine Force Pacific, Victor Krulack, estimated that it would "cost something like 175,000 [American] lives to reduce the enemy manpower pool by a modest 20 percent."[44] Both President Lyndon Johnson and his successor, Richard Nixon, knew that under no circumstances would the American public support this level of loss in Vietnam. Shortly after his election, Richard Nixon redefined America's goal in Vietnam as "peace with honor" and set in motion the forces that would eventually result in the withdrawal of U.S. forces from Vietnam.

The U.S. defeat in Vietnam was political, and it was definitive. Based on this, many veterans on the Run contend that the U.S. military was never defeated in Vietnam. Instead, they portray a military that was first forced to fight with less than its full power, and then later forced to quit. This image leaves open an alternative scenario in which the war is fought in the absence of politics, and the U.S. military is free to use every weapon in its arsenal, including an invasion or the nuclear destruction of North Vietnam.

There is a second and related source for the idea that America could have won a military victory in Vietnam. Many Vietnam veterans divide Vietnam-era America into two groups, with good soldiers on one side, and bad politicians and antiwar civilians on the other. In this bipolar view of Vietnam-era politics, bad politicians, and unsupportive civilians, Vietnam veterans who feel they have been unfairly labeled incompetent warriors or violent aggressors can challenge these images by presenting themselves as good soldiers who were betrayed by those at home. In the now classic post–Vietnam War film *First Blood, Part II,* Rambo becomes the poster child for this interpretation of America's loss in Vietnam when he says, "This time, sir, do we get to win?"

What makes the belief that America could have won the war in Vietnam a contradictory one is that nearly all the combat vets we know speak about their time in Vietnam as one in which they saw little in the way of victory, and a lot in the way of confusion, failure, death, and loss. Their own experiences often seem disconnected from their view that America could have won the Vietnam War. They did not see victory themselves; there was never a light at the end of the tunnel as long as they were in Vietnam. Yet the belief that this light could have been made to appear, if only politicians and citizens had supported them, remains strong for many Vietnam battle veterans.

Like so many other questions about the Vietnam War, the issue of whether or not the United States could have won can never be resolved. Scenarios about how the war might have ended in victory for America and South Vietnam will remain forever hypothetical. They are, however, the source of a particular irony. While these scenarios help explain the U.S. defeat in Vietnam, they actually work against creating an acceptable national memory of the war. It is one thing for a nation to see its soldiers as brave warriors defeated by a superior enemy. It is quite another to remember them dying while losing a war that presumably could have been won. Serbs, as well as descendants of the Confederate States of America, for instance, have forged unifying narratives around noble defeats by more powerful enemies.[45] The U.S. losses in Vietnam, however, offer no such opportunity. A satisfying memory of war must arrange the events of that war into some *sensible* story, but it is hard to make sense out of a war if you believe it was lost for no reason. So the memory of the Vietnam War remains restless, compelling Americans to continue their search for a meaningful way of remembering that conflict. One form taken by that search is the POW/MIA movement.

THE POW/MIA MOVEMENT: REMAKING THE VIETNAM VETERAN

Almost as soon as the United States stopped fighting on the ground in Vietnam, public controversy shifted from the war itself to the U.S. government's handling of matters concerning POWs and MIAs. With the war over, many of those who had actively opposed U.S. military involvement in Vietnam resigned from the domestic debate about the war, a debate they saw as over. However, a new group of angry Americans emerged to take their place. Initially, this group consisted primarily of family members and comrades of U.S. fighters still unaccounted for in Southeast Asia.[46] In the immediate aftermath of the war, questions multiplied about whether live POWs were knowingly abandoned by the U.S. government at the end of the war, whether the Vietnamese and their allies were withholding information about American MIAs, and whether there is a shadow government working to keep the truth about live POWs hidden from the American public, providing the basis for a POW/MIA social movement.

The POW/MIA movement in the United States is a consequence of America's loss in Vietnam and the subsequent conflicts over how the nation would remember the Vietnam War. If the Vietnam War had been a popular and unifying victory for the country, it is unlikely that questions about the fate of POWs and MIAs would have sparked an intense social movement, particularly considering that the U.S. government, with the help of the Vietnamese, has managed to account for a larger proportion of Americans lost in the Vietnam War than for any other war in U.S. history. Despite this high level of accounting, anger over the government's failure to account for *all* of its missing blossomed into a nationwide social movement based on the proposition that the U.S. government abandoned and betrayed its fighting forces in Vietnam. By the 1980s this movement had grown to encompass many more Americans than just those whose relatives or comrades had never returned from Vietnam.

The growth of the POW/MIA social movement is linked to its ability to help forge new ways of thinking about the Vietnam War and the Americans who fought it. By suggesting that the U.S. government betrayed its soldiers in Vietnam, the POW/MIA movement helps keep alive the idea that the war could have been won if it were not for government officials. By focusing on those who might still be captive or whose fates are unknown, the POW/MIA movement also counters the label of Vietnam veterans as failures with the image of them as patriots who were victimized by a government that sent them to war without giving them the ability to win, and then abandoned them in Southeast Asia when the war was over. Finally, the POW/MIA movement provides symbolic recognition for Vietnam veterans who feel they were never truly brought home from the war, even though they returned to American soil.

The official flag of the POW/MIA movement is the central symbol of the betrayal and abandonment of the U.S. soldier. The silhouette of a lone prisoner is posed against a background of barbed wire and guard tower, signifying his captivity. His head bends slightly with the weight of sadness and confinement, but his back and shoulders remain upright as a symbol of his will to endure. For many, the unnamed soldier on the flag has come to stand not only for U.S. soldiers held captive in Southeast Asia, but for all Vietnam veterans who feel they have never been truly brought home to the country they left behind when they went to fight in Vietnam.

The ability of the POW/MIA movement to evoke these kinds of sentiments makes it a significant part of the struggle to reframe the public's image of the Vietnam veterans as long-suffering patriots. For instance, when the Run for the Wall, with POW flags flying from several hundred motorcycles, rides into towns on its route across America, it challenges mass media images of U.S. soldiers destroying villages and killing civilians with images of long-suffering prisoners of war, of brokenhearted families still waiting to know what happened to their loved ones, and of veterans unselfishly devoting their time, money, and energy to a pilgrimage on behalf of their fallen and miss-

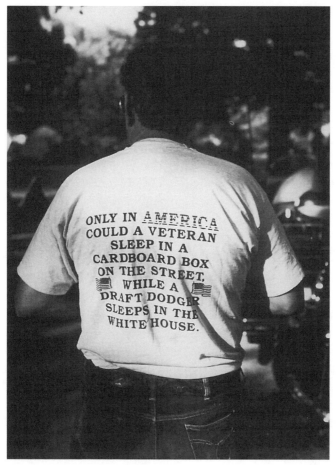

FIGURE 17. Bitterness over antiwar protests and draft dodgers is a common theme on the Run.

ing brothers and sisters. In this sense, the Run for the Wall, like the larger POW/MIA movement, operates on two levels: as an obvious political movement on behalf of Vietnam veterans who remain unaccounted for, and as a more subtle effort to redefine what it means to have fought in the Vietnam War—and by extension, to give a new meaning to the war itself.

Understanding the Run for the Wall requires appreciating at least the basic framework of the POW/MIA debate, why this debate remains so intense almost thirty years after the end of the war, and how it has generated a broad-based national social movement that has given rise to manifestations such as the Run. We begin with a brief look at the U.S. withdrawal from Vietnam.

An Unsatisfactory End

In July of 1967, Secretary of Defense Robert McNamara, who at least a year earlier had privately decided that the Vietnam War could not be won, told the press and President Johnson that the United States was not stalemated in Vietnam, and that the U.S. military was making "substantial, measurable, and evident progress" toward winning the war. Barely six months later, on January 20, 1968, the Viet Cong and North Vietnamese launched what came to be known as the Tet offensive, a coordinated attack on nearly every major city, airfield, and military base in South Vietnam. The Tet offensive was America's largest military victory of the Vietnam War and yet, ironically, probably its most disastrous political defeat. American and South Vietnamese forces achieved a ten-to-one kill ratio over their adversaries, losing 4,335 soldiers killed in action during the month-long Tet offensive to an estimated 45,000 communist fighters killed. In terms of the body count, by which U.S. military leaders measured success in Vietnam, Tet was a stunning military victory for the United States and its South Vietnamese allies.[47]

On the political side, however, the Tet offensive touched off a sharp downhill slide in public support in the United States for continued involvement in Vietnam. According to the Gallup Poll, in 1965 only 24 percent of Americans felt that sending U.S. troops to fight in Vietnam was a mistake. By 1969 this number had more than doubled, to 58 percent. Nor, contrary to popular wisdom, was this opposition to the war strongest among the young who were at risk of fighting it. Throughout the Vietnam War the proportion of those between the ages of twenty-one and twenty-nine who said they opposed the Vietnam War was *equal to or lower than* the proportion of other age groups that opposed the war. In the fall of 1969, for instance, 58 percent of those in the age group from twenty-one to twenty-nine said they felt the Vietnam War was a mistake, while 63 percent of those over fifty said they were opposed to the war.[48]

For many Americans who had believed McNamara's claim in 1963 that the United States could expect victory in Vietnam no later than 1965, the Tet offensive was the straw that broke the camel's back of government credibility. Barely two months before the beginning of the Tet offensive, General William Westmoreland, commander of the U.S. forces in Vietnam, had told the National Press Club in Washington, D.C., "We have reached an important point when the end begins to come into view." In the aftermath of the Tet offensive, Westmoreland's words sounded to many Americans much worse than unwarranted optimism; they sounded like a lie.[49] The Tet offensive became a lighting strike to the tinder of the U.S. antiwar movement. People and organizations who had been uncertain about the war swung solidly into the antiwar "Get out now" camp, joining already committed activists in highly visible antiwar demonstrations, letter-writing campaigns, and draft resistance.[50] Before 1968, a largely pro-government mainstream press had portrayed antiwar forces as mostly a campus-based movement of young men hoping to avoid military service. After 1968, as housewives, priests, ministers, doctors, and educators publicly proclaimed themselves in opposition to the Vietnam War, it had become increasingly difficult to ignore the fact that the antiwar movement had deep roots in other segments of American society.[51]

In May of 1968, under pressure from the growing U.S. antiwar movement, and assailed by his own doubts about the Vietnam War, President Lyndon Johnson limited the bombing of North Vietnam, accepted an offer from the Democratic Republic of Vietnam to begin preliminary peace discussions in Paris, and announced he would not seek reelection. In November of 1968, Richard Nixon won the presidential election as the "peace candidate" with a "secret plan" to end the war. Nixon's secret plan came to nothing, and the Vietnam War dragged on for another five years, during which Nixon's administration focused not on winning the Vietnam War, but on finding a negotiated way out that would give the United States "peace with honor." Finally, on January 27 the Paris Peace Accords of 1973 were signed. In the end, more Americans and Vietnamese were killed in the period after Richard Nixon was elected than in all the years of the Vietnam War before his election. The treaty terms that ended the U.S. war in Vietnam were essentially the same as the 1954 Paris Peace Accords that ended the French war with the Viet Minh: withdrawal of all foreign forces from North and South Vietnam, no foreign military intervention in the affairs of North and South Vietnam, and a complete exchange of all prisoners of war. In the end, after fifteen years of war, the United States was further away from its goals in Vietnam than it had been in 1954. In 1954 the United States still had a chance to make an ally out of North Vietnam and its leader, Ho Chi Minh. After nineteen years of anticommunist efforts, the United States had ensured that Vietnam would rest solidly in the communist camp.

On February 12, 1973, the Democratic Republic of Vietnam, the Viet Cong, and the Laotian Communist guerilla force, the Pathet Lao, released a total of 588 American prisoners of war during Operation Homecoming. After the release of two additional POWs, on March 29, 1973, President Nixon declared, "For the first time in many years, all the prisoners are finally home." Two weeks later Roger Shields, the head of the Pentagon's Prisoner of War Task Force, echoed this sentiment when he said that there were "no more live American soldiers loose anywhere in Indochina."[52] While this signaled the end of America's war in Vietnam, it was only the beginning of America's domestic battle over the fate of U.S. POWs and MIAs.

Counting POWs

The belief is widespread that POWs were abandoned by the U.S. government at the end of the Vietnam War and are still being held somewhere in Southeast Asia. According to a 1990 Gallup Poll, 64 percent of the U.S. public believed there were still live POWs being held in Southeast Asia. A year later a CNN/*Time* poll recorded that 70 percent of those polled agreed with the statement that Vietnam was still holding American POWs.[53] Vietnam War historian H. Bruce Franklin has suggested that the belief in live POWs has become a matter of faith for many Americans: "A prudent person would not question the existence of live POWs at a public gathering or in a strange bar, for the belief in their existence, their suffering, and their betrayal often has all the intensity of a religion."[54] This is certainly true on the Run for the Wall. The Run's official position that Americans are still being held in Southeast Asia is clearly stated by a sticker found on many RFTW motorcycles: "We ride for our *live* POWs."

As we noted earlier, the belief that live POWs remain in Southeast Asia is a consequence of America's withdrawal from Vietnam, which meant that the United States had no physical access to the places in which the war had been fought. Nor did it have much political leverage with either the victorious Democratic Republic of Vietnam (North Vietnam) or the subsequent unified Socialist Republic of Vietnam, particularly after the U.S. government refused to honor Nixon's private promise to the North Vietnamese government to provide Vietnam with war reparations.[55] With neither physical access nor political leverage there was no way to verify the Vietnamese government's claim that all U.S. POWs had been returned at Operation

Homecoming, or that the Vietnamese government was doing the best it could to account for American MIAs. After more than twenty-five years of being told by U.S. political and military leaders that Communists were "masters of deceit," many Americans had little willingness to believe the proclamations of Communist officials.[56]

No sooner had the U.S. government declared that all POWs had been returned than dissident voices began to question the administration's truthfulness. These charges were initially based on what were termed "discrepancy cases," instances in which the U.S. and Vietnamese prisoner of war lists did not agree. At the time of Operation Homecoming there were ninety-seven U.S. servicemen listed as POWs by their commanding officers who were not among those eventually released by North Vietnam. Forty-two of these were subsequently identified as having died while prisoners of war, and their remains were repatriated to the United States.[57] This left a total of fifty-five discrepancy cases involving men who had been listed as POWs but who were not accounted for shortly after Operation Homecoming. Since these men had been listed as POWs based on the best guess of their commanding officers as to their fate, some may not have lived to be taken prisoner or may have died of battle wounds shortly after being captured. There were also five other Americans who had been listed at one time by the Vietnamese as having been in custody who were neither returned at Operation Homecoming nor accounted for in any other way. Taken together, these discrepancies left unaccounted for about sixty Americans who had been listed as POWs either by the United States or North Vietnam. There is a high probability that most of these men did not survive past Operation Homecoming. As Bruce Franklin observes:

> Given the conditions of wartime in Indochina, one might expect that some men would die in captivity without the postwar government having any record of their identity and fate. In Laos, Cambodia, and South Vietnam, the insurgent fighters were under constant attack, ravaged by disease and malnutrition, and rarely able to provide long-term, uninterrupted, organized administration of large regions. As might be expected, the bulk of the discrepancies pertain to men known or believed to have been captured by guerilla forces in South Vietnam and Laos.[58]

In addition to the discrepancy cases based on POW lists, reported "live sightings" of American or other Caucasians in Southeast Asia added fuel to the debate over whether Americans had been left behind at Operation Homecoming. Between the fall of the Saigon government to North Vietnam in 1975 and 1999 there were 1,897 firsthand live-sighting reports. According to the U.S. government, 1,832 (96 percent) of these have been resolved. A total of 1,283 (68 percent) were determined to involve Americans who had been accounted for, such as civilians in prison for crimes committed in Vietnam, returned POWs, or missionaries,. Another 504 claimed sightings (27 percent) were determined to be fabrications, often motivated by the rewards that various POW support groups offered for information on captive Americans. Pre-1975 sightings accounted for another 45 reports (2.4 percent). Finally, 65 reports (3.5 percent of the total) were evaluated as possibly involving Americans in a captive environment. The frequency of these live-sighting reports shows a sharp decline over time. Sixty-four percent of the live sightings that were not ruled out as erroneous by the U.S. government occurred between 1973 and 1976, and 80 percent of all possibly valid live sightings were reported before 1985.[59]

For those who doubt that there are American POWs being held in Southeast Asia, the small number of sightings judged to have any potential value, and the rapid decline in the number of such reports after the fall of Saigon, are taken as clear evidence that no American POWs remain alive in Southeast Asia today. Indeed, in 1976 the House Select Committee on Missing Persons in Southeast Asia concluded that "there is no evidence that any of these missing Americans are still alive."[60] For those who believe in the continued captivity of Americans in Southeast Asia, however, these figures, and the House committee's conclusion, demonstrate just the opposite. The larger number of sightings between the U.S. withdrawal in 1973 and the defeat of the Saigon government in 1975 is seen as proof that the U.S. government left *some* Americans behind. The decline in reports of live sightings after the fall of Saigon is attributed to the defeat of America's former ally, South Vietnam. According to this view, the sharp decline in information that reached the United States after 1975 about possible American captives is due to the ability of the North Vietnamese victors to exert control over the entirety of Vietnam, not to a decline in the number of captives. Some POW activists also contend that the decline in live sightings after the fall of Saigon occurred because once the North Vietnamese communists consolidated their

political control over all of Vietnam, American captives with valu-
able technical information were transferred to China or Russia, never
to be heard from again. On this point, one Run for the Wall regular
said: "I don't know if any of them are still alive. It's possible. I do
know that once they were in Russia or China, these countries couldn't
afford the political fallout of admitting they were holding Americans.
So these men just disappeared." POW activists who agree with this
view can point to revelations from KGB files released in the 1990s
showing that U.S. prisoners were held by the Soviet Union after both
the Korean War and World War II, even though in the latter war the
United States and the Soviet Union were allies.[61]

The debate over POWs is often reduced to numbers and prob-
abilities. How many Americans did the U.S. government have reason to believe were still being held captive at the time of Operation
Homecoming? What are the odds that anyone taken captive in the
1960s or 1970s could still be alive today, given the conditions they
would have likely suffered as prisoners of war? From the perspective
of Run for the Wall activists, however, the purpose of their "mission"
is not defined by the number of Americans who might still be held
captive. As Skipper said in 1998, "It doesn't matter if only one American is being held captive; we'll ride until he is brought home."

Counting MIAs

Beyond discrepancies in U.S. and Vietnamese lists of American POWS
is the larger question of the fate of Americans missing in action as a
result of the Vietnam War. The problem of accounting for MIAs is
compounded by the fact that the United States did not fight the Vietnam War only in Vietnam. U.S. war efforts in Southeast Asia covered a theater of battle that included Cambodia and Laos as well.
Twenty-six percent of the 2,265 Americans the POW/MIA movement
typically lists as unaccounted for were lost in Laos (519) and Cambodia (81). Although these countries were officially neutral during
the war, both tolerated North Vietnamese and Viet Cong operations
within their borders, and both cooperated only minimally with U.S.
efforts to account for MIAs after the war was over.

Today, anyone who asks how many Americans remain MIA as a
result of the Vietnam War will find answers ranging from 2,265, to
1,100, to none. These wide variations result from two factors: the time
frame on which the answers are based and the varying definitions

that have been used to determine who remains missing. At the end of Operation Homecoming the U.S. government listed 2,265 American servicemen as MIA. Between 1975 and 1999 joint efforts by the U.S. and Vietnamese governments to locate and repatriate the remains of missing Americans reduced the number of missing to 2,069. Nevertheless, many POW/MIA activist groups continue to use the earliest postwar accounting of MIAs. On the Run for the Wall, many riders wear patches that list the number of American MIAs from each of the country's wars. The figure listed for the Vietnam War is typically the original 2,265. Using the highest possible number of cases is typical of most social movements. Anti-drunk-driving activists, for instance, typically report the total number of people killed each year in auto accidents in which "alcohol was involved," regardless of whether or not it was the driver responsible for the accident who had been drinking, or who was drunk. In a similar vein, POW/MIA activists will often report the number listed as missing in 1973 rather than in 2000.

A more difficult problem involves determining who should be considered missing.[62] At the end of the Vietnam War, the U.S. government listed 1,171 Americans as missing in action, and another 1,094 soldiers as killed in action/missing in action (KIA/MIA). This latter designation was given where there was strong evidence that a soldier had been killed in action, but his remains could not be recovered. Typical KIA/MIA scenarios involved incidents in which spotters reported that no one had escaped a disabled U.S. aircraft before it crashed, or planes were shot down over water but no bodies were recovered, or the bodies of soldiers who suffered massive wounds in battle could not be retrieved before Americans were forced to abandon their positions. Consequently, the often quoted 1973 figure of 2,265 MIAs was actually a combination of two groups, soldiers whose fate was truly unknown and others whose fate was fairly certain even though no body had been recovered. In order to clear up this confusion, the KIA/MIA designation was later changed to killed in action/ body not returned—KIA/BNR. In 1976 the Department of Defense decided to close the books on the Vietnam War by reclassifying all remaining MIAs as KIA/BNR, bringing the number of missing in action to zero by Department of Defense accounting. This was unacceptable to many MIA families because it constituted an official declaration that their loved ones were no longer alive. In response, the National League of Families, the most organized POW/MIA activist group at the time, obtained a restraining order to keep the DOD from "killing off" their loved ones. This restraining order, however, was rescinded in 1977.[63] For its part the POW/MIA movement saw this reclassification by the Department of Defense as a naked attempt to silence criticism of its handling of POW/MIA matters. Subsequent political action to retain the MIA designation led to congressional legislation establishing a Missing in Action Database under the authority of the Library of Congress. This database continues to list all Americans whose bodies were never returned to the United States as missing in action, whether they were designated by the Department of Defense as MIA or KIA/BNR, thus providing a degree of official sanction for the claim that more than two thousand Americans remain missing in Southeast Asia.

There are POW/MIA activists who claim that even the Library of Congress Missing in Action Database number of 2,069 MIAs is too low, arguing that the government continues to cover up the fact that Americans not listed in the database were lost in covert actions in Cambodia and Laos both during the Vietnam War and after the 1973 Paris Peace Accords. For instance, one of the organizers of the first Run for the Wall reports that he trained nineteen men who he knows were left behind during the Mayaguez Incident in 1975. For other POW/MIA activists, including the majority of those on the Run for the Wall, the numbers that really matter are not how many Americans are missing or possibly captive in Southeast Asia, but the number of mothers, fathers, wives, husbands, brothers, sisters, children, and grandchildren who have been left in limbo as to the fate of their loved ones, or who have no grave to visit other than the black granite marble of the Vietnam Veterans Memorial.[64] For them the Run is about ensuring that the U.S. government continues or intensifies its efforts to obtain a full accounting.

This demand for a full accounting has both political and symbolic dimensions. Demands for a full accounting of MIAs made by the Run for the Wall and other POW/MIA activists constitute, at one level, a straightforward effort to compel the U.S. government to continue pressuring Vietnam to cooperate with American efforts to locate the bodies of Americans lost in Vietnam. Beneath that message is a broader one that cautions the government to consider very carefully when and where it will send U.S. troops into harm's way. Or as

John Anderson, the RFTW national coordinator in 1996 said during a ceremony at the Run's lunch stop in Mount Vernon, Illinois, "If the U.S. government sends Americans to fight on foreign soil, it is responsible for seeing that no one is ever left behind when the war is over." Finally, the emphasis on a full accounting and on bringing the remains of the missing home to be buried in American soil is an expression of the centrality of the *individual* in American culture. This belief that the essential value of our country can be determined by how we respond to the needs of individuals is clearly stated in the slogan found on one RFTW vehicle: "If even one American is not worth the effort to be found, all Americans are at risk."

Organizing the POW/MIA Movement

The POW/MIA movement actually precedes the U.S. withdrawal from Vietnam and Operation Homecoming in 1973. On May 28, 1970, the National League of Families of American Prisoners and Missing in Southeast Asia was incorporated in Washington, D.C., with the goal of obtaining the release of all U.S. prisoners in Southeast Asia. The voting membership of the League consisted exclusively of the wives, children, parents, and other close relatives of Americans who fought in Southeast Asia and who had not been returned or otherwise accounted for. After Operation Homecoming, the League became a key clearinghouse for POW/MIA information and a focal point not only for families of those still missing in action, but also for a growing number of POW/MIA activists, particularly Vietnam veterans, who were not directly related to someone listed as MIA.

The League also created the key symbol of the POW/MIA movement. In 1971, two years before the war's end, Mary Hoff, a League member, designed and arranged for the manufacture of the League's official POW/MIA flag. Since then this flag has been a central image in the symbolic politics over America's missing in Southeast Asia. In 1988, it was flown over the White House as part of National POW/MIA Recognition Day, and a year later that same flag was installed in the U.S. Capitol rotunda, the only flag other than the U.S. flag ever to be displayed there. In 1990 the U.S. Congress designated the League's POW/MIA flag "the symbol of our Nation's concern and commitment to resolving as fully as possible the fates of Americans still prisoner, missing and unaccounted for in Southeast Asia." In 1998 Congress ruled that all U.S. post offices would fly the POW/MIA flag on national holidays. Today, the flag also flies in many other places, such as at rest stops along the New York State Thruway, on the flag-poles of businesses and private residences, on the sides of police cars in many communities throughout the United States, and on nearly every motorcycle, vest, and support vehicle on the Run for the Wall.

The League's successes in making the POW/MIA cause a national one also made it a target for criticism. Those outside the POW/MIA movement note that the creation of the League was closely linked with Richard Nixon's successful campaign to redefine the purpose of the Vietnam War. Although Nixon had promised an early withdrawal from Vietnam, both he and his secretary of state, Henry Kissinger, very much wanted a "peace with honor," that is, a way out that would not weaken America's image as the leader of the capitalist world. This meant a continued military presence in Southeast Asia until South Vietnam could be strengthened to a point at which it would be able to resist North Vietnam for a "decent interval," which would make it appear that North Vietnam had defeated only South Vietnam, not the United States.[65]

By 1969, however, the argument that U.S. men and women should continue to die in Southeast Asia in order to ensure a "free" South Vietnam was wearing thin among many key sectors of the pub-lic. To rally support for the war, political allies of the Nixon admin-istration helped form the Victory in Vietnam Association (VIVA). Shortly thereafter VIVA launched the POW bracelet project. As mil-lions of Americans began wearing bracelets inscribed with the name of an American POW, Nixon frequently played the POW card by de-claring that the United States would not withdraw from Vietnam until all American POWs had been returned. This claim was a political ploy, not serious policy, since Nixon and his advisors were well aware that wartime enemies have never exchanged all POWs prior to the end of hostilities. Nevertheless, it helped Nixon portray the North Viet-namese, who had said that they would return American POWs only after the United States had withdrawn from Vietnam, as a brutal, cold-hearted enemy against whom we should continue to fight. As the Vietnam War journalist Jonathan Schell observed, after 1970 the ma-jority of Americans thought we were fighting in Vietnam to get our POWs back.[66] It was in the middle of this political redefinition of the purpose of the Vietnam War that VIVA activists helped POW/MIA families form the League of Families, and were thereby linking the POW/MIA issue with continued support for U.S. military involvement in Vietnam.

After the war, the League was in the forefront of voices demanding that the United States defer normalizing relations with the Socialist Republic of Vietnam until it accounted for all American POWs and MIAs. The League maintains that the Vietnamese government has failed, and continues to fail, to cooperate fully with the United States in accounting for U.S. missing, and that the U.S. government should take no steps toward friendly relations based on what the League feels is the mistaken belief that this would lead to greater cooperation by the Vietnamese government. According to its own promotional material, "The League opposes steps in advance in the hope that Vietnam will act in good faith." The League's history of contributing to public support for continued fighting in Vietnam and its role in maintaining a hostile U.S. posture toward Vietnam has led some of its critics, including several former League activists, to suggest that the League has manipulated the legitimate concerns of those whose loved ones remain missing to orchestrate a right-wing chorus of support both for continued hostility toward Vietnam and for U.S. militarism in general.[67]

In recent years the National League of Families has also become a target of more radical sectors of the POW/MIA movement. The League's primary strategy has typically been to work with U.S. government agencies to obtain, as the League states on its web site, "the release of all prisoners, the fullest possible accounting for the missing and repatriation of all recoverable remains of those who died serving our nation during the Vietnam War."[68] Because of this, some POW/MIA activists have accused the League of being a willing collaborator in the U.S. government's efforts to hide the real truth about American POWs and MIAs in Southeast Asia. Between 1970 and 1990 the POW/MIA movement divided into two wings, or factions. One faction is best represented by the League and its focus on working with the government to obtain a full accounting. The other consists of Vietnam veterans and others who believe that the U.S. government continues to engage in a massive cover-up of the fate of American POWs and MIAs in Southeast Asia. This faction is best represented by a newer POW/MIA organization, the National Alliance of Families, formed in 1990.

The general outline of this suspected cover-up focuses on two types of illegal covert operations by the United States. The first was the ongoing violation of the neutrality of Laos and Cambodia. From the early 1950s until the fall of Saigon in 1975—two years *after* the United States had signed the Paris Peace Accords agreeing not to interfere in the affairs of Vietnam—the U.S. government used Cambodia and Laos as a base for secret CIA and National Security Administration intelligence-gathering operations, and as a launching point for incursions into Vietnam. U.S. planes regularly bombed suspected Vietcong and North Vietnamese supply routes in Cambodia and Laos, and U.S. troops operating out of South Vietnam conducted cross-border operations in Cambodia and Laos. The second type of covert operation involved using Cambodia and Laos as part of an opium distribution network through which U.S. operatives helped mountain tribes such as the Hmong and the Montagnards ship their opium crop via Thailand to markets throughout the world, in return for their support against the Vietcong.[69] Because these various covert operations violated both U.S. and international law, U.S. personnel who were involved, whether they were regular military or employees or contractors of government spy agencies, could not be acknowledged.[70] Even though by 1975 the struggle for a noncommunist Vietnam was over, there were several reasons why the United States could not risk revealing these covert operations by publicly acknowledging as MIAs those lost in carrying them out. First, the U.S. government could count on substantial negative political fallout both domestically and in the international arena if it admitted it had lied about its use of, and attacks on, Laotian and Cambodian territory during the Vietnam War. Second, the United States was a vocal critic of Vietnam's war against the Pol Pot regime in Cambodia. Admitting to its own violations of Cambodian territory would only weaken support for the U.S. position against Vietnam. Third, although U.S. involvement in the Southeast Asian drug trade *may* have ended with the fall of South Vietnam, some analysts suggest that because the money amassed from this trade provided a fertile funding source for other covert CIA actions against leftist insurgencies, revelations of the tainted source of this funding would jeopardize the political legitimacy of ongoing U.S. efforts to prevent socialist gains in countries such as Chile, El Salvador, Guatemala, and Nicaragua.[71] Although U.S. participation in these various covert actions is now widely known, the radical wing of the POW/MIA movement argues that because the government continues to officially deny them, it must also continue to cover up the names of those who were lost during such operations. Some POW/MIA activists, such as Monika Jensen-Stevenson and Red Daniels, argue that this continuing secrecy involves not only hiding information, but also intimidating, slandering, falsely prosecuting, or even killing those who threaten to reveal the POW/MIA cover-up.[72]

TRUTH, MISTRUST, AND POLITICAL ACTION ON A MOTORCYCLE PILGRIMAGE

The POW/MIA cover-up hypothesis enjoys wide acceptance both in the overall POW/MIA movement and on the Run for the Wall. Many of the people we have ridden with believe that American POWs are still being held in Vietnam *and* that the U.S. government has not told the American people everything it knows about who remained in captivity at the end of the war. Others may not believe that there is a cover-up of known POWs, but they do believe that the U.S. government has not spoken the truth when it claims to have done everything possible to obtain a full accounting of American MIAs.

This mistrust is the bitter harvest of the U.S. government's lack of honesty during the Vietnam War. From the end of World War II onward, political secrecy, disinformation, and even outright lies were key weapons in the government's struggle against left-wing and communist governments.[73] As early as 1946 the government began pursuing a strategy of political secrecy and covert military action to help ensure that Southeast Asia would remain within the orbit of the capitalist world. From that time until after the fall of Saigon in 1975, covert warfare, "black operations" run by military personnel "sheep dipped" to look like civilians, secret wars by proxy, and off-the-books missions in violation of treaties and international laws were a regular part of the U.S. effort to keep communist governments out of South Vietnam, and out of Southeast Asia generally.[74]

Many leaders of the national security community understood political secrecy and public dishonesty as an unavoidable evil in their fight against socialist and communist governments. They did not anticipate that these strategies would eventually become the basis for a spreading distrust of government both inside and outside the military. During the war, many soldiers learned firsthand to mistrust the government at whose request they were risking their lives. They heard presidents and defense secretaries telling the American people how close we were to winning the war, while they were fighting for their lives just to keep control of rural villages and remote fire bases in South Vietnam. They heard U.S. government officials deny that U.S. troops were fighting in Cambodia, even though, as one Run participant said, "I knew *that* was bullshit because I drove my tractor cab over the border into Cambodia hauling a trailer full of Rangers." The same was true for those who participated in the secret U.S. bombing of Cambodia. As one pilot friend of Ray's commented, "The only people it was secret from was you back in the States. I damn well knew where I was dropping those bombs, and I don't think it was a secret to anyone on the ground." For some soldiers in Vietnam, exposure to big and small lies by the government had a corrosive effect on their ability to believe in the wider sense and purpose of their mission.[75] In the end, many of them fought not because of what the government told them about Vietnam and Communists, but as we have heard so many veterans say, because they wanted to protect their friends and stay alive long enough to catch a "freedom bird" back to the world.

For those on the Run for the Wall, the mistrust of government sown by the Vietnam War extends beyond the question of what became of those who never returned. Many of the Vietnam veterans on the Run for the Wall feel that they, like the missing, were betrayed by their government. This perceived betrayal has many sources: government lies about the dangers of Agent Orange, their view that government leaders failed to make a serious effort to win the Vietnam War, the failure to honor them when they returned home, the erosion of veterans' benefits they felt they were promised when they entered the military, and a more subtle failure on the part of the government to help them find a path to follow toward their own understanding of what it meant to fight for the United States in Vietnam. The habit of mistrusting government created by the Vietnam War is so ingrained in many of the POW/MIA activists on the Run for the Wall that they would agree with Alabama senator and former POW Jeremiah Denton that "the motivation I have to believe there are Americans there, is the insistence [by the government] that they are not."[76] However, many of those on the Run would generalize this to most government proclamations, not just those pertaining to POWs and MIAs.

Today's POW/MIA activists on the Run have changed places with the antiwar protesters and "draft dodgers" of the 1960s and early 1970s. They have done more than just adopt the street politics and physical styles of antiwar protesters; they have also adopted their rhetoric about the U.S. government. POW/MIA activists who once supported the Vietnam War now say that you cannot believe anything a government official says, particularly when it pertains to the fate of U.S. soldiers left behind in Southeast Asia. Conversely, it is often now those who opposed the war who are most vocal in rejecting arguments that there are live POWs remaining in Southeast Asia, or that the U.S. government is still engaged in a cover-up of illegal actions there, or that the government has been insincere in its efforts to obtain a full accounting of American MIAs from Vietnam. Instead, many of these former government critics now take the position that the figures and explanations provided by the same government they characterized as wholly untrustworthy during the war should be believed.

In the middle of all of this are the real people who ride the Run for the Wall, or who help them along the way—people who are less concerned with large-scale political battles than with healing Vietnam War wounds that won't go away, including the sorrow of families who have never learned the fate of their loved ones, the continuing grief for dead comrades, personal demons that are their legacy of the war, and the need to make sense out of all this suffering. It is at this intersection, at this place where political action on behalf of POWs and MIAs and personal wounds connect, that the Run for the Wall becomes simultaneously a social movement and a secular pilgrimage to honor the dead and heal the living. Understanding the Run, however, requires more than simply appreciating the politics of remembering the Vietnam War, for the Run is a particular kind of pilgrimage—one that is made on motorcycles. Exploring why it is made on motorcycles, and how the larger culture of riders and bikers informs the Run for the Wall, is the next part of our journey.

4

"WE'RE NOT MOTORCYCLE ENTHUSIASTS. WE'RE BIKERS!"

Veterans, Bikers, and American Popular Culture

A warm October sun filled the living room of the house in southern Arizona where many of those attending a Run for the Wall reunion had gathered to watch a video replay of C-SPAN's coverage of Rolling Thunder '99. Interest ran high as the reporter made his way through the section of the Pentagon parking lot where Run for the Wall riders were staging for the parade. As familiar faces appeared on the screen, the watchers let out exclamations of recognition or made friendly wisecracks. About fifteen minutes into the tape, the reporter asked one of the Run for the Wall riders, "How many motorcycle enthusiasts are here today?" Immediately the room resounded with exclamations of "What?" "Are you kidding?" "Who is this asshole?" One of the men in the group summed up the collective indignation by saying, "We're not motorcycle enthusiasts. We're *bikers!"*

His statement captured the feeling of many at the reunion. They didn't just ride motorcycles; they *lived* motorcycles. As Som'r put it, "The difference between bikers and motorcycle enthusiasts is that enthusiasts own motorcycles, but bikers build their lives around them." Real bikers, she continued, are people who spend most of their free time cleaning, repairing, riding, or just talking about their "scoots," and doing most of their socializing with other bikers.

Her comments certainly applied to many of the RFTW riders in the room that day. For them, being a biker was not merely a pastime, it was a cornerstone of their identity. But what does it mean to be a biker? How is it that these two-wheeled machines have become a way of life for that subset of motorcycle riders who think of themselves as bikers? And what is the connection between biker style, Vietnam veterans, and the Run for the Wall? The answers to these questions are an important part of understanding what the Run for the Wall means to those who ride it, and even of understanding how the Run itself came to be.

The journey we detailed in chapter 2 is obviously not just a trip to Washington, D.C. It is a pilgrimage during which riders create a collective identity by sharing the political goals of the POW/MIA movement and carry out their personal search for a way to heal the emotional wounds left by the Vietnam War. But in addition, the Run for the Wall is a secular pilgrimage made *on motorcycles* and organized in accordance with a central feature of biker subculture—the *run*.[1] There are three themes in particular that link the Run for the Wall with biker subculture: the ways in which biker subculture developed initially as a form of resistance to the dominant post–World War II order in the United States; how this culture of resistance, once relegated to a relatively small segment of working-class riders in Southern California, came to dominate popular images of motorcycling; and finally, how Vietnam veteran bikers use this particular set of images to construct organizational and symbolic frameworks for the Run for the Wall.

MOTORCYCLES: FROM TRANSPORTATION TO SYMBOLS

When Otto Gottlieb bolted an engine to a two-wheeled frame in 1885, thus creating the world's first motorcycle, he was not trying to make a lifestyle statement. He was trying to solve a practical problem: how to apply the new technology of internal combustion engines to the business of locomotion. During the last decades of the nineteenth century and the first decades of the twentieth century, the motorcycle evolved alongside the automobile as a mode of *transportation*.[2] By the late 1920s, however, it was clear that the automobile, not the motorcycle, was the future of private transport. Even primitive automobiles carried more passengers and more cargo, provided better protection from the elements, and required less skill to operate than their two-wheeled counterparts.

FIGURE 18. A concern with veterans' issues is typical
of many hard-core bikers.

Once it became clear that self-powered four-wheeled vehicles were
more useful than two-wheeled ones, there were few *practical* reasons
to develop motorcycle technology any further. But the material world
is about more than utility. It is also about meaning. When the camera first appeared, for example, artists feared that painting would soon
be of little use because the camera could easily do what artists had
done for centuries—provide a visual record of people, places, and
events. Painting did not disappear, however. Instead, new schools
of painters—first impressionists and later surrealists—began using
the medium of paint and canvas to convey feelings not easily captured by the harsh realism of the camera's lens.[3] Similarly, motorcycles did not fade away when more convenient forms of transportation

appeared but instead changed their use and meaning. During the forty-year period from 1920 to 1960 the primary use of motorcycles in the United States evolved from transporting people to helping them construct and display identity. From the 1920s onward, the kind of motorcycle an American rode, the kinds of clothing associated with these motorcycles, and the kinds of behavior expected of those who rode them became increasingly important symbolically for both motorcyclists and those who watched them ride by.[4] During this same time the automobile was also becoming a symbol of identity and status, but in a way quite different from the motorcycle. Automobiles increasingly became symbols of upward mobility, membership in the upper and middle classes, and acceptance of the status quo, while the message of the motorcycle was moving in the opposite direction, as it became both a working-class symbol and an emerging tool for expressing varying degrees of rejection of the dominant order.

THE BIRTH OF THE OUTLAW BIKER

Part of the rejection of the dominant order associated with motorcycles rests with their ability to serve as an image of difference and danger. Compared to cars, motorcycles are inconvenient modes of transportation. Since the advent of the closed automobile, traveling by motorcycle has typically been dirtier, louder, windier, wetter, and colder or hotter than any comparable journey made by car. This raises the question of why someone would choose such an uncomfortable, and even dangerous, mode of travel—particularly in a society that assigns a high value to convenience and comfort.[5] There are three basic answers to this question: because it is a hobby, because it is cheap transportation, and because it has symbolic value.

Americans have a long history of pursuing rigorous forms of recreation.[6] So riding a motorcycle as a hobby does not necessarily mark the motorcyclist as someone who is outside mainstream culture, any more than does participating in other rigorous and sometimes dangerous forms of recreation such as skiing, mountain climbing, or skin diving. Such participation may be curious to the uninitiated, perhaps, but does not constitute a particular challenge to the dominant culture.[7] A similar claim could be made for much of motorcycle riding in America. For the majority of the current four million owners of road-going motorcycles in the United States, bikes are not a way of life, they are transportation, a way to spend a few weekend hours with friends riding local roads, or maybe a couple's magic carpet for a cross-country summer tour.[8] Probably fewer than a third of all motorcycle riders belong to any organized motorcycle association or club.[9] Despite their greater numbers, workers and students on utility motorcycles, wanna-be racers on "crotch rockets," and mature couples on decked out "luxo-tourers" do not dominate contemporary images of motorcyclists. In film, television, music videos, general distribution magazines, and pulp fiction, the image of motorcycles and their riders is generally that of threatening groups of black-leathered men on equally threatening machines, or loners from the margins of society heading down empty roads.[10] And this has been the predominant image for some time.

In the early days of motorcycling, and periodically since, there have been attempts to create a different image. Early ads, for example, sought to portray motorcycling as just another form of healthy outdoor exercise for adventuresome people of substance. One early ad even promoted the idea that riding in the wind was good for the "blooming complexion" of female motorcyclists.[11] These early efforts to market motorcycling as a benign middle-class pastime, however, were less than successful. As the contemporary dean of motorcycle journalists, Clement Salvadori, puts it: "For most of this century Americans have considered motorcycling to be a poor man's sport, a recreational pursuit enjoyed by the Great Unwashed, those with grease beneath their fingernails and bugs in their teeth."[12]

This link between motorcycles and dangerousness has deep roots in the fear of "the Great Unwashed" that has haunted well-off Americans since the beginnings of the industrial era in the United States. In his widely read book about the hereditary roots of deviant and criminal behavior, the social theorist Johannes Lange had this to say about motorcyclists in 1930: "I am particularly reminded of the great numbers of disgracefully careless motor-cyclists who not only make a nuisance of themselves to every one by the commotion they cause at all hours of the day, but who by their methods of driving provide constant danger."[13] This linkage of noise and danger was echoed by the police inspector for the District of Columbia in 1947 when he said: "Why do folks stand on the street corner and cringe every time a motorcycle passes? The answer is *noise*. The public associates noise with danger."[14]

But why? The simple answer is that we have a natural reaction to unexpected noise. But the fear created by the noise of motorcycles is far more than a natural response; it has longstanding cultural roots in the belief that the working class and the poor are dangerous, and this danger is manifest in and symbolized by the noise they make. Self-control is highly valued in American society, particularly within the middle and upper classes. The Protestant work ethic, so often praised as the root of America's success as a nation, is based on the proposition that the key to material and moral success is the ability to delay gratification, that is, to be in control of one's desires and passions.[15] Based on this proposition, successful Americans have a long history of blaming the existence of poverty on the lack of restraint among the poor.[16] Because we also assume that those who can control their desires are less likely to harm us or others, there has been a longstanding tendency to view the rich and the affluent as predictable and safe. By contrast, according to the Protestant work ethic, poverty suggests a lack of self-control. Thus, those who are not among the affluent are often presumed to be unpredictable and dangerous. Throughout late-nineteenth- and early-twentieth-century America, noisy public disruptions, whether boisterous drunks, screaming children, or loud domestic fights, were associated with the threat that growing waves of immigrant laborers and their families seemed to pose for the stability of American society. So-called better classes had enough self-control to avoid displaying their pleasures or sorrows in public. Those whom early-twentieth-century writers called the "dangerous classes," and whom today we call the "poor" or the "underclass," have always been associated in the minds of "solid citizens" with noise and disruption.[17] In this sense, the link between the noise of motorcycles and the danger some people imagine motorcyclists pose is rooted in the fear that American haves have always felt in the face of their have-not counterparts. Over the last seventy years or more, some motorcycle riders—particularly those who came to be known as "outlaw bikers"—have exploited this link as a way of irritating mainstream America. (Not that they are the only groups to do so, as anyone who feels assaulted by car stereos that vibrate buildings can testify.)

The connection between motorcycles and marginality predates World War II. In *Outlaw Machine*, an exploration of how Harley-Davidson motorcycles became icons of American biker culture, motojournalist Brock Yates observes that during the Great Depression, men from the industrial districts of Southern California, "embittered and disillusioned by the American dream," began to form into gangs to ride motorcycles, drink, and commit petty crimes together.[18] In the decade following World War II, the image of motorcycle-riding troublemakers would take on a new life, first with mass-media portrayals of outlaw motorcycle clubs during the '50s, '60s, and '70s, and then as a set of styles adopted by a much larger and more middle-class group—the "nouveau bikers" of the '80s, '90s, and beyond.

The late 1940s and early 1950s were characterized by the application of new military technology to the civilian world. This not only meant better cars and a whole new generation of improved household appliances, it also meant that motorcycles could be made more reliable, lighter, and easier to operate. The result was that motorcycling grew in popularity, particularly among working-class men. For the most part, until the 1950s, motorcycling was an innocent pastime that drew those who loved machines and the open road. Many rode touring bikes produced by U.S. companies like Harley-Davidson and Indian, outfitted with creature comforts such as windshields, saddlebags, and seats mounted on springs. These full-dress motorcycles, or "dressers" as they came to be known, were largely the province of respectable working-class men and women until shortly after World War II. But change was in the air, not so much in the overall reality of motorcycling in the United States, but in a shift to a new, darker *image* for motorcycling.

After World War II some alienated veterans came home, as Melissa Pierson puts it in *The Perfect Machine*, "to ride motorcycles in angry bunches."[19] In his now classic portrayal of the Hell's Angels, gonzo journalist Hunter S. Thompson similarly attributes the rise of outlaw motorcycle clubs in the 1950s to rootless West Coast veterans who could find no place for themselves in the idealized suburban, ranch-house, two-kids-and-a-station-wagon culture of 1950s America.[20] Instead, these veterans began using motorcycles as the foundation of a counterculture that was, in sociological terms, "retreatist" in character. Outlaw bikers are retreatist because their worldview rejects both the culturally dominant success goals of money and social status *and* the culturally approved means to achieve them, such as hard work, restraint, and submission to authority.[21] As writers such as Hunter S. Thompson, James Quinn, and Daniel

Wolf have shown, not only did outlaw bikers reject the 1950s version of the American dream, they saw those who enslaved themselves to the workaday world in pursuit of that dream as fools and "square johns." Instead of being diligent workers, these bikers tended to support themselves by casual labor or in some cases by petty crime, such as trafficking in stolen bike parts or illegal drugs. Instead of the rational pursuit of success, they preferred days passed in beer-soaked fogs. Instead of the safety of home and hearth, they preferred fast bikes and loose women. And instead of being busy chasing an illusive dream of suburban affluence, they opted for hanging around their motorcycles and their buddies, just having the time to ride, to "wrench," to drink, and to carouse.[22]

There was more to this emerging outlaw biker world, however, than creating an alternative lifestyle. These new outriders were not interested in simply leaving the everyday world behind the way hermits and monks have done for centuries. Instead, they wanted to confront the world they were rejecting. They wanted to annoy it. They wanted to make sure that the squares knew they were being rejected. It is in this sense that the outlaw biker subculture of the 1950s was a counterculture, a way of life designed as much to announce a rejection of the dominant order as to escape from it.[23]

In the emerging outlaw biker world of the 1950s, a certain *style* of motorcycle, and a certain *style* of presentation became prominent public symbols of this rejection of mainstream values. Instead of riding the chrome and comfort-laden dressers favored by respectable working-class riders, the new outlaw breed began transforming their bikes into minimalist machines by removing everything that spoke of luxury, comfort, and convenience: windshields, front fenders, factory saddlebags, luggage racks, and—most importantly—mufflers. As the minimalist outlaw motorcycle evolved, riders rejected the "glide" range of motorcycles equipped with rear shock absorbers that Harley-Davidson had introduced in the mid-1950s. Instead, they increasingly preferred what came to be known as "rigid" or "hardtail" motorcycles that bolted the rear wheel directly to the bike's frame without the benefit of suspension.

The image of spartan, loud motorcycles stripped of all the comforts of full-dress bikes, ridden by men who had likewise stripped their lives of many of the comforts cherished by mainstream Americans, brought a new edge to American motorcycle culture in the 1950s. As

Brock Yates puts it, "These veterans, feeling cast out of normal society, embraced the motorcycle not only as a recreational diversion but
as a weapon against the established order, a raucous, fire-breathing
barbarian of a contraption, the exhaust rattle of which was not unlike that of a .50–caliber machine gun. As weapons for wreaking havoc
among the citizenry, unmuffled Harley-Davidsons were adopted by
hundreds of restless young men flung into the ennui of the postwar
world."[24] The men who built and rode these motorcycles, and the
women who joined them, formed the basis for a new breed of motorcycle club. Club names like the Booze Fighters, Pissed Off Bastards
of Bloomington, Satan's Sinners, and the Winos announced to the
world that these were not the harmless hobbyist clubs of working-
class riders that had dominated the prewar scene.[25] These new clubs
had something to say to the wider society, and that was, "We don't
respect your world. We don't fear you. So fuck off."

In the late 1940s the emerging world of outlaw motorcycle clubs
was small and concentrated on the West Coast, particularly in Southern California, where the climate favored building a life around motorcycles. What began as a limited, local phenomenon, however,
quickly assumed a place in American popular culture vastly out of
proportion to its actual size. Analysts of U.S. motorcycle history typically credit the news media's portrayal of a relatively small-scale conflict between motorcyclists and police in Hollister, California, in 1947
as the detonating event that made the outlaw biker a fixture on the
American pop-culture scene. The reality of the Battle of Hollister, as
it came to be known, began when between two thousand and four
thousand motorcyclists rode into the small California town for a
weekend of camping and revelry centered around motorcycle dirt-
track races and hill climbs, sponsored by the very respectable American Motorcycle Association. On Friday night a group of four hundred
to five hundred riders began drinking in several bars along San Benito
Street, the town's main drag, and performing motorcycle antics in
the street and on the sidewalks. The small Hollister police force was
unable to restore order that night. In one instance, when the police
arrested some of the revelers, their buddies broke them out of the
local jail. The party continued in full swing throughout Saturday. Finally, on Sunday, the Hollister police called for backup, and with the
help of thirty California highway patrolmen and several members of
the Monterey County Sheriff's Department force, order was restored.[26]

The final toll from the Battle of Hollister was forty-nine arrests, some broken windows, and several serious injuries to motorcyclists who were the victims of their own stunt riding. The local press treated the matter as a troublesome, but not a calamitous, event. On the following Monday morning, the *Hollister Free Lance* detailed the primary offenses as "disregarding speed laws, driving motorcycles into bars, executing stunts in the middle of streets, and loosing beer bottle barrages." More telling, however, was the paper's reportage of the crowd-control strategy employed by the beefed-up police force, "Herding the cyclists into the block between Fifth and Sixth streets, the officers ordered them to disperse, and as a distraction, loaded an orchestra on a truck and had it play for the milling crowd. . . . As the cyclists stopped their 'play' to dance, officers remained, standing nearly shoulder to shoulder, keeping an eye on the dancers—nearly every cyclist had brought his 'moll' along."[27]

Any public disturbance that can be quelled by getting the troublemakers to dance hardly deserves to be called a "battle." Nevertheless, the *San Francisco Chronicle*, and later the Associated Press and *Life* magazine, reported the Hollister incident as if a new breed of barbarians had stormed the gates of civilization. The *Chronicle* headlined the story "4000 Touring Cyclists Wreak Havoc in Hollister," magically transforming *every* motorcyclist who came to Hollister that weekend into a hooligan, even though only an estimated 10 percent of the total four thousand were drinking in the town over the weekend, and an even smaller percentage were actually involved in causing trouble.[28] The Associated Press and *Life* magazine, in an early display of what would later come to be known as "pack journalism," repeated the *Chronicle*'s version that four thousand motorcyclists had terrorized the town of Hollister. They also ran a photograph taken by *Chronicle* photographer Barney Petersen that showed a drunken rider sprawled on his machine amidst a street littered with beer bottles.[29] Recent investigation by Oregon columnist and motorcycle historian Jerry Smith into the photo archives of the now dead Petersen turned up multiple versions of this photo that showed the rider arranged in different postures on his bike, and different arrangements of beer bottles, indicating that Petersen's emblematic photograph of the Hollister incident was probably staged.[30] In any case, it did not represent the bulk of the riders who came to Hollister that weekend. Yet the growing magic of postwar mass media transformed this picture into the defining image of American motorcycling for many people, both then and later.

The overblown media portrayals of the Battle of Hollister set the stage for the next step in refashioning the pop-culture image of motorcycling in America—the 1954 release of Stanley Kramer's film *The Wild One*, starring Marlon Brando as Johnny and Lee Marvin as Chico, leaders of rival motorcycle gangs who disrupt the peace and quiet of a small American town. This film introduced the theater-going public to Hollywood's image of the outlaw biker. Although Hollister was a relatively minor confrontation, *The Wild One* crafted the story into a broad warning against a new danger stalking the social landscape. To make sure audiences did not miss its message, the movie's opening scene shows an empty rural road, as an off-camera voice says, "This is a shocking story. It could never take place in most American towns—but it did in this one. It is a public challenge not to let it happen again." To some extent, the ability of the Hollister story and *The Wild One* to capture public attention reflects a larger set of beliefs in American culture. Ever since the United States began to transform from a nation of farmers into a land of industrial cities, a mainstay of American culture has been the belief that the nation's best qualities are rooted in a rural heritage that is constantly in danger of being corrupted by the disorder and sinfulness of city life.[31]

In addition to tapping the broad theme of rural purity versus urban corruption, *The Wild One* focused on a topic that concerned many adult Americans in the 1950s and 1960s—youth rebellion. In what is arguably the signature line of the film, when Johnny is asked, "What are you rebelling against?" he replies, "What've you got?" Three years later James Dean would perfect this image of aimless, disaffected youth in *Rebel Without a Cause*. In this sense, *The Wild One* was part of the larger 1950s concern with teenage rebellion and what many perceived as the nihilism of the younger generation. In the popular culture of the time, alienated youth were portrayed as dangerous youth. Along with the images of roughneck bikers, 1950s mass media introduced America to street corner hoods, fighting gangs, drag racers, and alienated young men on journeys to nowhere. The widely popular novel (and later a movie) *Blackboard Jungle* provided the public with images of street toughs taking over a New York City high school. Stories about gang rumbles were regular newspaper fare, while Leonard Bernstein's *West Side Story* raised images of gang warfare to the lofty heights of Broadway. *Rebel Without a Cause* helped crystalize public concern over angry young men risking their own lives and those of others by racing souped-up cars on lonely country roads. And Jack Kerouac's novel *On the Road*, a book that became a sacred text for some and a frightening sign of the times for others, offered up a blueprint for living life without a destination, the antithesis of success-oriented organization men in gray flannel suits.[32]

Two of the most prominent pop-culture images from this period were hoods and bikers. Although not identical, in the world of 1950s popular culture they provided parallel images of danger. Hoods were portrayed in urban settings, hanging around street corners and prowling the dark alleys of poor urban neighborhoods. Bikers, although they came *from* cities, were typically shown traveling empty stretches of country roads or terrorizing small rural towns. Despite this difference in settings, hoods and outlaw bikers were portrayed visually in very similar ways. The 1950s image of the urban tough was a young *white* man, a cigarette dangling from the corner of his mouth, a sneer on his lips, denim pants low on his hips, engineer boots on his feet, and a leather or denim jacket hanging open over his t-shirt—in other words, the same style of clothing worn by the bikers in *The Wild One* and in subsequent films about outlaw bikers.

The biker/hood image represented a significant change in motorcycle style. In many pre–World War II motorcycle ads and photographs of motorcycle clubs, male riders are typically shown wearing collared shirts, *neckties,* twill or gabardine pants tucked into knee-high equestrian boots, and military- or chauffeur-style caps. Women were often similarly dressed—minus the tie. By contrast, 1950s outlaw bikers and urban toughs are shown wearing dungarees (nobody wore "jeans" until the 1960s), heavy boots, t-shirts, and short-waisted denim or leather jackets—in other words, the everyday garb of working-class manual laborers. Also, while the leather jackets had a long history of popularity among motorcycle racers and some riders because of the protection they provided in case of a spill, those worn in films were typically more elaborate and less utilitarian than racing leathers of the time, stylistically linking them more closely to images of rule-breaking black-sheep fighter pilots of World War II than to the race track. These styles imbued hoods and bikers with an aura of danger because they hinted at social disorder. As Pierson observes, "At various times bomber jackets, aviators' caps, and cowboy and engineer's boots worn outside of their sweaty, risky, working-class applications have carried a potent charge of subversiveness. The vague twinge of fear they inspire in the ordinary citizen is due to the fluidity they recall, the refusal of the lower orders to stay in their place. The threatening symbolism of black leather motorcycle gear is only partly its kinky sexual associations; the rest is the terrible specter of the prole run amok."[33]

As the image of urban danger began to change from white working-class hoods to the unemployed black or Hispanic males in 1970s, the pop-culture style link between bikers and street toughs evaporated. But in the 1950s, if you were an angry young man, wanted to look like an angry young man, or wanted to make a movie about angry young men, the denims, t-shirts, heavy boots, and black leather jackets associated with outlaw bikers and hoods was the requisite uniform. From the 1950s and into the 1970s, this uniform was most closely associated with outlaw bikers. By the early 1980s, however, it had become the most popular style among more respectable bikers as well. Today, the majority of men and women riding on the Run for the Wall, like many other contemporary bikers, dress in styles reminiscent of early outlaw bikers. But how is it that a style that was once confined to the narrow subculture of outlaw bikers came to be the dominant style among American motorcyclists?[34]

From the release of *The Wild One* onward it is difficult to know whether art imitated life, or life imitated art. Did the popularity of *The Wild One* and the spate of bad-biker films that followed throughout the '60s help stimulate the growth of an outlaw biker culture in America? Or did these films simply reflect the fact that motorcycle barbarians really did pose a new threat to American society? The simultaneous appearance of outlaw bikers and the explosion of mass-media technology in the 1950s make it difficult to separate authentic outlaw bikers who embraced certain styles and behaviors as expressions of the actual conditions of their lives from those who copied movie and other mass-media images of how bikers *should* look and act.

There is fairly broad agreement among communications specialists that mass-media images began to play a powerful role in shaping American culture and styles in the 1920s, and that this influence

accelerated rapidly after World War II.[35] From the flapper era of the
1920s, to the hippie styles of the 1960s, to the cap-backwards jock
culture of the 1980s, to the baggy-pants gang chic of the 1990s, many
young Americans have copied styles they first encountered reading
magazines, listening to the radio, going to the movies, or watching
television.[36] It is also clear, however, that not everyone responds iden-
tically to the same images. People are selective when it comes to incorporating mass-mediated images into their lives. Not all young
people today imitate urban gang chic, not all soccer moms drive
around in SUVs, and not every young motorcyclist dreams of becoming an outlaw biker, or even of looking like one. Nevertheless, popular images and styles exert a powerful impact on the culture because
they often represent something more than just the actual number of
people who follow them.

There is little doubt that mass-media characterizations of the
prevalence of outlaw bikers, street corner hoods, and nihilist youth
were overblown. The power of these images, however, came not from
their numerical accuracy, but from the fact that they symbolized important changes taking place in American social life. One of these
changes was that children and parents increasingly lived in separate
worlds. Parents often felt they neither controlled nor understood their
children the way their own parents had understood and controlled
them. And they were right. Postwar youth spent more years in school
and had fewer work and family obligations than their parents' generation, and they were spending more and more of their free time
outside the home. The automobile and the motorcycle contributed
to the growing generation gap by helping young people escape the
surveillance of parents or community members who knew them (just
as the automobile had contributed to the freedom of the young in
the 1920s—and the bicycle before that).[37]

Meanwhile, the expanding mass-media system was playing an
ever larger role in circulating new tastes and styles among young
people. The culture of the postwar teenager was born. One version
of this teenager that appeared in the popular media was dark and
threatening, typified by biker outlaws, hoods, and nihilists who represented not so much actual characters as they did the anxieties of a
changing society. Within a decade, however, yet another set of motorcyclists would emerge as an alternative to this dark image.

ENTER THE "NICEST PEOPLE"

As the postwar world developed, teenagers began to be seen less and less as new barbarians, and more and more as new markets. In the world of motorcycling, one of the most successful marketing campaigns ever was the "You meet the nicest people on a Honda" ads of the 1960s. Honda had two goals for these ads. One was to transform the 1950s image of motorcycle riders as black-leathered, working-class toughs into an image of clean-cut, middle-class students. The other was to use this sanitized image to expand the market for the small-displacement utilitarian motorcycles that were the only bikes Honda could produce in large numbers at that time.

The campaign was effective in attracting large numbers of baby-boomer men, and some women, into motorcycling. The 1960s saw an explosion in the sale of motorcycles, particularly smaller-displacement motorcycles in the 175 to 350 cc range offered by Honda and its major Japanese competitors, Yamaha, Suzuki, and Kawasaki. Real men continued to ride Harley-Davidsons, the aging stock of Indian motorcycles, and the British bikes in the 500 to 650 cc range offered by Triumph, BSA, and Norton. But it was college-bound young men and women riding what working-class bikers often disparaged as "Jap-crap" and "rice burners" who transformed motorcycling into a semi-respectable, middle-class activity in 1960s America.

While Honda and its competitors helped make motorcycles seem more utilitarian and less threatening, they retained a symbolic value in the minds of many of "the nicest people." For many baby boomers who began riding motorcycles in the 1960s, their bikes, small and Japanese though they might have been, gave them a feeling that they were somehow different from the masses, less bound, freer. In the 1960s many young men—Ray included—defended the purchase of a motorcycle to parents or wives as an economical alternative to a second car, all the while knowing that they really wanted a motorcycle not simply for what it could do, but for what is *was*—a ticket to *somewhere else*. Motorcycles symbolized the hope of keeping a grasp on the *male* ideal of freedom, of controlling one's own destiny, at a time when the patterns of daily life were being increasingly determined by corporate and political forces that seemed beyond an individual's control.

In 1969 the Honda motorcycle company transformed recreational motorcycling in America and gave a major boost to dreams of hitting the road with the introduction of a dramatic new motorcycle, the CB750. Equipped with the first disc brake on a mass-production motorcycle, with an in-line, four-cylinder, overhead camshaft motor that had more in common with sports cars of the day than with the twin-cylinder engines of the typical motorcycle, and with unequaled reliability, the CB750 changed the motorcycling standard. As one motorcycle commentator wrote in a thirty-year retrospective on the Honda CB750, "At that moment, motorcycle history was instantly split between that which came before the CB750 and what came after. From the fall of 1969 on, nothing would ever be the same . . . in 1969, no motorcycle on the road did anything, anywhere, and for as long as you wanted to do it, half as well as a CB750."[38]

Soon every other Japanese manufacturer was offering motorcycles of similar size and virtue, ushering in the era of the Universal Japanese Motorcycle, or UJM, as they came to be known. In their various configurations, UJMs were light enough for no-hassle commuting, powerful enough to haul two people and their gear for a weekend or a monthlong trip, smooth enough to ride for hours on end, and reliable enough to set out across long stretches of uninhabited countryside without fear of being stranded fifty miles from help. They also were the death knell for European motorcycles sold in the United States. Unable to compete with the UJMs, the British trio of Triumph, BSA, and Norton lost their U.S. markets and soon went bankrupt. Other European manufacturers, particularly Italian marques such as Ducati, Laverda, Morini, and Moto-Guzzi, either withdrew or seriously curtailed their U.S. operations. Out of all the foreign motorcycle companies in the United States in the 1960s, only BMW was able to maintain a serious presence, based on the near-cult status of their machines among experienced, long-distance touring riders. Harley-Davidson, the only U.S. motorcycle manufacturer operating at the time, staggered and almost collapsed under the weight of the UJM invasion and the company's home-grown problems of ineffective management and poor quality control. Between 1969 and 1980, Harley-Davidson's share of the U.S. motorcycle market plummeted from 80 percent to 30 percent.[39]

Whether they rode little Japanese runabouts, UJMs, Harley-Davidsons, Brit bikes, or BMWs, for many motorcyclists of the 1960s and 1970s their machines were a symbolic (and sometimes actual) ticket to somewhere more exciting, to a *journey*. Even if an extended physical journey was not possible, many riders came to feel that their motorcycles could take them on an inner journey to new levels of understanding and awareness. There was really nothing new about this desire for liberating journeys. The motorcycle has long been an enchanted machine, for it touches on important themes in American culture, among these the open road as the image of freedom, and the value of self-improvement through self-awareness.

FREEDOM AND THE OPEN ROAD

More than a hundred years before the motorcycle boom of the 1960s, Walt Whitman wrote:

> Afoot and light hearted I take to the open road,
> Healthy, free, the world before me,
> The long brown path before me leading wherever I choose.
> Henceforth I ask not good-fortune, I myself am good-fortune,
> Henceforth I whimper no more, postpone no more, need nothing,
> Done with indoor complaints, libraries, querulous criticisms,
> Strong and content I travel the open road.[40]

Like Whitman, Johnny says in the opening narration to *The Wild One*, "This is where it begins for me, right on this road." Indeed, if you change "afoot" to "astride" in Whitman's poem, it reads like the text of a modern ad for hitting the road on your motorcycle. One 1999 ad that appeared in a number of mainstream motorcycle magazines posed two motorcycles against the backdrop of the open West above the words "It's a free country. Act like it."[41] Another ad common that year was even more explicit in its portrayal of the motorcycle as an escape pod for the American male from the constraints of everyday life. The visual image is a motorcycle cockpit, gloved hands on the bars, an open road ahead. The copy reads, "Monday's gaining on you ... with all its responsibility and commitment. It whines in your ears and nips at your heels, but you've got 1500 reasons not to turn back, a virgin stretch of highway and a three day beard.... So roll on the throttle, Monday can kiss your saddlebags goodbye. Don't stop!"[42]

Such images resonate with an idea that has played an important historical role in American ideology and popular culture—the concept of the frontier, a space that is open, empty, waiting to be explored and conquered. While such a frontier has long disappeared (and indeed the frontier as an empty space never really existed in America in any case, as these "empty spaces" were already populated by native peoples), it can be recaptured through modes of travel that create the illusion of exploring new space by moving down the road.[43] Thus, while leather-clad bikers and senior citizens living full time in their RVs would seem to have little in common—the one traveling on the most minimal of vehicles, the other literally taking their houses with them—they share a sense of being frontiersmen and pioneers. Among RVers who "boondock"—that is, camp out in the open, away from the amenities of RV parks and hookups—there is a particularly strong sense that they are recreating the life of their ancestors. As one RVer put it, "To me, we are the pioneers of our century."[44] RVers also share with bikers some other important characteristics: an emphasis on freedom and self-reliance, a sense of community with others who share their particular mobile lifestyle, and a feeling of living on the margins of the larger society (in the case of RVers, based on both their gypsy life and their age).

This image of the motorcycle (or RV) as the key to the open road captures an important characteristic of the American idea of freedom. Within American culture the dominant image of freedom is what political analysts refer to as *negative* freedom, that is, a *freedom from* constraints that individuals or governments might place on us.[45] The evolution of freedom as both a historical and legal force in American society has focused primarily on limiting the ability of governments to interfere with public or private speech, the press, the practice of religion, and the use of private economic power to one's own best advantage.[46] With the rise of consumer culture in the twentieth century, the idea of freedom has also come to include the right to appear and behave in whatever way expresses one's chosen lifestyle without interference from others. Motorcycles are perfect vehicles for pursuing this conception of freedom.

In a culture that understands freedom as freedom from constraints imposed by others, aloneness, or at least the image of aloneness, has a powerful appeal. As Philip Slater noted some time ago, American culture embraces the "pursuit of loneliness," in the sense that we often search for ways to be free from the limitations that relationships place upon our freedom to do what we want, when

we want to do it.[47] Of course, if we have no relationships to constrain us, we are also completely alone. The importance of the open-
road image in American culture has much to do with the desire to
be free from the constraints of others. The road has come to symbolize a place where all possibilities lie ahead, where nothing in our past
can stop us, and where our aloneness ensures that there is no one to
intrude on our private journey. This is why scenes of empty roads
stretching into the distance are typical fare whenever movies, TV
shows, or advertisements want to say something about freedom. There
are no houses, no other vehicles, no signs of civilization, nothing to
intrude. This same set of cultural images links motorcycles and freedom in biker culture.

Whether it is in ad copy, motorcycle journalism, or just conversation among bikers, no word is used more frequently to describe the
experience of riding a motorcycle than "freedom." This is certainly
true on the Run for the Wall. Whenever riders on the Run talk about
why they ride, the conversation inevitably revolves around the idea
that the road is the one place where you are free from the stresses
and constraints imposed by everyday life. Motorcycles can deliver, if
only for a brief time, an idealized sense of aloneness. Pierson puts it
this way: "It is possible to feel more alone on a motorcycle than anywhere at rest. . . . On a bike there are people all around, in a car in
the next lane and not five feet away, but they can't get you. You can
ride away alone. You are spared the burden of words, the responsibility of a cogent reply."[48] Gary Garripoli, practitioner of the Chi-
nese healing art Quigong and author of *The Tao of the Ride: Motorcycles
and the Mechanics of the Soul*, offers a similar description of the
motorcycle's ability to deliver freedom through aloneness: "There is
something about being alone on a bike, cruising down the road in
the silence of a loud engine and pounding wind. In these moments
everything can seem perfect. . . . No one and nothing can touch
us. . . . When you shed the restraints of what other people expect from
you, you are free. Isn't that one reason why people like to ride motorcycles? No restraints, no safety net, nothing to hold you back?"[49]

Many of those on the Run for the Wall are very explicit about
the idea that the freedom of the road is the freedom from the pres-
sures and unpredictability of daily life: "Being on my bike is the one
place where I feel like I'm in control of my life." "When I get out on
the road I feel like I've just gotten out of jail." "There's nothing like

it. It's the only place I'm free from all the bullshit around me." Comments like these are routine whenever Run for the Wall bikers talk about riding. One Run for the Wall friend, Revvv, who is both a dedicated biker and staunch anti-helmet-law activist, signs all of his written communications, "There is freedom in the wind," communicating both his general belief that motorcycling is freedom, and his more specific political opposition to any government that would interfere with his freedom to ride in the wind by forcing his head into a helmet.

The link between freedom and aloneness in motorcycle culture may mean an escape from the demands of others. But it also means that no one but the rider is responsible for the decisions he or she might make. This ideal resonates well with the American belief in individual responsibility and the related view that people deserve to suffer the consequences of their foolish actions, as well as to reap the rewards of their wise ones. The link between freedom and responsibility on the road was captured in a debate concerning where the following year's Run should begin among those attending the 1997 RFTW October reunion in Payson, Arizona. Some riders supported the traditional starting point of Ontario, California, while others argued in favor of beginning at the Queen Mary in Long Beach. The main objection raised to starting in Long Beach was that taking a group of riders through morning rush-hour traffic in the greater Los Angeles area would expose the long line of bikes to more risk of accidents than leaving from the outskirts of Los Angeles. In response to these concerns, Skipper, who would be leading the upcoming year's ride, said it did not really matter whether or not people would be riding through the L.A. area in a group, because "in the end, everybody rides their own ride."

MOTORCYCLING AND THE INNER JOURNEY

While the road has long been a prominent symbol of freedom *from*, in more recent years it has also become a symbol of a positive freedom *to*, in this case to develop self-awareness or find emotional peace. This idea of a motorcycle journey as a pathway to awareness or inner peace resonates with the American concern with the self, and also with the idea of spiritual search, especially in the wilderness—an idea that reaches back to many early- and mid-nineteenth-century Ameri-

FIGURE 19. Run for the Wall road guards get instructions before riding to Rainelle, West Virginia.

can thinkers, particularly the transcendentalists such as Ralph Waldo Emerson, Walt Whitman, and Henry David Thoreau. This attention to self-improvement derived from the belief that in a rapidly developing industrial society filled with new opportunities, people can and should work to make themselves better than they are. Throughout the balance of the nineteenth century and the first half of the twentieth century, much of the attention on self-improvement was externally focused, that is, on acquiring the education, skills, and personality that would lead to advancement in the work world.[50] Beginning in the 1950s, the concept of self-improvement developed an equally strong inward-looking component. From the 1960s onward, a rapid growth in the professions of psychiatry, psychology, and counseling, and the emergence of an annual flood of self-help books aimed at people who want to change some part of their "inner self," made therapeutic approaches to life a prominent part of American culture. The essence of this approach is the belief that most of the difficulties in our lives result from some kind of psychological or emotional dysfunction, or, alternatively, from not being true to ourselves. If we look inward, we can discover and then rectify this dysfunction and rediscover our "true selves," thus resolving the problems that rob us of peace of mind.

Motorcycling followed this therapeutic turn with an emphasis on riding as a psychological and emotional journey. *Zen and the Art of Motorcycle Maintenance*, first published in 1974, introduced America to the pop-culture notion of inner discovery through the motorcycle journey. Interestingly, this book continues to be displayed in many major bookstores in the psychology or self-help section. Since then the idea that motorcycles lead us not only down the road but also into ourselves has become a mainstay of motorcycle culture in America. Nearly every book about extended motorcycle journeys treats the inner journey as an important part of the story being told, from Ted Simon's *Jupiter's Travels,* which detailed his world tour on a two-cylinder Triumph in the 1950s, to Ed Culberson's tale of riding the Pan-American Highway in the 1970s, *Obsessions Die Hard,* to *Investment Biker*, the story of an upscale banker's motorcycle journey around the world in the 1990s.[51]

Unlike the search for freedom from others on the road, the inner journey is not necessarily a self-absorbed one. For many riders the inner journey is about the connection to the physical world that results from intense experiences of such things as smells, visual images, heat, cold, or wetness that envelop them as they move through space unprotected by the body of a vehicle. Ray's own story of his first motorcycle ride is a good example of this sensuality. In the pre-dawn hours of a spring morning in 1967, he circled the island of Manhattan on a borrowed motorcycle. The way the smells changed as he rode past one neighborhood after another gave him a deeper appreciation for the ethnic complexity of life in New York City than anything he had ever experienced before and made him a lifelong motorcycle rider. This sense of connection to the outer world frequently turns up in the daily conversation of riders on the Run for the Wall. It is the rare gas stop or lunch break that does not involve at least some conversation about how it "felt" out there. The heat, the cold, the wind, the rain, and, on some occasions, the snow fill large blocks of talk time. Nor is this just chatting about the weather. By talking about these common experiences, riders forge bonds with one another as comrades who share a world of experiences that differentiate them from people who ride around in "cages."

Another component of the heightened awareness of physical surroundings that happens on a motorcycle is an increased sense of danger and vulnerability. The knowledge that a flat tire, the sudden appearance of a deer in the road, the unpredicted actions of another driver, or the rider's own error could turn a pleasant journey into a nightmare is always present. We have yet to meet a rider who does not know someone who was killed or seriously injured in a motorcycle accident. At the same time, this sense of danger is an important part of both the inner journey and the heightened connection to the world. As Gary Garripoli writes, "How exposed I am, how sensitive the controls are, how close I am to the pavement. It wakes me up and brings me to a place of sheer connection with everything about who I am, my mood, my fragility, and my incredible sensory system that even allows me to ride this 650 pound beast."[52] There is an attraction for many people in being made aware of this fragility, in sensing the smallness of their existence. They feel it creates both a deeper appreciation of life, and a liberating sense that we are only a small part of something very much larger. The exhilaration of getting off the bike safe and sound after facing the dangers of a day's ride is a feeling that every motorcyclist knows. And like any drink or drug that alters our consciousness of the world, it is an experience that riders continually seek to repeat.

For at least some of the Vietnam combat veterans who ride the Run for the Wall, this inner journey is not about self-development; it is about not going crazy. For them the road is where they find temporary peace, as the roar of the wind and the thunder of the bike overwhelm the voices from their past that make peace of mind rare and precious. These moments are not a luxury; they are essential. Corporal, an RFTW regular whose post-Vietnam life has been a long struggle against the physical and emotional wounds left by the war, put it this way: "I ride my bike to stay sane. The last time they let me out of the loony bin, I got this bike. It's just about the only thing that makes sense to me. Without it, and the stuff I take for pain, I'd be locked up somewhere again." Another RFTW rider, whose high-stress career collapsed with the onset of PTSD nearly a quarter century after he left Vietnam, put it this way: "When I wasn't working, I was out riding my bike at a hundred miles an hour in the dead of night. It was all that kept me together. It was the only place I could escape the pressure. When I couldn't take the stress, I'd go out and ride. Now I'm dealing with different things, but that's still the only place where I can find some space when everything seems like it's closing in." Yet another Vietnam combat veteran, Puma, who also lost his ability to practice his profession as the result of PTSD, said: "It's hard not being able to work at a regular job. Isn't that what you're supposed to do? What am I supposed to do with myself? When I'm riding, I feel like I'm doing something." For these Vietnam veterans, and so many others like them we met on the Run for the Wall, motorcycles are no more optional than the Valium or Prozac so many other Americans take to quiet their personal demons. And barring a crash, their inner motorcycle journeys are probably less physically destructive than chemical sedatives.

THE "NICEST PEOPLE" BECOME THE NICEST OUTLAWS

The link between popular images of motorcycles and core American values, along with the sanitizing of motorcycle culture that took place in the 1960s and 1970s, would suggest that the bad-boy image of motorcycles and their riders has faded into the past. But instead, something curious has happened. Beginning in the 1980s, what had once been the outlaw biker subculture became part of mainstream American motorcycle culture. Loud, low-slung, V-twin motorcycles customized with quantities of aftermarket accessories, black leather jackets or denim vests, back patches that mimic the colors of outlaw biker clubs, long hair, tattoos, and male jewelry are now the dominant motorcycling fashion for many middle-class and solid working-class Americans.

By the mid-1980s the term "biker" had come to encompass those for whom riding a Harley-Davidson (or Harley look-alike) and dressing in semi-outlaw fashion had become an important source of their identity, even though they were not living on the economic or moral margins of the society. For many Americans, one's true identity is increasingly expressed through one's choice of leisure activity rather than through work or profession. Avocation, rather than vocation, becomes the statement of self and is reflected in the dedicated pursuit of one's chosen recreational activity and in a diverse array of symbolic objects, from clothing to bumper stickers ("I'd rather be golfing," "I'd rather be sailing," etc.). In addition, recreational activities often serve as the basis for the construction of community, replacing or supplementing other forms of community based on geography, class interests, or ethnic and religious identity. Whether it is white-water rafting, model railroading, rock climbing, or motorcycle riding, recreational activities bring people together on a regular basis, allow them to share a common interest, and provide the context for forms of interaction and community that may go well beyond the specific activities themselves.

HARLEY-DAVIDSON, THE NEW AMERICAN ICON

It is more than clothes and other accessories that create the biker. The key element of the growing biker culture is the motorcycle itself. The "real thing" in biker culture has always been Harley-Davidson motorcycles. Hunter Thompson's BSA motorcycle was tolerated by the California Hell's Angels he wrote about, but real Hell's Angels rode Harleys. More recently, Daniel Wolf in *The Rebels: A Brotherhood of Outlaw Bikers* offers this quote from a Texas biker: "To some a Harley is just another motorcycle. To a biker a Harley is magical, for only a true biker can bring a Harley to life, and in return, only a Harley can bring life to a biker."[53]

This devotion to Harley-Davidson motorcycles is not because they represent cutting-edge motorcycle technology. In fact, their appeal is quite the opposite. For many contemporary riders the appeal of Harley-Davidsons is not their technological efficiency but their *symbolic* utility. For Harley lovers, nothing symbolizes the true history and the true values of American society better than a Harley-Davidson or—for those who cannot afford the real thing—a Harley-Davidson look-alike. This is why Harleys are seen as more desirable than either the latest high-tech crotch rocket or comfort-laden luxo-tourer. For a time, writers in the mainstream motorcycle press were puzzled and at times even expressed annoyance that so many riders seemed to prefer Harley-Davidsons over motorcycles from Japan and Europe, even though these foreign bikes were typically more reliable, more powerful for their size, better handling, and less expensive than Harleys. They were even further confused when Japanese manufacturers, hoping to cash in on the Harley phenomenon, began to deliberately take quiet, powerful, vibration-free engines and modify them so they would shake and roar like Harleys, in the process turning them into less powerful, less efficient, and generally cruder engines than they had been. For those who valued the ideals of smoother, faster, and more efficient, this backward-looking design trend was the height of technological insanity.[54]

During the 1960s and 1970s, Harley-Davidson motorcycles had acquired a well-deserved reputation for unreliability and poor quality control. Pre-1980s Harleys were so notorious for their mechanical shortcomings that even Harley riders told jokes about them, such as "Buy Harley, get the best. Ride a mile and walk the rest," or "Ninety percent of Harleys ever made are still on the road. The other 10 percent made it home." At one motorcycle gathering we attended, the band leader in the lounge at the local motel told his audience, "I'm a biker myself. I know the Harley position." With that, he squatted down, looked straight ahead as if staring at a motorcycle engine, put on a mournful face, and said, "Awwwww, shit!" Another common joke asks, "What do Harley-Davidsons and hound dogs have in common?" The answer is, "They have the same initials. They both spend a lot of time riding around in pick-up trucks. And they both always mark their spot"—this last comment is a reference to the tendency of pre-1980s Harleys to routinely leave small, and sometimes large, puddles of oil under their engines.[55]

The main cause of Harley unreliability was vibration. The design of Harley-Davidson engines, with two cylinders set at a forty-five-degree angle, creates strong primary vibrations, and the larger the cylinders, the more vicious the vibration. This constant shaking tended to loosen fasteners and destroy electrical components. During the 1996 Run for the Wall, for instance, a 1970s-era Harley riding in front of us lost a rear turn signal assembly, which barely missed hitting us as it bounced down the road. At the next stop we learned that the problem occurred when the bolt that held the assembly to the rear fender had vibrated loose.

In 1983 Harley Davidson replaced its cast-iron shovelhead engine with a new aluminum motor, the first new engine design for Harley since 1936. Although retaining Harley's signature forty-five-degree V-twin layout, the Evolution engine, or Evo, as it came to be known, benefited from modern design and materials, plus a new system of mounting the engine to the frame with composite rubber bushing that isolated the rest of the motorcycle from the potentially destructive vibrations of the engine. Although they helped substantially, these improvements still did not yield the level of reliability typical of most four- and six-cylinder Japanese motorcycles. At the

Columbus Day RFTW western reunion in 1999, for instance, a gathering of riders were talking about their Harleys. One of them asked the group how many had either replaced their motors or had faced major engine work. Six of the eight Harley owners there had experienced one or the other, and in most cases these repairs took place on motorcycles with less than fifty thousand miles behind them. In contrast, many other brands of touring motorcycles, such as Honda Gold Wings, Yamaha Ventures, and BMW RT models, commonly run eighty to a hundred thousand miles or more with only routine maintenance. But, as those assembled said, the pleasure of a Harley is not in its reliability. It is in the history, the look, the feel, the sound, and for the male riders, the admiring looks you get from female "hard bellies" as you ride by, even if you are a graying, middle-aged man.

For many bikers, the automobile-like reliability of foreign motorcycles is not even desirable. For them motorcycling is about an intimate relationship with a machine, a relationship that is itself part of the rider's identity. Perfect motorcycles may not be the ideal counterparts for imperfect people. A perfect motorcycle does not invite the rider into a mechanical, grease-under-the-fingernails relationship with it, or with other bikers. Biker-author Bob Bitchin put it this way: "The fact that Harley's broke a lot was an asset. You'd be parked at the side of the road, working on a busted chain or bad coil, and sure enough, another biker would stop and help. You'd meet all kinds of good friends that way. It was a brotherhood built around a machine that wasn't perfect, just like the people who rode them."[56]

In addition, being able to work on your own motorcycle, to modify it to your own needs and tastes, and to display your knowledge about bikes are important in demonstrating that you are a real biker, someone who is competent and self-reliant. As Daniel Wolf points out, riders earn status by being able to work on their own motorcycles: "Club bikers take their motorcycles seriously . . . conversely they take a dim view of an individual who would flaunt the symbol of their lifestyle without having earned it." In this sense, "customizing is an exercise in identity construction. A biker builds a very personal bond between himself and a mechanical reality that he designs, creates, and then maintains."[57]

The way that bikers value Harley-Davidsons for their symbolic rather than their technological attraction reflects a wider trend in contemporary American life, the search for identity through objects. In

The Tourist, social analyst Dean MacCannell observes that "modern materialistic society is probably less materialistic than we have come to believe." Rather, the value of material objects increasingly derives from how they make us feel about ourselves rather than from what they are or what they do.[58] Wolf echoes this idea when he writes, "A biker is a man who has turned to a machine to find himself. He has learned how to find both meaning and pleasure in the man-machine relationship, and he uses his motorcycle to create peak emotional experiences that are worth living for."[59]

For many who have adopted outlaw style, their Harleys are what makes it possible for them to feel like bikers, in large part because others ascribe that identity to them as they ride by in a flash of leather, chrome, and noise. None of the rationalist, technological critiques of Harley-Davidsons really matter in the face of the identity a Harley bestows on its owner. As one motorcycle magazine commented, "Hard-core Harley riders aren't like other people. They display a dedication to their American-made iron as dogged as Kenneth Starr's to crucifying Clinton."[60]

Such dedication comes from a number of different sources. Two of the most important are patriotic belief in America's moral superiority as a nation and the continuing value attached to individuality in a mass-market society.

Patriotism

The valorizing of Harley-Davidson motorcycles within American biker culture has always been closely tied to nationalist sentiments. The veterans who first forged this outlaw culture in the years after World War II typically rode American or British motorcycles.[61] Even though early outlaw clubs favored Harley-Davidsons, many would accept those who rode Triumphs and BSAs as members. More important than riding a Harley was that you did not ride a motorcycle built by one of America's recent enemies. For men who had fought for America against Germany, Japan, or Italy, riding motorcycles made in these countries seemed like collaborating with the enemy. For a time, motorcycles made by America's British allies were acceptable, although eventually even these were prohibited as outlaw clubs began to mandate that their members ride Harley-Davidsons.[62]

One of the seeming ironies about outlaw biker culture is that, while it may symbolize rejection of mainstream American lifestyles, it remains deeply attached to traditional American ideals and to a patriotic vision of the United States. From the mid-1950s until the late 1990s, when Harley-Davidson was the only U.S. motorcycle manufacturer operating in a market increasingly dominated by Japanese imports, riding a Harley-Davidson was almost as patriotic as saluting the flag, in the eyes of many hard-core bikers. In addition, Harley-Davidsons have always been working-class symbols. In the minds of many they symbolize an industrial system built by generations of working-class Americans. From this standpoint, buying a foreign motorcycle was a betrayal of America's working class in much the same way that driving a Toyota or a Honda was seen as an insult to U.S. auto workers in the 1960s and 1970s. As one Harley rider put it: "It's an attitude and ego thing. If you're an American, you have an attitude, and if you have an ego you don't want to be seen riding foreign junk."[63]

In addition, while foreign motorcycle manufacturers of the 1960s and 1970s were pursuing the art of building small, efficient machines, Harley-Davidson continued to produce motorcycles in "the American tradition followed by Lincoln and Chrysler, with more chrome and bigger size and the motorcycling equivalent of Buick's portholes, and lots of sheet-metal surfaces to accept gorgeous paint."[64] In this sense Harley-Davidson motorcycles attracted a dedicated American following because these machines remained true to the American ideal of expansiveness.

Despite the patriotic loyalty to Harley-Davidsons among the faithful, the company fell into increasingly hard times beginning in the late 1960s and continuing into the 1970s. In part this reflected problems with the motorcycles themselves, but it also reflected a wider disenchantment with the view of the United States as the ideal country. The unsuccessful end of the Vietnam War, the oil embargo, and an era of stagflation during which the cost of goods and loans rose far more rapidly than wages eroded the confidence that many Americans once had that they were living in the best nation on earth. In this context, U.S. products—motorcycles included—lost some of the halo they had long enjoyed in the eyes of U.S. consumers.

There was a substantive reality behind this decline in Buy America sentiment as well. The United States had emerged from World War II as the only major power whose industrial base had not been heavily damaged. This gave U.S. industry a powerful competitive advantage in the marketplace. By the 1960s, however, Britain, Germany, Italy, and particularly Japan had rebuilt their industrial base with new technology and new strategies for production, while in many industries the United States lumbered on with production technology that often dated back to the 1940s or earlier. As a result, in the eyes of a growing number of American consumers, U.S. products—particularly vehicles—began to look shoddy and unreliable in comparison to foreign ones. First Volkswagens and Volvos, and later Toyotas and Hondas, began to replace Chevys and Fords as symbols of reliable everyday transportation. Sony and Panasonic, rather than RCA and Motorola, became the sought-after name brands in radios, televisions, and stereos. American products lost some of their ability to confer social status on their owners, as well. In many upper-middle-class neighborhoods, Mercedes-Benz sedans, and later, upscale BMWs and Volvos, replaced Cadillacs and Lincolns as signs of having arrived. Similarly, while outlaw bikers and other working-class riders remained loyal to their Harleys, it was Hondas, Yamahas, and Kawasakis that became objects of desire for many middle-class riders in the '60s and '70s. This shift also reflected the fact that the postwar World War II generation saw little stigma attached to owning German and Japanese products, unlike many of the older generation who remembered when the makers of these products had been the enemy.

Then in the 1980s, this pattern began to reverse itself. By the late 1980s U.S.-made Harley-Davidsons had become the new status symbol in motorcycles, just as American-built trucks and what eventually came to be known as SUVs had become the new symbols of status in the world of four-wheeled vehicles. This change is the product of both material and symbolic factors. At the material level, in the 1970s the United States began a radical transformation of its economic system that involved the relocation of many industrial jobs overseas and the development of powerful, computer-based systems of production, distribution, and management that made it possible for U.S. corporations to control new worldwide economic empires from strategic global cities in the United States.[65] This transformation jump-started the U.S. economy. The rapid growth of upscale suburban neighborhoods in the developing cities of the New South, the highways filled with new, ever-more-expensive vehicles, and the boutiques and name-brand coffee shops of revitalized urban centers were, in the eyes of many Americans, evidence that happy days were here again.

By the 1990s most Americans believed that the nation as a whole had returned to good times, whether or not their own fortunes had improved. [66] One consequence of this return to economic growth was a renewed pride in American-made products.

In addition to the material gains of the 1980s, the United States underwent a rebirth of patriotic sentiment that began with the election of Ronald Reagan. In many ways, Ronald Reagan, the cowboy actor, took America back to its pre-Vietnam glory days when men were men and the United States ruled. Reagan spoke the language of the frontier, of an imaginary world in which there is "no society, only individuals," of self-reliance, and of America's natural right to dominate the world. Reagan backed up this promise with an embarrassingly small but very successful "war" against Grenada, a proxy war against the socialist government of Nicaragua, and the most costly peacetime military buildup in the nation's history, which forced the Soviet Union into a financially ruinous arms race. Reagan's frontier rhetoric and his quick-draw military policy helped restore national confidence in U.S. military might and bolstered the belief in the minds of many Americans that we really are the good guys.

And then in 1990, George Bush sent U.S. troops to "kick some ass" in Iraq. Their success in turning what Iraqi leader Saddam Hussein had promised would be the "mother of all battles" into a killing field of Iraqi dead restored U.S. fighting men and women to the status of heroes, an accolade that had fallen into disuse during and after the Vietnam War. As one Vietnam veteran on the Run for the Wall said, "When I saw those troops being welcomed home from Iraq, I knew it was okay to be a veteran again. It made me angry that I wasn't welcomed home like that, but I was glad too." The Reagan-Bush era and the U.S. success in the Gulf War certainly did not eliminate the lingering political and cultural consequences of the Vietnam War, but it did create a climate in which more people felt proud of the United States and its military endeavors abroad. And for many motorcycle riders, this pride is expressed by riding the motorcycle that symbolizes American industrial history, the Harley-Davidson.

Individuality

During the '50s, '60s, and '70s, long, low, custom-looking motorcycles had been the exclusive province of working-class men who spent nights and weekends in backyards, garages, and gas stations, where they modified stock machines. However, in the early 1980s, under the design influence of Willy G. Davidson, grandson of one of Harley-Davidson's original founders, the company began mass producing and marketing motorcycles with a custom look. The genius of Harley-Davidson's strategy was to combine visual elements of actual choppers and custom bikes with mass-media images of outlaw motorcycles. Now you no longer had to be a mechanic or an outlaw to ride a bad-ass bike. One of Harley's most popular models has been its soft-tail line. These bikes are designed around a hidden rear-suspension system that mimics the hard-tail look of outlaw choppers without the discomfort and control problems common to hard-tail hemorrhoid specials.

Another part of Harley-Davidson's success in selling mass-produced custom motorcycles is the extensive array of add-on parts available from both Harley-Davidson and aftermarket distributors. With these, owners can transform their mass-market machines into something that feels more like an expression of personal style.

By the end of the 1990s, retrospective articles in motorcycle publications frequently credited the Harley-Davidson Motorcycle Company with "saving" what had been a dying motorcycle market in the United States.[67] During the 1980s, the number of registered motorcycles in the United States had dropped by one third, from six million in 1980 to just over four million by 1990. The years since then, however, produced a remarkable turnabout, with motorcycle sales growing by double digits each year from 1991 to 1999. This explosive growth was due largely to the expanding appeal of Harley and Harley-like cruiser bikes, and the entry or return of many now middle-aged riders to motorcycling.

The real appeal of the cruiser motorcycle lies in its ability to resolve a fundamental tension between American culture and its social system. The American culture prizes individualism and values those who are able to express their individuality. The country's social system, on the other hand, is organized around the production and distribution of look-alike, mass-market products and a highly routine, bureaucratic way of life. Although there is nothing really custom about the motorcycles that Harley-Davidson and its imitators sell, with a little more money and a few pieces of billet chrome accessories, owners can feel as if they are riding a unique machine that is indeed an expression of their individuality. Nor do today's bikers need to spend much time with wrenches in their hands to achieve this satisfaction. On the Run for the Wall in 1999, for instance, Ray was admiring a new Harley-Davidson that had been customized into an attractive piece of rolling art. In conversation with the owner he said that he understood the satisfaction that comes from having a successful "garage project." The owner replied honestly, but a bit sheepishly, "I didn't do it myself. I just paid my dealer to put that stuff on."[68]

Overall, Harley-Davidson transformed a style of motorcycle that had once emerged from the handiwork of owners into something available to anyone who could afford it, and it was a formula that worked. By 1998 Harley-Davidson accounted for more than 50 percent of the heavy-cruiser motorcycle market, which itself had grown to represent more than 50 percent of all motorcycles sold in the United States. In 1999 Harley-Davidsons were the top sellers in eight out of ten categories of motorcycles.[69] From the late 1980s onward, the demand for Harley-Davidsons regularly outstripped the company's annual production, and prices spiraled into the $20,000 range for many highly desirable top-of-the-line models.

MIDDLE-AGED REBELS

Although Harley-Davidson and other cruiser-style motorcycles patterned after outlaw styles may symbolize important American values such as patriotism, freedom, and individuality, that does not entirely explain why the majority of those who purchase them are middle-class men (and some women) who have little intention of adopting the economically and culturally marginal lives of authentic outlaw bikers. It is easy to parody these graying, middle-class professionals riding mass-produced custom motorcycles. Indeed, much fun has been made of RUBS—Rich Urban Bikers—ever since public figures such as Malcolm Forbes Sr., Arnold Schwarzenegger, and Jay Leno became visible symbols of the growing number of affluent middle-aged men dressed in biker style, riding Harley-Davidsons. The lives of these new bikers were far more conventional than the one-percenter outlaws who originally populated clubs like the Hell's Angels, the Pagans, and the Outlaws.[70]

Sociologist Stephen Lyng has suggested that this "squaring of the one-percenter" represented by middle-class bikers imitating outlaw style is primarily the result of clever marketing of the Harley-Davidson and its imitators.[71] Certainly marketing, film, and television have all played a role in popularizing outlaw biker style. But that is not the whole story. When forty- and fifty-year-old middle-class men forsake golf shirts and martinis at the nineteenth hole for sweaty chaps and Budweisers at the end of a long day's ride, and when their wives pass up tennis lessons and rounds of bridge to attend biker rallies, where they sometimes respond to calls of "Show us your tits," something more complex is happening than just marketing. As Schouten and McAlexander note in their study of the subculture of RUBs and other outlaw-imitating bikers, Harley-Davidson marketing may have tapped a longing among middle-aged men for a way to transcend the routines of daily life and to find community and brotherhood, but it did not create those desires.[72] These desires, we suggest, emerge from the desire for personal connection and the lack of transcendence or spirituality experienced by many people, particularly middle-class professionals, whose lives are dominated by the rationalist, hyperspeed demands of the postmodern world.

It is also important to keep in mind that the image of the affluent middle-class RUB styling on his or her Harley is as much overblown as was the 1950s image of outlaw bikers terrorizing small towns. At $17,000 to $20,000 for top models, new Harleys are often out of the price range of the kinds of working-class riders who once made up the core of motorcycle riders in the United States. And it is also true that Harleys have become status symbols for some upscale Americans. Our experience suggests, however, that a fair share of the men and women riding Harley and Harley-clone motorcycles do not fit the RUB profile. Rather, they are people earning modest wages, or in the case of some RFTW riders, Vietnam veterans living on disability pensions, who have decided to devote a very large part of their income to owning a motorcycle as their one important possession. One close friend from the Run who is both unable to work and unable to obtain full veteran disability owned nothing but his Harley at a time when he would have been homeless had he not been able to live in VA hospital housing. The relatively unchanging appearance of Harley-Davidson motorcycles also contributes to an overestimation of the size of the RUB population. Only experienced bikers who can recognize the subtle differences in motorcycle design and styling can readily distinguish a 2000 from a 1980 model Harley. So while new bike prices may exceed $20,000, many older bikes are available for $10,000 or sometimes even less, putting them in range of at least a portion of working-class Americans.

Whether one is a RUB or a working-class rider, however, the attraction that cruiser bikes and outlaw styles hold for Americans who are supposed to be living conventional lives is an expression of three things: the rise of conservative ideology, the related appeal of populist sentiments, and the desire among many middle-aged baby boomers to rebel against the surprising ordinariness of their lives.

Much of biker culture is conservative in a general sense because it embraces conservative views of what individualism and freedom mean. The essence of conservative thought in the United States is the belief that if people are allowed to pursue their self-interest with few restrictions, they will create a natural system of checks and balances as the basis of a well-ordered society with the maximum amount of liberty for every individual.[73] Among bikers, this translates into the right of individuals to do and say what they please, whether that might be running unmuffled exhausts, riding without a helmet, or making jokes that more liberal Americans might find offensive. Like other conservatives, many (although not all) bikers tend to see government intervention as the primary threat to individual freedom. Thus, laws requiring that motorcycles meet noise restrictions or that motorcyclists wear helmets are seen as government intrusions on freedom, rather than, as liberals might see them, issues of public order and safety legitimately overseen by government for the good of the community as a whole. The conservative understanding of freedom manifests itself on the Run for the Wall in such things as scheduled stops just over the border of states without helmet laws so the riders can "exercise their freedom of choice" by removing their helmets.[74] Also, while motorcycle rallies such as Americade, the largest rally for touring motorcycles in the United States, or Wing Ding, the national rally of Honda Gold Wing riders, urge their participants to conform to local noise laws, the Run for the Wall makes no such suggestion. On the contrary, at least half if not more of the motorcycles on the Run for the Wall operate with modified exhausts that would probably not meet state or federal noise regulations.

The link between biker culture and conservative politics is also more than a matter of belief. It is a basis for political action. In recent years a number of motorcycle rights organizations have worked closely and successfully with conservative legislators to change federal policy that penalized states that did not pass mandatory helmet laws, and to overturn existing helmet laws in twenty-four states.[75]

While biker culture tends toward the conservative end of the political spectrum, it also reflects the influence of populism on American culture. Although both conservative and populist ideologies are suspicious of large central governments, populism tends to see solutions to daily problems as based in community obligations and mutual aid, rather than autonomous individuals pursuing their own self-interest.[76] The values that populists attach to community and mutual assistance are linked to the frontier and immigrant history of the United States. The earliest colonial communities were close-knit arrangements where individual freedoms were clearly circumscribed by community will and community need.[77] The experience of nineteenth- and twentieth-century immigrants to the United States also contributed to the growth of populist sensibilities. Rather than collections of autonomous individuals, immigrant neighborhoods often consisted of family members or people who came from the same village in the Old World, who pooled resources and provided mutual assistance in the face of trouble or hard times. An equally powerful populist experience in U.S. history was the labor solidarity that shaped the struggle for workers' rights from the 1870s through the 1940s. During these years, U.S. miners, factory workers, and their families often stood together as brothers and sisters against the insults, truncheons, and even bullets of those who felt these workers had no right to improve their lot in life through collective action.[78] Thus, while American culture in general, and conservative ideology in particular, attach great value to the individual, ideas of mutual aid and collective responsibility run deep, if more hidden, in American society as well.

The populist values of mutual aid and collective responsibility are reflected in biker culture through the commitment to *brotherhood*. Within the outlaw biker world, brotherhood expresses the most fundamental responsibility of club membership—the obligation to provide other members whatever support they need, when they need it, whether it is the loan of a few dollars, motorcycle parts, help with repairing a bike, a sympathetic ear in times of trouble, or backup in a fight. For outlaw bikers, brotherhood *is* the club. For members of outlaw clubs, the experience and responsibility of brotherhood is the defining element of their social lives. It is the social glue that keeps the club together as a place of identity and safety for its members. Onion, a member of the Rebels Motorcycle Club, explained it this way: "Brotherhood is love for the members of the club . . . you know there is going to be a brother to give you a hand when you need it."[79] Thus, while outlaw biker culture may seem to occupy the fringes of American society, its value system is actually built around beliefs that are deeply rooted in American culture.

The concept of brotherhood that keeps outlaw clubs together is also a part of the wider culture of motorcycling. However, just as the motorcycles that typify this wider culture are less hard-edged than full-fledged outlaw machines, the vision of brotherhood among the wider motorcycling community is less all-consuming than the outlaw code. Motorcyclists in general share norms of support and sociability. A motorcyclist working on a disabled bike by the side of the road is cause for any other rider to stop and offer assistance. Similarly, motorcyclists who happen to arrive at highway rest stops, restaurants, or motels at the same time will typically exchange talk about where they came from, where they are going, and what the day's ride was like. Unlike brotherhood in motorcycle clubs, however, the exchange of sociability and aid on the road among motorcyclists in general is not based on ongoing social relationships and thus has few structured expectations of direct reciprocity except a belief in the circulation of aid—just as someone may have helped me, I should pass the favor on to the next rider in need that I might encounter. The role of brotherhood on the Run for the Wall, as we will discuss later, falls somewhere between the strict obligations found in outlaw clubs and the looser rules of aid and sociability among motorcyclists in general.

While part of the appeal of biker culture is its symbolic connection to both conservative and populist values, another important part of this appeal rests with the ability of biker culture and biker style to help many middle-aged baby boomers reclaim their youthful expectations that they would not grow up to lead what they saw as the boring, conventional, straight-jacketed lives of their parents. Many of those who came to adolescence in the period from the mid-1950s to the mid-1970s were influenced by a spirit of rebellion bred of both general societal change and more specific struggles, including the sexual revolution, the battle for equal rights for ethnic minorities and women, and the antiwar movement. It was a generation that came to believe it would always march to the beat of a different drummer. Through the normal progression of education, maturation, work, marriage, and family responsibilities, however, most of this generation came to live routine adult lives. Now in their forties and fifties, some male baby-boomers find they can recapture the youthful feeling of being different from the mainstream by exchanging their everyday world for the community of bikers, even if only on weekends. This desire was effectively captured in one Harley-Davidson ad that showed a custom motorcycle above the caption, "Those who don't know me think I pretend to be a biker on weekends. Those who know me, know I pretend to be a banker during the week."[80]

It would be easy to dismiss the middle-aged biker as simply another instance of male midlife crisis. We suggest, however, that this paradoxical search to be different by adopting the highly *uniform* styles of motorcycles and clothing is an expression of the tension between individualism and community, between conservatism and populism, in American culture. As the political, economic, and ideological framework of U.S. society has come to increasingly emphasize the individual as an autonomous being struggling against others to succeed or just to survive, many people long to be part of something more communal, to experience some sense of solidarity with others somewhere in their lives. For many men this solidarity was once found in places like the union hall, the grange, or the barracks, while women often found equivalent solidarity in extended families and community organizations.

As work has become more individualized and competitive, as families have become more geographically dispersed, and as neighborhoods have become increasingly populated by transient strangers, people have sought new ways of finding community and solidarity. The world of bikers is just one of the many expressions of this contemporary search. Bikers can find conversation, support, and sometimes lifelong friends through their shared interest in motorcycles, riding, and the image of difference that bikers project. More than a generation in midlife crisis, the rise of a new group of middle-aged bikers is an expression of fundamental changes taking place in U.S. society as people look for new ways to experience populist solidarity in a conservative culture.

BIKER CULTURE, VIETNAM VETERANS, AND THE RUN FOR THE WALL

Among the combat veterans who returned from Vietnam in the 1960s and 1970s were some who shared important characteristics with the hard-core bikers of that era. Both groups were small and socially isolated. Both were patriotic and promilitary, although not necessarily progovernment. Both were strongly focused on the notion of freedom. Both believed deeply in brotherhood. For these reasons, many Vietnam veterans who had been motorcycle riders before the war, or who were drawn to motorcycle riding after it, found a comfortable social world among bikers. It is from the blending of the values and rituals of these veterans with the values and rituals of the biker subculture that the Run for the Wall was born.

Small, Visible, and Isolated

There are no reliable statistics on the total number of hard-core bikers, either outlaws or independents, but it is undeniably small. Even today, after years in the media limelight, the most prominent outlaw club, the Hell's Angels, numbers only around five hundred. Despite being few in number, outlaw bikers have been the source of an *image* that has had a powerful impact on American culture even while the outlaws themselves remain outsiders, unwelcome in the offices and living rooms of mainstream America. Similarly, media stereotypes of the Vietnam combat veteran have come to occupy a popular niche much larger than their actual numbers would suggest. As indicated in the previous chapter, fewer than 4 percent of draft-age men served in Southeast Asia.[81] Nevertheless, the men who fought in Vietnam became symbols of deep divisions in the society. Some saw them as heroes, some saw them as villains, and some saw them as victims. And, like bikers, many Vietnam veterans found that their status as veterans often prevented them from occupying a routine place in society. They had become strangers at home, outsiders to their own culture.[82] For some of these men, the social marginality they experienced after the war made it easier to enter another marginal subculture—the world of bikers. This is not a new phenomenon. As we noted previously, after every major war of the twentieth century, some veterans gravitated toward socially marginal biker lifestyles.

Patriot Bikers

Because the subculture of bikers has contained a large portion of working-class veterans, it has been fertile ground for patriotic, pro-America, and promilitary values. Even before the popularity of the film *Easy Rider*, outlaw bikers were decorating choppers with American eagles and representations of the Stars and Stripes. From the late 1960s onward, these symbols became even more common on biker machines. These pro-America, promilitary themes within biker subculture became more than decorative abstractions during the Vietnam War. In 1965, the Hell's Angels, then the most visible outlaw club in the United States, took an open political stance by attacking an antiwar march from Berkeley to the Oakland Army Terminal that was being led by beat poet and antiwar activist Allen Ginsberg. Although the Hell's Angels called off their plans to attack another march planned for the following month, they captured national attention when Angels president Sonny Barger issued the following statement: "Although we have stated our intention to counter-demonstrate at this despicable, un-American activity, we believe that in the interest of public safety and the protection of the good name of Oakland, we should not justify the Vietnam Day Committee by our presence because our patriotic concern for what these people are doing to our great nation may provoke us to violent acts. Any physical encounter would only produce sympathy for this mob of traitors."[83]

For some returning Vietnam veterans who felt that their patriotic support of the U.S. government made them unwelcome guests in a society where many of their own generation had begun to wonder whether real patriotism lay in opposing rather than supporting the war effort, the patriotic world of bikers often seemed more comfortable than the local bar, bowling alley, and even, in some cases, the VFW hall.[84]

Riding for Freedom

The biker ideal is built around the open road, one of the most powerful symbols of individual freedom in America, as we mentioned earlier. Bikers ride to be free. U.S. soldiers are taught that their purpose is to fight for freedom. Throughout the Vietnam era, presidents argued that the Vietnam War was a fight for freedom: first the freedom of the South Vietnamese people to live in a capitalist rather than a communist society, then the freedom of U.S. citizens that would

FIGURE 20. Brothers Vietnam, one of the many Vietnam veterans biker groups.

presumably be threatened if Vietnam and then the rest of Southeast Asia fell under communist rule, and finally, in the latter years of the war, the freedom of U.S. soldiers held captive in Southeast Asia. The meaning of freedom for Vietnam veterans is not necessarily identical to its meaning for bikers, however. For soldiers the struggle is not about individual freedom, but about the freedom of peoples and nations. For bikers it is about individual freedom to take to the road unrestrained by rules and obligations.

Bikers and veterans are nevertheless closely linked because the American idea of a free nation resides in the image of a society in which individuals are free to engage in their personal pursuit of happiness. In this sense, the Vietnam veteran who believes he fought for freedom and the biker who believes in a life passionately devoted to the freedom of the road share a common universe. They understand one another. They feel comfortable with one another.

Brotherhood

Those who have been to war tell us that there are few bonds as powerful and compelling as those between comrades who face death together. Indeed, the language used to capture the intensity of the warrior bond is often very similar to the language of love. As the narrator of de Bernières's *Corelli's Mandolin* says:

> Soldiers grow to love each other; and regardless of the matter of sex, this is a love without parallel in civil life. . . . You come to know every nuance of each other's moods; you know exactly what the other is going to say; you know exactly who will laugh and for how long over which particular type of joke; you acquaint yourself intimately with the smell of each man's feet and perspiration; you can put your hand on someone's face in the dark, and know who it is; you recognize someone's equipment hanging on the back of a chair, even though his is the same as everyone else's. . . . You become accustomed to seeing each other frankly, and nothing is hidden.[85]

The intensity of the bond between warriors is also often heightened by their youth. War is a young man's endeavor, for the most part. This means that fighters bring all the passion of their youth to battlefield relationships with comrades. As one rider who witnessed the death of far too many friends in Vietnam said: "I was young [seventeen]. These were the first real friends I had made as an adult. It made me afraid to get really close to anybody after that. I thought, 'If I do, they'll just be taken away.'"

The warrior is no stranger to what bikers mean when they talk about brotherhood. This is one of the powerful attractions of biker culture for Vietnam veterans. It is a world in which they can relive, even if in a pale form, the bonds of brotherhood and shared risk that they experienced when they were warriors and young. Among Run for the Wall riders, the ideals of brotherhood include giving other riders any assistance they might need in dealing with a disabled bike, giving money to those having financial problems getting to D.C. or back home, and most importantly, providing emotional and moral support for riders troubled by wartime memories, the pain of wartime losses, or fear of seeing the Wall.

As in outlaw clubs, brotherhood on the Run focuses primarily on supporting members of the group. At the same time, brotherhood on the Run does not extend as far as the demands of the outlaw code. One outlaw described the obligation to stand up for a brother club member this way: "Right or wrong, I'd be there. If wrong, though, I would take it up with him later about what the hell he was doing. But I wouldn't let him take a licking and then say: 'Well, that's why I didn't help.' I'd help him and then tell him: 'You know, I think you're an asshole! Think about that when we get to court.'"[86]

While there is a strong code of brotherhood on the Run, it does not extend to risking injury or jail because someone else acted like an "asshole." Also, reciprocal obligations among those who participate in the Run for the Wall are less encompassing than the brotherhood of an outlaw biker club. The Run is a rolling event, not a club based in a fixed location where members meet on a regular basis. Consequently, the Run provides a looser structure of obligations than motorcycle clubs that are part of a rider's day-to-day life. At the same time, the Run for the Wall links far-flung individuals into a community support network through which many members will respond to calls for help from other RFTW bikers.

Shared Rituals and Symbols

In addition to a common devotion to freedom and brotherhood, biker and military subcultures share certain symbols and rituals. For both bikers and soldiers, the *parade* is the primary vehicle for displaying their unity, coordination, and power. For bikers, their parade is the *run*. Motorcycle runs differ from both recreational group riding and charity rides. Recreational group rides are simply about enjoying the pleasure of motorcycle riding in company, which usually involves a combination of riding and hanging out together at some destination point, usually a bar, restaurant, or some other place where riders eat and drink together. While there may be pleasure involved in runs, they typically are organized to serve a serious organizational or political purpose. For outlaw motorcycle clubs or other closely knit motorcycle organizations, the annual or biannual run is their central defining event. It is through their runs that these groups demonstrate to both themselves and others their core identity as a *motorcycle* organization. Within the world of outlaw motorcycle clubs, the run is so symbolically important that participation is often mandatory.

There are also some important differences between runs and the increasingly common charity rides. Unlike purely recreational riding, charity rides have a serious purpose. This may range from rides where the bikers bring toys to be given to poorer children in their city or town during the holidays, to large-scale regional or national charity events, such as the Love Ride to raise money for the Muscular Dystrophy Foundation, or the Ride for Kids, which supports research into pediatric brain tumors. Charity rides typically have few requirements for participation other than the willingness to give money or a toy to the cause. Thus, while participation in charity rides is often large, the bonds among participants are relatively few compared to those in the run. True motorcycle runs also usually involve at least an overnight stay at some destination, where the riders spend a considerable amount of time together. Charity rides, by contrast, typically involve short distances and some brief event, perhaps a lunch, and then the riders disband to ride home on their own or in smaller groups. Finally, charity rides are normally not colored by a sense of gravity, even if money is being raised for a grave illness. They are more about having fun on a brief ride while donating to a worthy cause; the run, like a military parade, is typically organized to deliver a more serious message to both those who participate and those who observe. For this reason, the idea of a run, such as the Run for the Wall, resonates with veterans who understand the significance of these kinds of serious public performances.

In addition to the parallels between military parades and motorcycle runs, veterans and bikers share another common experience—designating one's membership and experience by wearing uniforms, patches, and pins. Veterans are experienced in symbolizing their unit, rank, and accomplishments through decorated clothing. For the biker, the unit is symbolized by colors, or by club or association patches. Status and accomplishments are represented not by signs of rank and medals or ribbons, but by patches or other insignia indicating positions such as road captain or road guard, and by pins and patches representing journeys made and rallies attended. In this way the biker's uniform is more similar to a soldier's uniform than is almost any other type of civilian dress.

On the Run for the Wall, the RFTW back patch and individual bars indicating which years riders participated on the Run, and whether they went all the way or were participants (that is, rode only part way), are important parts of the rider's uniform. As we will discuss in subsequent chapters, there are other rituals, such as those associated with honoring and remembering the dead, that also bring soldiers and bikers onto common ground. It is such connections between biker culture and military culture that shape much of the character of the Run for the Wall.[87]

5

"PILGRIMS FOR AMERICA"
The Power of Ritual

MAY 22, 1999: LIMON, COLORADO

Dusk was falling over the KOA campground as we gathered once again for the Task Force Omega ceremony.[1] The thunderstorm that had passed through earlier had cleared, and the cool air was filled with the scent of damp earth. A "V" of candelaria had been set in the space where the ceremony was to be held, the light of the candles in the paper bags glowing warmly as the sun sank behind the mountains to the west. As in the previous year's ceremony, we were to read the names of all the missing soldiers from Colorado. This time, however, we formed into couples, and each couple was assigned a month and given a list of names of those who had gone missing in that month. As each month was called, the woman read the names on her list and the man responded in the gathering darkness with the words, "Still on patrol, sir!" After all the names were read, we joined hands in a healing circle.

CREATING AN AMERICAN RITUAL

The ten days of the Run for the Wall's journey across the country are punctuated with rituals like this one we participated in with Task Force Omega. These rituals range from prayers offered for the group's safety before each day's Run to elaborate ceremonies devised by the various groups that host the Run along the way, from individual rites carried out beneath the names of comrades and loved ones at the Wall to group rituals such as the healing circles at Limon and Salina, from public events to private prayer. In addition, the Run for the Wall as a whole can be seen as a ritual event, one in which participants not only seek healing and engage in political protest but also assert American patriotic values, create a sense of community, and (re)construct both personal identity and collective history.[2]

Many Americans see their own culture as lacking in ritual compared to other, more traditional societies, and to some extent, this is true. The United States has few unifying, societywide rituals in which all or most of the population takes part. (This may be one of the reasons for the widespread popularity of sports events such as the Super Bowl.)[3] Yet rituals are by no means absent from U.S. life. Americans mark a wide variety of occasions with ritual, from political events such as inaugurations and victory parties, to rites of passage such as graduations and weddings, to religious celebrations such as Easter services and Passover. Some rituals are family events such as Thanksgiving dinner and decorating the Christmas tree, while others are mass-mediated performances such as the Super Bowl or rock concerts. As society changes, and as old meanings fade and new ones are created, individuals and groups often respond by inventing new rituals or modifying old ones in order to fill "ritual gaps." For example, recently Americans have invented rituals for life passages such as divorce and menopause, events for which rituals did not previously exist.[4] Ritual events such as the Run for the Wall can also serve as a means of protesting existing conditions and as vehicles for social change. These new rituals are not created from scratch, but often draw on familiar cultural elements as a framework for expressing changing individual and collective values and needs. In so doing, such rituals also demonstrate that, far from being rigid and traditional, rituals are creative and flexible ways in which individuals and groups both respond to and initiate social change.[5] This chapter examines the reasons that a particular form of ritual, the pilgrimage, lends itself especially well to the needs of veterans and others who participate in the Run.

WHY RITUAL?

Rituals can be described as symbolic, repetitive acts that are predictable (to some extent, at least) and that say more than can be said by other means. Rituals also seek to accomplish certain things: to create meaning out of chaos or disorder, to bring about personal and collective catharsis, to create commitment, to transmit knowledge, to mark changes in social or spiritual status, to create or affirm identity. Often, rituals are tied to narratives about the past (whether mythical or historical, sacred or secular). Or they may seek to construct new narratives or reconstruct existing ones—as in the Run for the Wall and other rituals that present a particular narrative about Vietnam and the men who fought there. Part of the reason rituals are effective in doing these things is the power of the symbols and of the physical acts that are intrinsic parts of all rituals, and of the emotional and cognitive processes that these symbols and acts set in motion.

Symbols might be defined as objects and acts that carry and condense meaning. Symbols not only stand for things, they also create complex webs of significance, drawing together history, cultural values, and personal meaning; they represent, as Clifford Geertz puts it, a people's "most comprehensive ideas of order."[6] The U.S. flag, for example, represents not only the United States as a political state, but also (for many people, at least) values such as freedom and the American way of life. For others, the flag may have a more negative meaning, as a symbol of U.S. imperialism, for example, or a representation of a chauvinistic patriotism.

Symbols are not merely intellectual or abstract. Victor Turner, an anthropologist who devoted much of his work to the study of ritual, saw symbols as having two poles: the sensory and the ideological. On the one hand, the symbols used in rituals activate one or all of our senses (the sensory pole) and frequently involve activities that engage our whole bodies, or parts thereof (gestures, kneeling, dancing, moving in certain ways, etc.).[7] Viewed in this way, rituals are actions, performances that command the attention of both participants and audience.[8] On the other hand, the symbols used in rituals also convey important messages about cultural values (such as one's relationship to the ancestors or one's obligations to God). This is the ideological pole of ritual. It is the combination of the ideological and the sensory that makes rituals so powerful. For this reason

FIGURE 21. A Task Force Omega ritual in Limon, Colorado.

people sometimes find themselves moved by the rituals of other groups or cultures, even when they themselves do not necessarily share the values of those performing the ritual. So, for example, during the annual ritual at Limon described at the beginning of this chapter, we found ourselves moved to tears despite our own uncertainty about whether there are actually any POWs left alive in Southeast Asia. The candles flickering in the gathering darkness, the names of the Colorado missing read aloud, joining hands in a healing circle, all made these men real for us and made us hope for their survival. The ritual also allowed us to experience, in some small part at least, the grief of those who are still waiting for these men to return or be accounted for.

This brings up another point about symbols: They are capable of multiple interpretations even among those who participate collectively in a ritual. Whatever our personal doubts about the existence of live POWs, we were able to feel the ceremony at Limon as an expression of the unresolved losses of Vietnam and of lives in which the still uncertain status of a loved one missing in Vietnam will always prevent closure. That we can place our personal interpretations on the ceremony does not make it any less valid as a collective ritual. On the contrary, it enables us to participate emotionally in the ritual activities and brings us closer to the others in the group.

As we have said, the Run for the Wall is a ritual event filled with sensory experiences: the motion and roar of the motorcycles, physical discomfort (and occasional moments of fear) as well as the joy and sensual pleasure of riding, the thrill of seeing riders in a formation that sometimes stretches out of sight, wearing ritual clothing, touching names on war memorials, hugging other participants while saying "Welcome home," joining hands in a healing circle. These experiences reinforce and lend emotional power to the ideological messages of the pilgrimage. A man dressed as a POW crouching in a bamboo cage, for example, evokes a visceral and emotional response that a speech that calls upon the government to "bring them home" cannot. Rituals thus say more than words.

An important part of the sensory dimension of ritual is material objects. Almost any material object that humans have devised, along with objects found in nature, can become a symbol, from the sacred deer of certain Native American cultures to the Christian cross to a motorcycle. But objects are more than symbols that condense meanings in tangible form (though they are certainly this as well). Objects also contain memory. As C. Nadia Seremetakis puts it: "Memory cannot be confined to a purely mentalist or subjective sphere. It is a culturally mediated *material* practice."[9] In other words, objects and acts can call forth memory in a powerful way and can evoke emotions associated with these memories. Memory is thus a sensory process, and material objects are one of the things that both contain and activate this process. This is one reason that pilgrimages worldwide are dense with objects of healing and remembrance. Objects both represent the pilgrims' experiences and embody the spiritual, sacred, and emotional qualities of the pilgrimage site. They thus become more than passive material items. Rather they *participate* in the ritual process by evoking memory and grief, while at the same time helping to ease pain. For example, participants in the Run often carry (or wear) objects that connect them to their Vietnam experience, such as division patches (First Cav, Airmobile, jump wings), service ribbons and medals (particularly those certifying service in Vietnam), patches with the names of fallen comrades in whose memory they ride, and Agent Orange patches (including one with a skull that states "Agent Orange Health Club—Life Member").[10] In addition, people carry objects to and from the Wall that represent not only their own relationship to those whose names are inscribed there and their own memories of the war, but also objects given to them by individuals and groups along the way. These objects serve to make the pilgrimage in the donor's stead and embody the slogan on the Run for the Wall back patch: "We Ride for Those Who Can't."

And, finally, there is the Wall itself, a material object that brings both grief and healing. Here riders from the Run, like thousands of others who have visited the memorial, can leave their offerings of memory and can reach out to touch the names of fallen comrades and relatives. Here the memories, the grief, the names spoken in the riders' minds take on tangible form and become part of the sensory experience of the pilgrimage. As Morris points out, "memorializing is . . . necessarily concrete . . . because it is something one can experience and something to which one can refer, and because it frequently yields something we can call a memorial."[11] Yet memorialization, even in its most concrete form, is never static. Not only is it the outcome of a process of choice that has established what is memorable,[12] but the acts of memorializing themselves help create the memorial's significance and add layers of meaning to its original conception. This process is part of what has made the Vietnam Veterans Memorial the national shrine that it has become. And part of this process has been the amazing array of objects that have been left there by visitors, including the participants in the Run for the Wall.[13] These objects range from flowers to army medals, from letters to photographs, from combat medals to cross-stitches, from packets of cigarettes to a brand new Harley-Davidson brought one year on the Run. Such objects can have both personal and public meaning, for while they represent individual biography and individual grief, they also symbolize a collective loss.[14]

While objects are aids to, and repositories of, memory, and in this respect both represent and evoke emotion, rituals themselves are also part of remembering. Rituals serve to recall those who died and to call forth memories of the war. But they do more than this. Rituals can also create the past by shaping the memory of it and by helping to place individual memory in the context of a collective one. What Morris says of memorializing and tradition could well apply to the various rituals of the Run for the Wall: "Tradition enables the past to speak through the present by encouraging and enabling those in the present to see themselves as part of a whole."[15] But the Run also creates memory in another way, for it creates its own tradition and provides a set of memories that may stay with participants well

FIGURE 22. Some people ride in memory of a specific lost loved one.

after the Run itself has ended. Recalling the various ceremonies that have taken place during the Run brings back some of the emotion that these rituals evoked and keeps alive, at least in part, some of the Run's emotional power during the day-to-day life that marks the time until the next year's pilgrimage.

RITUAL, PROTEST, AND DEATH

Although participants in the Run for the Wall ride "for our *live* POWs," they also ride in memory of those who died in the war, and those who have died since, whether of war-related trauma, accident, or natural causes. In this respect the Run is similar to other pilgrimages in which death is an important theme. In many societies, death itself is viewed as a form of journey, and pilgrimage may be regarded as a form of symbolic death and rebirth.[16] Ritually, the pilgrim dies to the everyday world, entering a different reality, that of the pilgrimage journey. In such a reality, communion may even be made with the dead. In addition, places that are sites of tragedy or that commemorate the dead may be visited by those who seek to make some sense out of such death and tragedy.[17]

Once the funeral and memorial ceremony conducted after a person dies are over, there is little ritual space or social support provided by American culture for prolonged mourning or memorializing of the dead. This is especially true in comparison to what is found in many other societies.[18] Indeed, Americans are expected to get on with their lives; lingering over the dead or our memories is considered inappropriate or even unhealthy.[19] This lack of ritual, as we will see, is important in understanding some of the emotional power of the Run for the Wall and of the Vietnam Veterans Memorial. Both provide a place and an occasion for dealing with the still unhealed grief—and anger—over the losses of war. Not only does the Run enable individuals and groups to construct rituals of healing and protest, but it also provides a context in which they can seek to give meaning to the deaths of those whose names are on the Wall.

Even when new rituals are created, however, or when they seek to protest or change existing conditions, they still draw on familiar cultural materials for their construction. Biker culture, for example, while it protests mainstream society and its values, at the same time uses symbolic forms that are well recognized by that culture: the symbolism of the open road, the long hair and beard that identify an individual as outside society, the wearing of distinctive clothing (leather, boots, head scarves) that marks the biker off from those who inhabit a more ordinary world.[20] Indeed, any culture or ritual of protest must use recognized symbols if it wishes its protest to be heard and understood.

At the same time, there are characteristic ways in which rituals are organized that are common across a wide range of cultures. These ways of organizing rituals, and the purposes to which rituals are put, result in certain categories of rituals that are found in most, if not all, societies. These include rituals of healing, rites of passage, ritual journeys, and rites of memory and mourning. Thus while the initiation ritual into the Rebels motorcycle club described by Daniel Wolf "is a creative event" and although he states that "no two outlaw-club initiations are ever the same," the activities he describes would be familiar to any anthropologist as a classic rite of passage.[21] In Wolf's account, the bikers ride their motorcycles together into the wilderness, where the "strikers" (initiates) are overpowered, stripped, spread-eagled and tied on the ground, then doused with ashes and buckets of oil, feces, and urine, while being ridiculed by other club members. After this ordeal, the initiates are dressed in the club colors and welcomed into the group with all-night drinking and feasting, dope and sex, thus becoming full-fledged members of the club. The separation from normal society, the hazing, the ritual death and rebirth of the initiates, the bonding through a communal meal, and the donning of symbols of the initiates' new status are all symbolic elements that would be readily recognized by any tribal society that practices initiation rites. But these outlaw bikers did not have to read anthropological works on rites of passage to construct their ritual; all the necessary elements were already present in their culture and came readily to hand.

Similarly, it was not necessary for those who devised the first Run for the Wall to read works on classic Western pilgrimages in order to construct their own ritual journey, as they were already well aware of what a pilgrimage was and what it entailed. All that was necessary for them to do was to shape this ritual journey to their own needs and purposes.[22] In so doing, they have paid particular attention to areas in which rituals were lacking or inadequate, including the lack of public homecoming ceremonies for veterans, as well as rituals for mourning dead comrades. They also drew on rituals of mourning and forms of memorialization that were already well established in biker culture.

Biker funerals and memorial rides are occasions for the expression of biker solidarity, and such funerals often make news when they are held for outlaw bikers killed in violent encounters. Attendance at the funeral of a fellow biker, is, as one biker friend put it, "an expression of community," and the bylaws of outlaw biker clubs such as the Pagans make the attendance at the funerals of fellow members mandatory. Patches worn in memory of the dead by fellow club members become part of the process of memorialization. Similarly, those on the Run riding in memoriam for a dead comrade will often indicate this by wearing patches on their vests or bracelets bearing the name of the dead person, or by placing the name of their comrade on the motorcycle itself. And insofar as some bikers see themselves as fighting society and its conventions, the deaths of brothers, whether through violence or accidents on the road, may be viewed as similar to deaths in combat.[23]

While in many societies communication with the dead is a normal practice, and the deceased may even play an active role in the lives of the living (in the form of spirits, ancestors, ghosts, etc.), in mainstream American culture a sharper line is drawn between life and death, and consequently there is little in the way of culturally approved means for continued interaction of the living with those who have died. This lack often does not accord, however, with the feeling that many people have that the dead are still with them.

Many societies believe that in cases of premature or unnatural death—such as death by a violent act, or the death of someone young, for example—the spirits of the dead may come back to haunt or trouble the living. In Vietnam, most of the Americans who died were young. In this respect, they all died premature deaths. And most died violently as well. Moreover, many of the combat veterans had the traumatizing experience of seeing contemporaries, and often close friends, die suddenly around them, in horrible ways.[24] Whereas most Americans do not experience violent death firsthand and often only see dead people embalmed at funerals, combat veterans have experienced something that civilians encounter only if they are subject to war or natural disaster—the sudden, violent deaths of a large number of people close to them.

In addition, the conditions of the Vietnam War provided little context for grieving, which added to the difficulty of coping with the sudden deaths of close friends. Most of the dead were whisked away from the combat zone as quickly as possible and the bodies flown back to the States. Instead of being handled and viewed by those close to them, the bodies were handled by strangers.[25] Bodies left in the field might be used as booby traps by the enemy or as bait for ambushes, or they might be mutilated or degraded, adding to the horror of the death of comrades. In addition, little space was provided in the combat zone for mourning, and expressions of grief were discouraged. As Shay notes: "American military culture in Vietnam regarded tears as dangerous but above all as demeaning, the sign of a weakling, a loser. To weep was to lose one's dignity among American soldiers in Vietnam."[26]

While those at home could mourn the individual deaths of friends and relatives, they had not actually seen them die as the soldier's comrades had. Nor did the veteran necessarily return to a community that shared his sense of loss, as most of his dead comrades were scattered, buried in their own hometowns (or perhaps missing in action, with no grave site to visit). Thus there was usually neither a place nor a time where he could mourn. In addition, sometimes these dead comrades were known to the returned veteran only by the nicknames or "handles" that had identified the soldiers to each other during the war. This burden of grief, often coupled with survivor guilt, is one reason that so many vets have reported a sense of alienation and disorientation on their return from Vietnam.[27] Once they returned, there were no rituals of mourning available to provide emotional outlets or possible closure for the deaths of their comrades. Thus, many have continued to be haunted by the dead.

Beyond unhealed individual grief and unresolved guilt over those who died lies the issue of the meaning of the collective dead. As Shay points out, "In victory the meaning of the dead has rarely been a problem for the living—soldiers have died 'for' victory." Such meaning, however, is decided after the fact. "At the time of the deaths, victory has not yet been achieved, so the corpses' meaning hovers in the void until the lethal contest has been decided."[28] The lack of an American victory in Vietnam has left that war's dead permanently in such a void, in which it is difficult for the survivors to attach meaning to their comrades' deaths.

Grief, guilt, and the struggle to find meaning in the deaths of more than fifty-eight thousand young Americans are some of the reasons that the Wall has become such a powerful shrine of mourning and remembrance. Here, both veterans and the relatives of those who died in Vietnam not only can mourn the dead, but also can communicate with them, through speech and prayer, through letters and objects left at the Wall, and through the touching of the names on the black granite surface. The Vietnam Memorial "enables pilgrims to remember the individuals they once knew; it enables them to interact with the names in their own private rituals—tracing the names onto paper, taking photographs, placing flowers."[29]

FIGURE 23. The Remembrance Table awaits the start of a familiar ritual on the Run.

Memorials like the Wall assert the continued importance of the dead for the living. Like the pilgrims to war grave sites in Europe, pilgrims go to the Wall to "pay their respects to the ones who have died, to affirm that their death was not in vain, that they are not forgotten."[30] At the Wall, one confronts the losses of war: "Grief for a young husband, or for a twenty-year-old brother, is . . . grief for what might have been; grief not for a lost past, but for a lost future."[31] And those who never knew the dead, such as those who were babies or even unborn when their fathers were killed in Vietnam, also come, seeking to mourn or to find some meaning or healing in a life lived with a perpetual absence.[32]

For many Vietnam veterans, the Wall, rather than the graves where physical remains are buried, is the real final resting place of those who died in Vietnam. Thus the Wall, like the tombs and monuments of other cultures where the deceased are believed to reside, becomes the meeting place between the living and the dead.[33] The granite surface of the Wall is deliberately designed to reflect the living among the names of the dead. One of the most famous pictures of the Wall shows a veteran leaning against the black marble, the shades of his comrades-in-arms reflected in the monument's gleaming surface.[34] On the Wall, "each of the dead has a name and cannot be compacted into an heroic symbol, an abstracted abstraction,"[35] so that "the presentation of so many thousands of names . . . draws attention to individual loss, individual grief, individual pain, individual suffering, individual sorrow."[36] For some, the voices of "the thousands of names that will not remain silent" speak to them from the Wall.[37] One veteran who regularly rides the Run described it as a jumble of voices he could not even understand, as if all of the dead were speaking to him at once. The relationship between the dead, the living, and the Wall is also reflected in a piece of Wall folklore: the belief that touching the names of the dead on the Wall brings back their souls. "For these men," said one veteran's wife, "touching those names, it's like touching a heart or soul."[38]

Part of the power of the Vietnam Veterans Memorial lies in its ability to absorb and reflect multiple meanings. As Sellers and Walter suggest, it "is one of the few war memorials . . . that allows, yet does not force, repentance for our part in the war as well as honour for those who died."[39] By drawing people together, the memorial is both a place that evokes pain and one that helps to heal. Here the dead can be mourned, and pain and grief given expression and form, regardless of one's view of the rightness or wrongness of the Vietnam conflict, or of war in general.[40] At the same time, as Berdahl suggests, the Vietnam Veterans Memorial, along with other Vietnam memorials, "has created a dominant memory of Vietnam that focuses on individual experiences and tragedies of the war."[41] For many of the veterans on the Run, this is summed up in the slogan discussed earlier, "Forget the war, remember the warrior," that, by focusing on the individual, seeks to separate both the living and the dead from the pain and shame caused by the war.[42]

While the Wall speaks eloquently of the dead, it is only some of the dead—the American dead—who are remembered there, not the many Vietnamese, both civilians and soldiers, who also perished in the tragic conflict. Thus the Wall speaks to us only of our own sacrifice, though in so doing, it can be argued, the memorial speaks of the sacrifice that is experienced in *all* wars.

But the ritual power of the Run lies not only in the physical destination of the Wall, but also in the journey itself, that is, in its nature as a pilgrimage.

THE RUN FOR THE WALL AS PILGRIMAGE

We are sometimes asked why we refer to the Run for the Wall as a pilgrimage. The simplest answer is that this is the term the participants themselves use. At a deeper level, however, the term "pilgrimage" is justified by the fact that the Run for the Wall contains many, if not all, of the elements that students of ritual would see as characteristic of any classic pilgrimage. At the heart of a pilgrimage, after all, is the idea of a journey, and at the heart of the journey is the idea that traveling to a different or special place will bring about a change in one's life, in one's viewpoint, in one's state of being. The physical journey is thus paralleled by a spiritual or psychological one; it is not mere travel. And while the destination is important to pilgrimage, so is the journey itself.

The only thing that seems to differentiate the Run for the Wall from classic forms of pilgrimage is that it is not based in a particular religious tradition. But pilgrimage need not be religious. The Run for the Wall can be seen as a secular pilgrimage, that is, one that takes place outside a specific religious tradition, and that does not have as its goal a religiously defined destination such as a famous shrine or miracle site.[43] This does not mean, however, that secular pilgrimage cannot have a spiritual dimension. The Run for the Wall, in addition to incorporating Christian rituals (such as morning prayers before each day's journey), includes Native American and even some New Age spirituality, as well as a more general sense of spiritual mission.

Although some pilgrimages are required by religious tradition (such as the Muslim pilgrimage to Mecca or a medieval penitent's journey to Rome), many, if not most, are undertaken out of individual initiative, desire, or need. Pilgrims may seek to acquire spiritual benefits from visiting a sacred place, to find healing for physical or psychological problems, to atone for sins, to honor the holy places of their religious traditions, to establish or affirm their own religious, cultural, or personal identity, and to engage in social or political protest. While pilgrims in the past often went to sacred places to be healed of physical ailments, today's pilgrim usually seeks psychological or emotional healing rather than physical cure, or looks for some sense of fulfillment or completion of a life cycle.[44] British widows visiting the battlefield graves of husbands killed in the World Wars, for example, report "that now their life is complete and they can die in peace."[45] In such cases, the physical journey of the pilgrimage becomes symbolic of life's journey as well.[46]

One of the characteristics of pilgrimage is its long history as a popular ritual, sometimes officially encouraged or required, other times undertaken despite official indifference or even resistance. As Victor Turner said, "Pilgrims vote with their feet" (or in the case of the Run for the Wall, with their wheels). Therefore, engaging in pilgrimage is a particularly appropriate way for veterans to express their anger at government indifference and neglect as well as their grief at the death and suffering rendered by America's longest war. At the same time, pilgrimage is a recognized ritual form, thus tying Run participants to other rituals past and present, giving it ritual legitimacy.

Central to pilgrimage is the *meaning* of the journey, and it is this meaning that distinguishes pilgrimage from more ordinary trips. For example, one could ride a motorcycle into Washington, D.C., to visit the Vietnam Veterans Memorial just because it is a famous site. This would be a very different journey from traveling with the Run for the Wall, whose participants see themselves as people with a mission. In the first instance, the visitor is a tourist; in the latter, a pilgrim. And while anthropologists and others have debated whether there is a difference between pilgrimage and tourism (and whether tourism is the characteristic pilgrimage of the present age), the difference is clear to participants in the Run for the Wall. As one Vietnam veteran stated, "I'm a pilgrim, not a tourist."[47]

Part of what makes a journey a pilgrimage thus lies in the intent of those who participate. Those who take part in the Run see a definite distinction between their journey and more ordinary rides. On the 1998 Run we sometimes heard scornful comments about the "day riders" along the way who had no sense of the serious nature of the Run and its mission but who joined us for a short period because they thought it would be a kick to ride their motorcycles with a bunch of other bikers. In contrast to those along the way who regularly join the Run for part of its journey every year and are committed to the cause, some of these day riders would cut in and out of the pack, drink beer or liquor at stops, and in general behave in more rowdy and less serious fashion than those who perceived the Run as a true pilgrimage.[48] At the same time, not all those who go on the Run for the Wall begin their journey as pilgrims. Some participants start out seeing it as "just going for a ride." After they have experienced the emotional power of the Run and its rituals, however, they too become pilgrims and supporters of the Run and its cause.

Pilgrimage, far from dying out in a secular, modern world, is, if anything, enjoying increasing popularity. Greater affluence and improved and more convenient modes of travel are only part of the reason that pilgrimage is so popular in the contemporary world. More important may be pilgrimage's flexibility, its ability to meet a wide range of individual needs and to fit within a range of religious and nonreligious cultural forms. Because pilgrimage can accommodate a wide variety of goals and motivations, whether religious or secular, traditional or newly established, it is a flexible form of ritual that may be particularly suitable in a society such as the United States that emphasizes individual choice and distrusts rigid ritual forms. Such flexibility has become especially important for those who seek spiritual activities that fit their particular needs rather than those structured by traditional religious institutions (although traditional religious pilgrimage also continues to flourish); it can be seen in what Walter terms "the spontaneous creation of personal rituals within an overall historical framework" during pilgrimage.[49] Although he is speaking of war grave pilgrimage, his description applies to many other kinds of pilgrimage as well, including the Run for the Wall: "Thus although pilgrimage is an old practice, pilgrims can use their journey to address such current problems as drug addiction and safe airplane travel. . . . Pilgrimage rituals can constantly be reinscribed with meaning, in part, perhaps, because they are often created by and depend upon individual desire and popular practice, and hence are always in process."[50]

Since it was established, the Vietnam Veterans Memorial has been the object of pilgrimage, beginning with its inauguration and continuing unabated to the present day. Sometimes the pilgrim's journey to the Wall is solitary; sometimes it is made in the company of others, whether family, friends, or fellow veterans. Veterans' hospitals may organize groups of patients for such a journey, seeking healing for those struggling with PTSD.[51] Or veterans may organize themselves, as in the Run for the Wall. Whatever the form of their journey, most veterans undertake this pilgrimage with many of the same goals and fears as those that characterize the participants in the Run.[52]

PILGRIMAGE AS A LIMINAL PASSAGE

The power of the Run for the Wall as a ritual is clear from both our own responses to it and those of other participants. The fact that many are drawn back to repeat the journey year after year is further testimony to its power. But what makes the Run such a compelling journey? To answer that question, we need to examine the ritual structure and the symbolism of pilgrimage.

Anthropologists Victor and Edith Turner suggested that pilgrimage can be seen as a rite of passage, a ritual that carries individuals from one stage or condition of life to another. As in any rite of passage, one of the important ritual elements is leaving ordinary life and entering what Victor Turner called a "liminal" state. In effect, one is in a different time and place, symbolically speaking, from ordinary life. This state is characterized by what Turner termed "communitas," in which the ordinary divisions and distinctions of society are dissolved, at least for the time, and participants enter a state of equality and shared experience. The desire to experience such communitas, according to Turner and Turner, is a major motivation for pilgrimage.[53] During the liminal time of pilgrimage, various transformations can take place, a different sort of life can be led or envisioned, one can come in touch with other, different worlds. One may also encounter something that lies outside the bounds of ordinary life—healing, connection (with others, with the divine), or even miracles.

While the symbolism of a journey plays a part in a number of different kinds of rituals, in a pilgrimage, the central feature of the ritual is an actual movement through space.[54] The pilgrims are physically removed from their ordinary life and exist, for a time at least, in another reality, the reality of the ritual journey with its focus on the pilgrimage destination. In the case of the Run for the Wall, the reality is composed of a hundred or more veterans and supporters intensely focused on the act of riding their motorcycles, on the physical hardships of the journey, on the rituals that mark the way, on the issues of the Vietnam War, on POW/MIAs, and on their final destination—the Wall.

In the Run for the Wall, it is with the riding of motorcycles that the liminality and communitas generated by the Run begin, as participants separate themselves from ordinary life by the very mode of transportation taken to make the journey. Riding a motorcycle differentiates participants in the Run from others on the road, and this difference is heightened by the general biker culture sense of apartness, which distinguishes bikers from more ordinary people, who ride in "cages." Riding a motorcycle is a way of making what has become a relatively safe and routine (and even boring) trip across the country more extraordinary, difficult, and even dangerous.[55]

It is a not uncommon characteristic of pilgrimage—and especially of a worthwhile or particularly meritorious pilgrimage—that it be difficult. In the past simply making the pilgrimage was difficulty enough, with the long distance pilgrims had to travel (usually on foot), the dangers posed by local transportation, bandits, and others who preyed on travelers, poor food and lodging, unsanitary conditions, disease, and so on. Nowadays, with greater affluence and improved means of transportation, travel to most of the world's pilgrimage sites is not the difficult journey it once was. However, one can *make* the journey difficult, through financial sacrifice, through ritual abstinence, or through making at least part of the journey in physically difficult ways (walking many miles to a shrine when one could drive, approaching a church barefoot or upon one's knees). In a similar fashion, the Run for the Wall elevates the merit of the pilgrimage by having its participants make the trip on motorcycles rather than in some more convenient or comfortable way.[56]

What is the purpose of hardship and danger? From a psychological perspective, hardship and suffering add worth and value to the end gained. They also serve to focus the mind and the emotions on the ritual and its purposes.[57] Enduring hardships on the Run also links the riders to important American values about masculinity, and particularly the equation of maleness with the common man that is rooted in American ideas of equality and democracy. The "real man" is a working man. Real men make their way in the world by subjecting their bodies to hard use, from the farmers and woodsmen of the colonial militia to the cowboy gunfighters of the Old West, to the twentieth-century warrior—whether real, as in the case of Audie Murphy, or fictional, as in the case of Rambo. Toughness, that is, the ability and willingness to endure discomfort and pain without complaint and without slacking off, has long been an element of the American ideal of the heroic male.[58] By enduring the hardships of the Run without complaint, male riders proclaim—to themselves and others—that they are real men, different from the wimps riding around in "cages" (and also from the "draft dodgers" who refused to go to war).[59]

Difficulty and danger also can increase the sense of accomplishment once the journey has been completed and can strengthen the bonds among the pilgrims. The nerve-wracking trip through a snowstorm on the way to Flagstaff during the 1998 Run not only provided a topic of conversation for days to come, but also created a sense of unity among those of us who had been together on this section of the Run. Some even spoke of creating a special snow-squadron patch to commemorate the event and to mark those who had shared this experience.[60] In addition, the exhaustion and buzz that are produced by long days of riding and by the roar and vibration of the motorcycles make participants particularly receptive to the ritual messages of the journey.[61] This is combined with the repetition that is characteristic of ritual—similar messages regarding POW/MIAs, why we ride, and so on, are communicated in a number of ritual forms throughout the journey—and inscribes a powerful ritual message upon participants in the Run.

The hardships and danger endured by veterans on the Run also might be seen as a symbolic form of self-sacrifice that pays homage to the dead and to those who are believed to have been left behind in Vietnam. While we never heard anyone on the Run say this explicitly, the difficulty of the journey may also re-create for the riders some of the hardships, and the resulting camaraderie, of the Vietnam experience itself, for the wartime experience was also one of liminality and communitas. Those fighting in Vietnam were removed from ordinary life and placed in circumstances from which there was a risk that their only exit would be through death or injury. And in the warrior ideology (if not necessarily in actual experience), all are equal under conditions of combat. In this ideal image of combat, distinctions are made only on the basis of character and personality, not according to social status, occupation, wealth, or ethnic background.[62] This sense of communitas is strengthened and solidified in the face of a common enemy and the ever-present danger and excitement of combat conditions. As one veteran told us, "When the world is exploding all around you, and you are running like hell pumping out rounds, you're scared shitless, but there is no high like it in civilian life."

In this sense the Run for the Wall not only brings back memories of the pain and horror of the war experience, it also recreates an idealized past, the communitas of warriors who side by side faced both the horror and the thrill of imminent danger and threat of death. What Walter says of former soldiers' return to battlefield grave sites in Europe might apply equally to many Vietnam veterans: "The war often provided 'the best years of my life' for those for whom the rest of life has offered little. . . . Or . . . the ex-serviceman may come to feel that the world that he fought for and that his mates died for had been lost anyway, so he clings to those other veterans who can affirm the old values, and to the memory of those who sacrificed themselves for those values."[63]

In the Run for the Wall, a veteran can recreate, if only for a few weeks and only in a muted form, the emotional intensity and communitas of that wartime experience. This is probably a major reason for the comments we have heard from several veterans: "The Run is the highlight of my life," and "I live for the Run; I plan for it all year."

Hardship is not only physical, however. The psychological and emotional pain that pilgrimage entails may be more difficult than physical obstacles: "Grief-centered pilgrimages have their share of pain and suffering, and such emotional pain is often a vital element in the development of a pilgrimage."[64] More difficult than the hardships of a cross-country motorcycle trip for many of the riders are the pain and grief that the trip evokes. This sickness of the soul is eloquently captured in one patch that reads "Not all wounds are visible." The unhealed emotional wounds of the war are what bring many veterans to the Run. At the same time, it is also this pain, and not any physical hardship, that has kept several people we have met from completing, or even attempting, the Run.

LIMITS TO COMMUNITAS

While the Run for the Wall, like many other pilgrimages, espouses an ideology of common purpose, the Run also mixes communitas with more individualistic motives and actions. As Eade and Sallnow have pointed out, pilgrimages are complex phenomena, with sometimes conflicting and contested meanings and motivations.[65] The views of individual pilgrims may or may not fit with the articulated collective goals of fellow pilgrims, and some pilgrims undertake their journey concerned only or mostly with their own motivations and feelings, rather than with a sense of collective endeavor or purpose. "Often, even within group pilgrimages, the meanings and messages transmitted to individual pilgrims may be personal and special to them alone . . . every pilgrim has a story to tell."[66]

As discussed earlier, those on the Run are bonded by three common goals: riding across the country to the Wall, promoting the POW/MIA cause, and healing the emotional wounds of war. The degree of commitment that individual riders have to these three goals, however, may vary substantially. For some, the Run is a desperate effort to force the government to obtain freedom for aging comrades or relatives still in captivity in Vietnam. For others, the primary goal is to ensure that those who are still missing are finally returned home to be buried in their own country. For others, the main concern is simply the struggle to arrive at the Wall. For still others, the focus of the Run is to support and be supported in the long difficult process of healing the wounds of war, and to acknowledge and be acknowledged in their identity as veterans. For us, the Run has been an opportunity to support and connect with those who were sent to war at a young age and who had their lives changed forever, and to confront our own grief and anger over a war that devastated so many of our generation.

Yet although people bring their personal goals to pilgrimage, even the most inwardly focused pilgrim is often affected by the communal ritual of the journey. "The individual on a personal quest is touched by and drawn into the social processes of the pilgrimage. . . . The outward, physical journey may be an inner, spiritual one, but the inner spiritual journey may also involve an outward search for belonging, community, and social identity."[67] Thus, many who undertake the Run for the purpose of personal healing or mourning find themselves, by the end of the journey, bound up with the Run as a communal event and committed to the cause to which it is dedicated.

But it is not only the individual concerns and inward focus of people on the Run that conflict with or modify feelings of communitas. Social differences among pilgrims are not necessarily dissolved in the act of pilgrimage but may continue to divide pilgrims even as they are engaged in a common ritual.[68] Sometimes these differences center on differing expectations and goals for the pilgrimage itself, or differing ideas of how it should be organized and conducted. Such

differences can loom especially large in a folk ritual such as the Run
for the Wall, which has no formal centralized authority that dictates
the way rituals will be carried out.[69] Other differences arise from distinctions made among those with different experiences of the Vietnam War, for example, between in-country combat vets and those
who served in other military roles during this period, between officers and enlisted men, between different branches of service, and, of
course, between veterans and nonveterans. In addition, there are personality conflicts that emerge in the course of the journey and that
can be exacerbated by the emotional and psychological problems that
many in this particular group of vets have experienced.

Thus while the ideology of the Run for the Wall is one of brotherhood and a common goal—and this is an ideology that receives
far more than lip service, as riders provide each other with financial,
emotional, and mechanical aid in the long journey across the country—this ideology exists in tension with the divisions that are not
completely dissolved in the ritual communitas of the Run. Such tensions may even lead to groups splitting off to make separate, parallel
runs, joining up here and there with the main pack but setting their
own times and routes and even arriving ahead of the others at the
Wall, as has happened several of the years we have been on the Run.[70]

In the final analysis, however, one of the remarkable things about
the Run for the Wall—as with many other rituals, including pilgrimages—is its ability to bring together people of diverse backgrounds,
values, and goals in a common activity. In this, it is not only the
common journey that plays a role, but also the Run's destination—
the Wall. To quote Eade and Sallnow: "The power of a shrine . . . derives in large part from its character . . . as . . . a ritual space capable
of accommodating diverse meanings and practices. . . . This . . . is what
confers upon a major shrine its essential, universalistic character: its
ability to reflect and absorb a multiplicity of religious [and secular]
discourses, to be able to offer a variety of clients what each of them
desires."[71]

THE RUN FOR THE WALL AS AN AMERICAN PILGRIMAGE

It is clear that the Run for the Wall exhibits many of the features
commonly associated with pilgrimage: a journey, communitas and
liminality, a special place that is the object of the journey, and so

on. But the Run is also a very *American* ritual, and it is this that both gives the Run its distinctive cultural form and helps create some of its emotional power.

A key symbol of the Run, that of coming home, embodies important American values. This symbolic theme is apparent in the greeting that veterans give each other, and that they receive from individuals and communities in the places where they stop in the course of the Run.[72] But "coming home" is reflected not only in the belated welcome and acceptance contained in the phrase "Welcome home, brother." Pilgrimage itself represents a kind of return: "Although pilgrimage is, in physical terms, concerned with going out, it is also, in a very real sense, a return, a going back, not just in the physical return home, but in emotional terms. One theme that constantly occurs within pilgrimage . . . is that of holding on to the past, to what appears to have been lost to the present, and of reconstituting that past in an idealised and romanticized way."[73]

In the Run for the Wall, the idealized return is reflected in two ways: the return to the camaraderie and communitas of the wartime experience, and a return to the kind of American values that are felt to be epitomized by the small communities along the way that welcome the returned warriors with expressions of support, appreciation, and patriotism. The welcome they receive represents to many on the Run "what we were fighting for" and assures them that there really was a homeland that they were defending. Such a homeland offers a symbolic alternative to the society experienced by many of the veterans on the Run when they returned home from Vietnam, a society torn apart by dissension over the war and seen by many vets as hostile to them. After the stop in Rainelle on our first Run in 1996, one veteran commented, "My reception in Rainelle made up for my reception when I returned from Vietnam."[74]

In addition, the symbols of patriotism that are deployed during the Run (American flags, the Pledge of Allegiance, the national anthem, eagles, Native American designs, and so on) invoke American values of freedom, patriotism, bravery, and sacrifice for love of country. These symbols are incorporated into the various rituals that punctuate the journey and are displayed on the bikes and the persons of the pilgrims themselves.

Pilgrimage also accommodates two other important elements of American culture—individualism and community. In the Run for the

Wall, participants join in a common cause but also ride in order to realize individual ends. It is here that the flexibility of pilgrimage as a ritual comes into play, for the Run's population fluctuates as individuals feel free to participate or to withdraw if the Run does not meet their needs. Individualism and community are also both perfectly expressed and experienced in the group act of riding. Participants on the Run are able "to do their own thing." As the group heads down the road, each rider is encased in his (or her) own world: "On a motorcycle feeling, experience, and thought are united. The rider is wholly at one with his world."[75] At the same time, one is riding as part of a group, with the motorcycles only a few feet away from each other in side-by-side formation, dependent upon other bikers to ride safely. Other riders are also there to give aid when needed. Thus through shared interests, and through the act of riding together, a sense of community is created and everyone works together to make certain that anyone on the Run who wants to will be able to "go all the way." This is expressed through the biker concept of brotherhood (and to some extent, sisterhood), and the wider American cultural concept of "family" (see chapter 7).

But there is more to joining a group like the Run for the Wall than mutual aid or working for a common cause. One of the paradoxes of individualism in American culture is that it is often through joining a community that the individual may most fully realize his or her identity. Thus many of those who join the Run for the Wall find themselves developing new identities as veterans through their experience. Many veterans we have met on the Run have not been active participants in mainstream veterans' organizations such as the American Legion and the Veterans of Foreign Wars, particularly vets who experienced rejection by such organizations when they returned from Vietnam. Stories of being told by some World War II veteran that they had not fought in a "real war" are common when Vietnam veterans get together to talk about their homecoming. On the Run, veterans can share their experiences with others who understand what they have been through, and in a context in which it is not only acceptable but even a matter of pride to be a veteran. The Run has also introduced veterans to others in their city or state who are not only fellow Vietnam veterans but also bikers. Such contacts can become the basis for a new social world, and a new identity, once they return home. In Arizona, for example, the Run has served as the catalyst for the creation of a group of Run for the Wall activists centered in Phoenix, many of whom had not known each other before the Run. There are others we know who had never been involved in any veterans' group or activity relating to veterans who became active in various veterans' organizations *after* they returned home from the Run, organizations ranging from the Vietnam Veterans motorcycle clubs to the American Legion. Such actions represent a significant change in these individuals' identity. Until then, they had not actively embraced an identity *as* veterans, either because they were reluctant to acknowledge their veteran status in the face of social prejudice or because their war experiences were so traumatic they simply did not want to think about them and instead focused on their postwar lives. For some, the Run itself becomes central to the maintenance of that identity, both during and between Runs, and such individuals may become heavily involved in the annual planning for the Run.

"NOT ALL WOUNDS ARE VISIBLE": THE RUN AS HEALING RITUAL

The wounds of Vietnam that afflict the participants in the Run for the Wall are, for the most part, not the obvious ones. They are less visible ailments such as PTSD, the effects of exposure to Agent Orange, addictions, guilt, anger, and loss. Participants often speak of their pilgrimage as a journey of healing. But how, exactly, does such a ritual heal?

Medical anthropologists generally distinguish between "curing" and "healing."[76] Curing refers to the effects of the biomedical system that eliminate or correct the source of the biomedically caused disease. The patient may still remain ill, however, continuing to suffer from the psychic, social, and cognitive consequences of the disease, even after the physical cause has been eliminated or corrected. Healing, on the other hand, involves dealing with these consequences and restoring the patient to emotional, psychological, and social wholeness. As Danforth states: "Healing, like becoming sick, is at once a cultural, social, psychological, and physiological process. In all cultures powerful sets of symbols mediate between the sociocultural world, on the one hand, and psychophysiological states on the other. Meaning, in other words, ties together social relationships, emotional states, and physiological conditions."[77]

In a society dominated by a biomedical approach to human ailments, this healing process is often downplayed or neglected. Thus, while a cancer patient, for example, may be cured through surgery and radiation or chemotherapy, other consequences of the disease and its treatment, such as the fear of death, the changed view of one's body, or difficulties in personal relations, usually are not directly addressed by the biomedical system.[78] This is one reason for the rise of the American cultural phenomenon of support groups. Such groups not only seek to heal the consequences and ongoing problems of diseases such as cancer or lupus, but also address personal traumas for which there is no biomedical cure (such as rape, incest, or the death of a child). In this respect, the Run for the Wall can be seen as a support group that provides its participants with healing for "the wounds that are not visible," including grief and loss, guilt, alienation, PTSD, and other effects of participation in the Vietnam War.[79]

But how do rituals actually heal? And specifically, in the case of the Run for the Wall, what are the "powerful sets of symbols" of which Danforth speaks that mediate the healing process?

Rituals are often seen as healing through a process of catharsis, itself viewed as "the key to successful ritual."[80] The release of emotion, it is argued, brings both psychological relief and physical healing. In this respect, it is not uncommon for healing rituals to first heighten the anxiety of the person being healed, increasing the power of the emotional release. Thus the pilgrim on the Run for the Wall feels increasing anxiety and pain as the Wall draws closer, climaxing in confrontation with the Wall itself and with the dead whose names are inscribed there. Most of the rituals during the journey remind the riders of their final destination; the Run accumulates ritual objects to be taken to the Wall from those along the way; and the morning prayers ask God for strength as the Wall grows closer. The confrontation when the group arrives at the Wall is painful and emotional. With tears streaming down their faces, veterans locate the names of dead comrades on the Wall and lay their offerings beneath the names. Or they wander the Wall's length, seeking to absorb the tragedy of over fifty-five thousand names engraved in the polished black granite. Some kneel in prayer. Others, unable to bear the pain, collapse on nearby benches, accompanied by supportive friends. The pain is highly personal and individual, yet collective as well. "We will not leave until everyone is ready," John and Linda Anderson, the leaders on our first year of the Run, told us when we arrived at the Wall, affirming the support that the Run as a whole promises to suffering individuals.

While catharsis may be one element of ritual healing, however, it by no means completely explains the process. Nor is the journey to the Wall, even in the company of other veterans, all that is involved in the healing.[81] While we have no way of measuring the healing that takes place among those who take part in the Run for the Wall, by participants' own accounts it is a more effective healing process than a private visit to the Wall might be.[82] There are several reasons that can be suggested for this.

First, the Run is a ritual, and as we previously discussed, rituals have a particular power not found in other activities. Second, the Run is built around a set of American cultural symbols with powerful, positive meaning for many of the vets: the "Welcome home"; the riding with other veterans and supporters; the POW/MIA issue; the ceremonies along the way that commemorate the veterans, the dead, and the missing. As Thomas Csordas states, "The key to the therapeutic effectiveness of systems of religious healing is precisely this ability to reorganize or restructure the conceptual worlds of people who are ill."[83] On the Run, such restructuring involves, in part, replacing the veteran's hostile homecoming reception with the positive "Welcome home," and the shame at having fought in an unpopular war with a sense of pride. Third, because it is more than a one-shot ride, the Run is able to sustain a sense of brotherhood and community among many of its participants beyond the pilgrimage.

While a cure is something definite, marking the end of the therapeutic process, healing can be ongoing and can need regular renewal. In this sense, the Run for the Wall is similar to some of the ritual therapy groups found in other cultures, as well as to more secular American support groups, such as Alcoholics Anonymous.[84] Such groups tend to have certain things in common. First, they often address physical and psychological problems that cannot be addressed by the society's conventional systems of healing (including the Western biomedical system). Second, the individuals involved in such groups are often socially marginal in one respect or another or are in difficult situations in which they feel they have little control over their lives.[85] On the Run, such individuals find themselves with others who have had similar experiences and who can provide understanding and support. In addition, through association with the group, a person is offered a framework of meaning within which suffering can be understood. And finally, when the support group includes participating in some extraordinary experience, whether it is entering a trance state, walking over hot coals,[86] or riding a motorcycle across the country, sufferers can achieve a sense of self-worth and empowerment, thus "moving . . . from a negative state of illness to a positive state of health through a persuasive rhetoric of empowerment and transformation."[87] It is in the ritual and symbolic elements, and especially in the engagement in an extraordinary experience, that the Run for the wall differs from groups such as AA or support groups in VA medical centers.[88]

All this does not happen overnight, of course, or even in the course of a single Run for the Wall. Like individuals in other societies who become lifelong members of their ritual therapy groups, many of those who participate in the Run for the Wall feel the therapeutic need to return for the Run year after year: "Although the pilgrimage is fixed in temporal terms, the processes of pilgrimage do not stop at the return. Many people return incessantly in their memories, keeping alive those special moments that changed their lives. . . . For some the experience (and the desire to recreate the community within which that experience was felt) is such that they attempt to reconstitute it, and to return again to that idealised past, by going on pilgrimage again and again."[89]

Like other pilgrims, those who have made all or part of the Run, return to it—or to memories of it—many times. Like other support groups, the Run is concerned with individual healing; however, its central focus is on a collective experience (the Vietnam War) rather than on purely individual experiences (such as childhood trauma) as the source of the problems it tries to address.

Experience, Meaning, and Memory

Central to the healing process is the construction of meaning. Out of inchoate individual suffering, collective meaning is created through the ritual process. For many Americans, both civilian and in uniform, the Vietnam War created a void of meaning. Those who could not accept official rhetoric that justified the war or the sensibility of its strategy, as well as those who later could not reconcile their image of America with the idea of losing a war, had to redeploy the conceptual tools of their culture to construct new understandings. This was easier for civilians, for if they could not accept the official meanings offered by the government, they could either define the war as unimportant and go about their lives, or join the antiwar movement as activists or simply as someone who supported a swift U.S. withdrawal.

These options were not available to those in uniform, particularly those serving in Vietnam. They certainly could not define the war as unimportant and simply go about their business. For many, the war *was* their daily business. Nor could they easily pursue the war-resister route, even had they wished. While some who served in Vietnam became antiwar activists after returning home (and some even protested while still in uniform), for most, the war was a reality to be actively pursued or at least survived, not an opportunity for political action.[90] More importantly, those in the middle of a war have a great need to understand what they are doing as moral and meaningful. Defining a war as immoral or meaningless while you are fighting it comes at a great price. When men and women who have been taught that killing is wrong are asked to kill in the name of their country, they need to believe that their country is justified in asking them to do so. When people are asked to risk death in the name of their country, they need to believe that there is some tactical or strategic purpose that will keep their possible death from being meaningless. And when people are asked to step outside their normal lives in service to their nation, they need to believe that they will return as honorable and welcomed citizens who did their duty. When the meaning system that enables soldiers to believe in the morality, purposefulness, and honorableness of their sacrifices breaks down, they face a crisis not just of the mind but of the spirit. This is precisely what happened to many of the Vietnam veterans who have found their way to the Run for the Wall.[91]

Many U.S. combat soldiers experienced the day-to-day conduct of the Vietnam War as senseless. They could not frame a larger purpose behind much of what they themselves were doing. They experienced the intense pursuit of enemy body counts with no apparent strategic goal in mind. Trained to fight to win, soldiers found themselves fighting and bleeding for pieces of terrain that were abandoned only to be fought and bled for again. Pilots leveled vast stretches of nearly empty jungle yet were not allowed to bomb obvious military targets in North Vietnam. Soldiers found themselves risking their lives—and seeing their comrades killed and wounded—unsure if there was any purpose to their fighting other than staying alive. If they found another motivation, it was often revenge for the death of a close comrade; in other words, they were motivated simply by the consequences of the war itself.[92]

In addition, many of the young men who fought in Vietnam had their faith in themselves—and in the values of their culture—shaken by the experience. As one veteran traveling to the Wall put it, "You're taught to believe in God, you don't harass anyone, you don't kill. . . . You have some values, and all of a sudden it just don't mean nothing."[93] As Jonathan Shay points out in *Achilles in Vietnam*, "The most ancient traditions of Western culture instruct us to base our self-respect on firmness of character," and we want to believe that our own moral courage will hold firm even under the most difficult circumstances.[94] Such a belief in their own good character was challenged by the actions many soldiers found themselves committing while in combat situations, creating the fear that such actions might in fact represent their real character.[95]

Once the veterans returned home, their belief that those who take up arms in defense of their country are performing heroic service and will be welcomed with honor was challenged by the indifference or hostility that many of them felt they received. Many veterans report that the civilians they encountered didn't want to hear about the war, even when they asked the vet what it was like. Moreover, the behaviors that had been appropriate, necessary, and commendable in the combat conditions of Vietnam were regarded with disgust and horror by many civilians back home. As one VA counselor working with Vietnam veterans put it: "One of the jobs of combat training is to remove some of the conflict over aggression, so that you can be aggressive. In wars like World War II, society helped remove this conflict. In these wars, society tells soldiers that their aggressiveness is good. When the war's over, society welcomes them back home. But that's not what happened with the Vietnam War."[96]

Some of the veterans on the Run have told us that they had "got on with their lives" after returning home and for many years felt there was nothing to confront or deal with from their Vietnam experience. Often it was some particular event that awakened memories and emotions of that experience and brought them to participate in the Run for the Wall. This event might be a physical or mental breakdown, a life-altering event such as a death or divorce, a "midlife crisis," or an encounter with a place or situation connected with the war. As we noted previously, visiting the memorial at Angel Fire had this kind of powerful impact on several of the Vietnam veterans we know, just as seeing the news of the dedication of the Wall had a similar effect on others. Still other Vietnam veterans have suffered a variety of physical and mental problems since their return from the war: drug and alcohol problems, broken relationships, PTSD, the effects of Agent Orange, and so on. To these is added the lingering—and often surprisingly fresh—grief that many of these veterans still feel for their dead comrades all these years after the war.

Many Vietnam veterans also harbor strong feelings of guilt, not only for acts that they might have committed in the heat of combat, but also for "failing" to save comrades. In some cases there is guilt that they served in Vietnam as clerks or support personnel, roles that did not expose them to the danger of death and injury experienced by those in combat but subjected them to being called REMFs (rear-echelon motherfuckers) by those who did face battle. And many suffer from survivor guilt—they have lived to go on with their lives when so many thousands did not. "My name should be up there" is something we have heard several veterans we know say when confronting the Wall.

The role of post-traumatic stress disorder deserves a special mention here, as it is the diagnosis applied to a range of difficulties suffered by many of the veterans on the Run. The literature on this subject, especially as applied to Vietnam veterans, is vast, and sometimes contradictory and controversial, and we do not have the space to review it here.[97] However, the idea that traumatic experiences during the war, and especially in combat, have led to later life problems plays an important role in the biographies and self-images of the veterans. PTSD is a diagnosis recognized and treated by the Veterans Administration medical system, and a number of people we know receive full- or partial-disability income based on this diagnosis.

The Diagnostic and Statistical Manual of Mental Disorders III was the first edition to include PTSD as an identifiable, discrete disorder, and it listed a set of observable post-traumatic symptoms, including re-experiences of the distressful event in the form of flashbacks and dreams, loss of interest in formerly pleasurable activities, sleep disorders, irritability, persistent mobilization for danger, and so on.[98] The

PTSD diagnosis is "inextricably connected with the lives of American Veterans of the Vietnam War, with their experiences as combatants, and, later, as patients of the Veterans Administration (VA) Medical System."[99] This diagnosis was not made immediately after the war, however. It was at least a decade after most soldiers were discharged that the PTSD diagnosis became official, and even longer before the VA offered specialized treatment for the disorder. By this time, "the 'crazy Vietnam vet'—angry, violent, and emotionally unstable—had become an American archetype."[100]

Although diagnoses of shell shock and similar conditions among combat troops date back to the nineteenth century, not everyone accepted PTSD as a recognizable syndrome. Those who denied the existence of such a syndrome felt that "no new diagnostic classification was needed to account for the psychiatric disorders affecting Vietnam veterans."[101] Advocates of the diagnosis, however, made a compelling moral argument: "The failure to make a place for PTSD would be equivalent to blaming the victim for his misfortunes—misfortunes inflicted on him by both his government and its enemies. It would mean denying medical care and compensation to men, who, in contrast to their more privileged coevals, had been obliged or induced to sacrifice their youths in a dirty and meaningless war. Acknowledging PTSD would be a small step toward repaying a debt."[102]

In a sense, then, the PTSD diagnosis sought to make sense out of the experiences of veterans who were suffering from a variety of symptoms related to their combat experience by saying, in essence, that they were not crazy but suffered from a genuine disorder, with real identifiable causes. In doing so, it offered at least the possibility of a cure (though a cure seems to have proved elusive).

But the PTSD diagnosis offers meaning only at a clinical level. And it does not address the less severe, but nonetheless disturbing, memories and problems of other veterans who have not been so diagnosed. To see why another level of meaning may be necessary for healing, we turn to the relationship between healing and narrative.

Narrative and Healing, Narrative as Healing

An early writer on what was at the time called "traumatic memory" points out that memory is an action: "*It is the action of telling a story*. . . . The teller must not only know how to do it, but must also know how to associate the happening with the other events of his life, how to put it in its place in that life history which for each of us is an essential element of his personality."[103] Such stories can be part of a shared cultural identity, such as the identity veterans can develop *as* veterans. John Braithwaite, in his analysis of cultural communication among Vietnam veterans, refers to these stories as "myth," not in the sense of myth as falsehood, but as a speech form that "provides speakers with a way to apply and express significant aspects of their cultural identity." These stories deal with a variety of phenomena common to many, if not all, veterans (not just experiences of the war, but homecoming, dealing with the VA, etc.):

> The stories told by Vietnam veterans regarding these common topics provide a ground for the speaker's beliefs in what moves them and their world. The stories allow the Vietnam veteran storyteller to articulate to himself and his listeners the way he, *as* a Vietnam veteran, sees and experiences the world. The stories told about the problems encountered by one veteran, which are common to all veterans, help us to understand the forces transcending the fate of any particular man. . . . The stories help to establish a sense of "place" for the speaker within a particular cultural milieu.[104]

The self is thus fit into a larger narrative.

Recent discussions of the role of narrative in experience have suggested that there cannot even *be* experience in any meaningful way unless we can construct a narrative. This narrative, however, is constructed in a cultural context. If there are past experiences that are difficult or impossible to talk about, it may be not so much that language is inadequate, or that memory is too painful, but rather that "sometimes there are situations or events . . . that are the occasions of 'experiences' that cannot be expressed in the terms that language (or, more broadly, the symbolic order) offers *at that moment*."[105] Such a situation has been reported for Holocaust survivors, as well as for survivors of individual rather than collective trauma, and this has also been a problem for Vietnam veterans, many of whom felt unable to talk about their war experiences. Part of the reason for this is that the Vietnam War itself "had no conventional narrative structure—a war without a clear beginning or end, without well-articulated goals, fought sometimes with scant regard for geographic boundaries, and indeed, remaining undeclared, technically not a war at all."[106] Because the Vietnam War lacked a recognizable narrative structure, that is, a way to talk about it that fit with stories of other wars, many veterans found it hard to tell others about what they had experienced. Isak Dineson observes that even the greatest sorrows can be endured if we can put them into stories.[107] Unfortunately, this avenue of relief was closed to many Vietnam veterans by the seeming incoherence of any story they might tell about the Vietnam War.

The Run for the Wall offers veterans a symbolic order in which a narrative can be created, and experience articulated and reclaimed. Through participation in the Run, veterans and their supporters create meaning out of psychological and emotional pain, and a new narrative is built that seeks to integrate the Vietnam experience into individual and collective biography. But this new narrative does not begin at an intellectual or cognitive level. It begins with the highly sensory act of motorcycle riding. As we have previously noted, the long motorcycle ride across the country and the successful arrival at the Wall take physical and psychological suffering and translate them into physical (and psychological) accomplishment. Painful emotions and memories may be aroused in the course of the journey, but they occur in the course of a pilgrimage that demands physical attention and skill, and in the company of others who can provide understanding and support.

But there is more involved in ritual healing than physical accomplishment and somatic mastery. As things come together in bodily motion, so they come together in a cognitive way as new structures of meaning are created. For the veteran on the Run, suffering is due to the experiences of Vietnam and the resulting trauma. Part of the trauma, at least for some, was the controversy over, and opposition to, the war on the home front and the lack of a positive reception upon the veterans' return. If, as Wagner-Pacifici and Schwartz suggest, "People may need more ritual to face a painful and controversial part of the past than to deal with a painful part of the past about whose cause and meaning there is agreement,"[108] then it becomes clear why rituals such as the Run for the Wall form such an important part of both the individual and collective healing process. A powerful part of the therapy of the Run for the Wall lies in the ritual "Welcome home" that is received on the Run, both from fellow veterans and from noncombatants and communities along the way. Individual suffering becomes transformed into meaningful shared experience made even more effective by the rallying of communal support. The veteran is not just a wounded suffering individual who feels inadequate because he has not been able to adapt or cope after his experience (or because after leading a normal life he finds himself in midlife reliving his trauma) and not just someone experiencing a personal problem or defeat. Rather he is a returned warrior who, with self-sacrificing patriotism, fought for freedom, and who, betrayed by the government that sent him to fight and the citizens he fought to protect, is finally receiving some of the recognition he deserves. At this level, the Run for the Wall fits the general model of religious healing described by Danforth:

> At the psychological and social levels religious healing often proves effective by virtue of its ability to address directly the psychosocial problems that constitute an illness. Healing rituals may reduce the stress, conflict, and tension generated by various social or political institutions or by disturbances in people's relationships with others in a variety of ways. They may, for example, provide group support for people who are isolated or alienated from others. As these people are incorporated into new social groups, they receive attention, comfort, and sympathy, which may be of therapeutic benefit.[109]

In addition to providing group support, ritual therapy may also allow or require the participant to assume a new social status. As we have discussed earlier, this new status can involve both seeing oneself *as* a veteran and experiencing the transformation from "spat-upon" soldier to honored hero. Beyond this, however, the veteran on the Run for the Wall may take on a new role, that of political warrior, someone who is still fighting—fighting for an accounting of the POWs and MIAs the government has shamefully left behind. By engaging in this struggle on behalf of others, Vietnam veterans can add weight to their claim that they went to Vietnam because they were selfless patriots. This commitment of many Run veterans to the POW/MIA issue is symbolically linked to what many of them feel is another type of abandonment—the U.S. government's past and present neglect of Vietnam veterans. From repeated denials about the toxic effects of Agent Orange, to shrinking veterans' benefits, to the bureaucratic nightmare many vets have experienced in trying to pursue disability claims, to the recent closings of VA hospitals, many Vietnam veterans feel abandoned by their government after serving in a war that left them damaged physically, emotionally, or both.[110] The link between the abandonment of the unaccounted for soldier and the rejection of the returned vet intensifies the feelings of frustration and anger of many of those on the Run, because they feel a sense of identification with the POW/MIAs, the sense of "it could have been me." In a larger sense, MIAs may represent the part of the veteran that *was* left behind, the loss of innocence and youth, the sense of a part of a life that will forever be missing.

Whether or not all participants in the Run experience such feelings, or experience them in the same manner or degree, the Run offers the possibility of a cognitive reorganization of the veteran's experience through its symbols and rituals and their communal reenforcement in the course of the pilgrimage. At the same time, the ongoing pain experienced by many veterans is not denied or glossed over but instead given a context and communal support that reassure the veteran that he is not alone in his suffering, nor is he wrong or inadequate because he has such feelings. As a pilgrimage to a monument where the war's dead are remembered, the Run relocates the veteran's emotional pain from the individual to a much larger context, framing it as the consequence of a troubled war fought by a troubled nation, and not as the consequence of personal inadequacy. In addition, the Run binds the veteran once again to a larger society through powerful rituals of reintegration—most of all, by speaking the words "Welcome home."

But who are the people who speak these words? And what is their role in the Run for the Wall?

"AMAZING GRACE": COMMUNITY RITUAL AND THE RUN

Individuals and communities along the Run's cross-country journey play an important role in shaping its nature as a healing pilgrimage, not only by offering food and hospitality, but also by constructing rituals, making personal contact with individual veterans, and extending a warm "Welcome home."[111] This reception is unexpected, and often overwhelming, to those making the Run for the first time. "You'll be amazed at the reception you receive," a woman in Flagstaff told us as we joined the Run for the first time. "In California they don't care, and the same when you get to Washington, D.C., but in between, you'll be welcomed with open arms." It is this "in between" that constitutes the symbolic "heartland of America," the communities along the journey where hospitality is warm and veterans are honored. To many of the veterans, the communities that

welcome them represent the real America, not the America that rejected them but the America that supported the causes for which the
veterans were fighting: patriotism, freedom, family, and community.

Much of the activity that occurs along the journey is at the in-
stigation of local organizations and communities. Such a reception,
we were told, was not expected by those who participated in the first
Run, who had seen their initial contacts with communities along the
way mainly in logistical terms—making certain that camping would
be available, that local authorities would be aware that the group was
coming, and so on. In fact, this outpouring of welcome was part of
what helped to establish the Run as an annual event.

The first Run for the Wall followed a more northerly course on
the early part of the journey. This was later changed to the present
route because of the uncertainties of May weather in those northern
states. (Though, as the 1998 experience in Flagstaff shows, even the
present route can experience weather problems at that time of year.)
Some of the stops along the way, such as Salina, Kansas, and Rainelle,
West Virginia, have been on the itinerary since the very first Run.
Others, such as Angel Fire and the Navaho reservation, are more recent additions. Still others have been dropped, as the Run's route,
schedules, or size have changed. In 1998, for example, the Run made
a stop at the Vietnam veterans memorial in Pueblo, not on the itinerary previously. In 1999, however, the national coordinator decided
that, given the increasing size of the group and the time involved in
getting riders off and then back on the road, this stop would be
dropped.

The decisions about where to stop, and about what ceremonies
are held, are the result of a combination of inputs. During the Run's
early years, the national coordinator made the final decisions on the
route. More recently, a system of state coordinators and a newly
formed board of directors have also come to play a crucial role in
decision making about where the Run would travel and where it
would stop. State coordinators set up events and arrange for meal
stops, police escorts, gas stops, and so on, in their respective states.
Local groups, such as motorcycle clubs and organizations, Harley deal-
ers, and veterans' organizations, arrange food, ceremonies, camping,
and sometimes entertainment at the various stops. Both state coordinators and local groups may lobby to have certain stops made in
their communities, and difficult choices must be made, for the Run

simply cannot stop at every Vietnam memorial or other place of ritual significance that may lie along its journey. (Sometimes, however, a new stop becomes an integral part of the Run, as is now the case with the Navaho Nation Vietnam Veterans Memorial.)

Who are these organizations, groups, and individuals who host the Run along the way? What do they offer to these biker pilgrims? And what do they receive when the Run for the Wall stops in their community?

Because the Run intersects several streams of American culture—especially motorcycle riding and veterans—certain kinds of organizations figure most prominently in local receptions of the Run for the Wall. American Legion and VFW halls are often the location of meals provided for the riders, and various veterans' groups (such as the Vietnam Veterans of America) may participate in ceremonies along the way. Motorcycle organizations such as ABATE (American Brotherhood Aimed Toward Education) and local chapters of the Harley Owners' Group (HOG) also provide hospitality.

While in some places that the Run stops it is a minor event, with only a small part of the local community even aware of its presence, in several of the small towns along the way, the communities themselves are the hosts for the Run. In Cimarron, New Mexico, the group is fed in the parish hall and the mayor has addressed the Run. In Rainelle, where the local school is the focus of the ceremonial events, the Run is fed in the local Moose hall, and riders who wish to camp can bed down in the school gym. In Mt. Vernon, Illinois, after being fed at a highway truck stop, the Run parades through the town and past the local school.

The symbolic content of the Run for the Wall, and the nature of the pilgrimage experience, is thus the outcome of an interactive process. The Run itself provides the ceremonial occasion for specific messages not only about the Vietnam War and Vietnam veterans, but also about war, veterans, the military, sacrifice, patriotism, and community more generally. These messages can vary widely—from glorifying the military to deploring the tragedy of war. Some ceremonies honor the various branches of military service, some address themselves to veterans of all wars, some speak to the POW/MIA issue. But they all have as part of their message the honoring of the returned warrior and the mourning of the dead and missing.

For the veterans, the welcome along the way plays a major role

FIGURE 24. Like pilgrims at other destinations, riders leave offerings at the Wall.

in the healing process, in part by its (re)construction of the meaning of the war. It also connects the Run participants not just with other bikers and veterans, but with everyday folk in these communities. At the various stops, the veterans are publicly honored and thanked— a contrast to the welcome they remember receiving when they returned from Vietnam. Thus healing begins not only with participation in a journey but also in the stops along the way.

Just as relationships and communication among participants in the Run may continue between Runs, so may relationships between the Run and particular communities. Rainelle, West Virginia, is an example of this. The people of Rainelle turn out in force for the bikers' arrival, with ceremonies at the school yard, autograph signings for the schoolchildren, free camping, and a meal serving hundreds of bikers. As Rainelle is a poor mining town with a high rate of unemployment, the hospitality is all the more moving and remarkable. But the Run serves the town as well and provides an event both children and adults look forward to all year. "It gives me chills to see all the bikes riding in," one local woman told us as we stood watching the ceremonies during the 1999 Run. "It makes me think about what you've gone through riding across the country to get here, what you went through in Vietnam," she went on. "I feel you are making a difference. You certainly have made a difference here, increasing awareness of Vietnam among the young people."

The Run itself also seeks to connect to others along the way, and in most years, the Run includes two or three stops at VA hospitals. But it is not only hospitalized vets that the Run seeks to reach. Individual veterans along the way often greet the Run, and "getting out the word" has also to do with proselytizing the Run as a healing event, supporting and encouraging those who might like to join but hesitate out of fear of their own painful memories. And for "those who can't," the riders on the Run for the Wall carry objects to the Wall or bring back rubbings of names, or simply ride in their place or in their memory. In this way, like a colorful strand of interconnected threads, the Run weaves a pattern of movement and love that ties together Run participants, local communities, and the dead who are memorialized on the Wall, while at the same time constructing a narrative that seeks to heal the still painful wounds of war.

6

ALL-THE-WAY WOMEN AND THEIR WARRIORS
Gender on the Run

Motorcycle riding is a male-dominated activity. Although there have been female riders and women's motorcycle organizations for as long as there have been motorcycles, men are clearly more prevalent both among riders and in media images of motorcycling.[1] Women represent only about 8 percent of the approximately four million motorcycle owners in the United States, and women rarely appear as writers or featured riders in most mainstream motorcycle magazines. The only place in the motorcycling press that women *are* featured is in so-called outlaw magazines such as *Easy Rider*, *Biker*, and *In the Wind*, in which nude or scantily clad models draped provocatively over customized Harleys are a major visual theme and an important element of these magazines' popularity.[2] And although women are welcome as riders or passengers in some biker organizations and gatherings, there are other motorcycle clubs and events at which they are greeted with hostility or scorn or at best, tolerated.[3]

The male-dominated nature of motorcycling, and the fact that most Vietnam veterans are men, gives the Run for the Wall a decidedly male-oriented character. Although women participate regularly in the Run, riding either as passengers or on their own bikes, they are a minority, typically comprising no more than 10 percent of the participants on any particular Run. In the years we have gone all the way, the number of "all-the-way women," women who traveled from

California to D.C., has usually numbered between fifteen and twenty.[4] However, despite their small numbers, these women play important social and symbolic roles in the Run.

Women come to the Run for a variety of reasons. Many are there in support of their partners, who are veterans. Others come as bikers who were initially drawn to the Run primarily as an opportunity to ride across the country. Still others are there as supporters of veterans and veterans' issues in general, as individuals who suffered the loss of loved ones in Vietnam, or because of their own history of serving in the military. In the following pages we will explore the various reasons women join the Run for the Wall, and examine the symbolic role of women on the Run, including the role of Jane Fonda ("Hanoi Jane") as a symbol of female betrayal. But first we want to set the stage by discussing the place of women in biker culture and the world of women bikers and their relationship to motorcycle riding.

WOMEN IN BIKER CULTURE

In the early years of the sport, motorcycle riding was portrayed as relatively gender neutral, an activity suitable for both men and women. As Barbara Joans notes: "In the twenties and thirties women rode. Nothing special. Milwaukee created motorcycles and women as well as men took to them. Women were pictured riding, passengering and hanging out in the biking world. In those early days, men and women both rode and while it took daring to do so, women as well as men were daring. But by the late forties the motorcycle world changed."[5]

The contemporary image of the hypermasculine male biker developed in the 1950s is the motorcycling equivalent of the larger postwar culture that was being built on images of an imaginary past in which men were men and women were either sexless moms or available chicks (see chapter 4).[6] Consequently, the dominant mass-media image of a biker today is a man who rides either alone or with a decorative woman on the back of his machine. This image emerged in large part with the development of the outlaw biker world and the wider biker subculture modeled after it. This association of motorcycle riding with hypermasculinity—especially working-class masculinity—was given a powerful boost by fiction and nonfiction stories about outlaw bikers and by biker-gang movies. Women were included in these media portrayals primarily to add sexual spice, either as the objects of male lust in seamy stories about biker gang bangs, or as outlaw hellcats or members of female biker gangs in films.[7]

Joans suggests that there are two general public images associated with women who ride. The woman who rides with a man on his bike is stereotyped as a "sexual outlaw," a sluttish seductress exemplified by the posed images of women in outlaw biker magazines. The woman who rides her own bike, however, is stereotyped as a "gender traitor" for not staying on the back of the bike where she belongs.[8] As Joans and others have pointed out, such images are as stereotyped as the image of the wild, leather-clad male biker. And while there is sometimes hostility on the part of the public—and male bikers—to female riders, they may also be viewed with curiosity, approval, or even admiration.[9] Moreover, while the idea of a woman having her own motorcycle might be greeted with disdain among some all-male groups such as outlaw biker clubs, there are also men who *want* the woman in their life to have her own bike so that she can share his passion for riding.[10]

Despite this, the image of women as disposable accessories is a commonplace theme in the stereotyped biker culture. One Harley-Davidson ad in the mid-1990s, for example, used this image to promote its "convertible" soft-tail model. The ad featured two pictures, one showing the motorcycle outfitted in touring style with a windshield, saddlebags, and a dual seat. The other showed the same motorcycle stripped of these features, including the dual seat. The fully outfitted bike was captioned "A Las Vegas Wedding," while the stripped-down model was headlined "A Tijuana Divorce." The underlying message: Women can be removed from your life as easily as motorcycle accessories can be taken off your bike. A more hostile version of this message is expressed by a patch sometimes seen on the back of biker jackets: "If you can read this, the bitch on the back fell off."[11]

Biker skin magazines may be filled with nude women draped across or sitting astride shiny new machines, but they seldom depict women actually riding motorcycles. If they do, the women are wearing such skimpy leathers that they would suffer a serious case of road rash if all that exposed flesh went sliding along the pavement in a crash. In these magazines, biker gatherings are commonly portrayed as orgies of drinking and (mostly female) nudity. For this reason, some RFTW participants experienced mixed emotions when they learned that an article on the Run had been published in *Easy Rider*, and that another, longer special supplement on the Run for the Wall was being planned for *Biker* magazine.[12] While many welcomed the publicity this coverage would provide for the Run and its message, they felt that the portrayal of motorcycling that dominated these magazines was inconsistent with the serious nature of the Run's mission.

The emphasis given to women as "biker chicks" in the world of motorcycling misrepresents the many roles women actually play there. Even in outlaw clubs, women's roles vary from unattached "broads" who occasionally "party" with (that is, have sex with) club members, to "mammas" who serve the club as a whole by cleaning, cooking, and providing money and sex to club members, to "ol' ladies" who "belong" to a specific patch holder and who are an ongoing and sometimes respected force in the social world of the outlaw club.[13]

While a woman may consider herself rebellious by virtue of her relationship with outlaw bikers, in the men's eyes she is only the companion, not the rebel. What's more, a woman on her own machine would threaten a fundamental element of masculine identity that motorcycling constructs and symbolizes, that is, the way in which the male relationship to his world and his machine is complemented and reinforced by the more passive and decorative female. In addition to their ability to threaten masculine identity, women also threaten the bond of brotherhood that is so central to the culture of outlaw bikers. Men who become more attached to their women than to their brothers may not live up to the value that, above all else, you are there when your brothers need you, whatever their need.[14] At the same time, outlaw clubs cannot ignore the reality that some of their members may establish a close bond with a particular woman. Additionally, a woman who becomes a "righteous ol' lady" for her man assumes "a supportive-role function; she becomes part of a team with her ol' man," thus adding to his stature within the group.[15] For this reason, club rules regarding the relationship of women to the club and its members are typically designed not only to preserve male privilege, but also to ensure that both members and their "ol' ladies" will always put the club first. This helps preserve the idea that the primary bond for any club member is that with his brothers. Thus, in the hypermasculine culture of the outlaw bikers, the women who fit in best are those who accept, and enjoy, traditional male and female roles. As Wolf puts it: "The women who successfully adapt to the ol' lady role appear to be those who accept masculinity as a positive male quality. Rather than showing envy or attempting to constrain its expression, they affirm, enhance, and ultimately enjoy the masculine power of their men."[16]

Outlaw clubs represent one extreme of the construction of gender roles in biker culture. Within other motorcycle cultures, a woman's role, even the passenger's role, is far less secondary. Because we were used to the more egalitarian, couple-oriented world of Gold Wing riders with whom we had been associating in recent years, we were somewhat startled by patches we saw when we attended our first Harley-oriented rally, the Laughlin River Run. Patches such as "Loud wives lose lives" (a take-off on the common "Loud Pipes Save Lives" patch), and "Women: You can't live with 'em, and you can't shoot 'em," seemed a far cry from the Gold Wing culture of riders and co-riders, as did the bikini-clad models selling products at various vendor booths and the calls of "Show us your tits!" that often resounded when a woman rode by on the back of a motorcycle.

Among Honda Gold Wing riders there is a preponderance of couples in their forties, fifties, and even sixties, and women are usually active partners with men in riding rather than second-class citizens. Although they usually ride on the back of their male partners' bikes, women are referred to as "co-riders" rather than "passengers." And women co-riders experience many of the same feelings about riding as those who have their own bikes. Letters, accounts of rides, and poems in *Wing World*, the magazine of the Gold Wing Road Riders Association, for example, testify to the rhapsody of riding experienced by the woman on the back of the bike.

WOMEN AND THEIR BIKES

In addition to women who ride as passengers, about 8 percent of all motorcycle owners are women who ride on their own machines, with or without the company of men.[17] There are also a number of all-female motorcycle organizations, such as Women on Wheels, Leather & Lace, Women in the Wind, and Ladies of Harley. Some of these, such as the Motor Maids, which was founded in the early 1940s, have been part of the U.S. motorcycle scene for some time. Thus, any consideration of motorcycles and gender roles needs to take account of the many different ways that women participate in the world of motorcycles.

There is a longstanding phenomenon of women riding their own bikes that goes back to the beginning of motorcycling. In fact, the proportion of motorcycle riders who are female has changed little since the early days of motorcycle riding, suggesting that earlier generations of women were not less liberated than contemporary women when it came to motorcycle riding.[18] Today, there are elderly women who have been lifelong riders, pioneers in the sport, some of whom are still riding their own motorcycles.[19]

For many women, the attraction of riding motorcycles is similar, if not identical, to the attraction that riding holds for men. Melissa Holbrook Pierson, for example, begins *The Perfect Vehicle* by rhapsodizing over the sensual pleasures of starting a day's ride: "In the neat dance that accomplishes many operations on a motorcycle—one movement to countered by another fro, an equilibrium of give and take—the squeezed clutch lever is slowly let out while the other hand turns the throttle grip down. The bike moves out into a brighter world where the sun startles the rider's eyes for a moment and washes everything in a continual pour."[20]

Like their male counterparts, many women who ride their own motorcycles see them as part of their identity. Ann Ferrar, for instance, describes female bikers as women who "live and breathe their motorcycles, who view their bikes as extensions of their personalities, and who steep themselves in a milieu."[21] Or as Pierson says: "A motorcycle becomes an extension of yourself, your body and faculties and hopes and pathologies."[22]

For a woman, riding her own motorcycle represents freedom in an even broader framework than it does for men. It means breaking free of conventions and restrictions placed on her *as a women*. It represents a challenge to the sexism that pervades certain subcultures of biking, a sexism that ranges from the exaggerated display of stereotyped gender roles to outright misogyny. A woman's motorcycling experience also differs from that of a man's in the particular satisfaction women get from the mastery of a machine in a world in which such mastery has traditionally been denied them. In some cases, the mechanical skills and knowledge are a matter of necessity. In her comparison of riders from Ladies of Harley and Dykes on Bikes (Women's Motorcycle Contingent), Barbara Joans noted that one of the things the groups have in common is their exchange of information: "They talk torques and taillights, chaps and patches. . . . Most especially, they talk techniques for bike chopping as most bikes are created with the male frame in mind and most women have to chop their bikes for comfort."[23]

While, like men, women who ride motorcycles assert an identity that expresses resistance to, or at least nonconformity with, mainstream culture, as female bikers, women also challenge gender stereotypes and traditional sex roles in ways that male bikers who adopt an exaggerated masculine persona do not. Although such challenges have become routine and accepted in some other areas of culture, in the often hypermasculine world of bikers, they can be problematic. As Ferrar points out, "When a woman decides to ride, often the act is more than it appears. Ever since the late nineteenth century, when women bucked tradition to ride bicycles, the sight of a woman on wheels has been tied to a slew of conflicting messages about her femininity, competency, power, and liberation. . . . Today, women bikers are still scrutinized in a way that our male counterparts are not."[24]

Some of the problematic nature of women's participation in the biker world can be seen in the relationship of women to some of the motorcycling organizations. The wider world of Harley riders, for example, shares some of the characteristics of the outlaw biker clubs and exhibits some differences regarding the position of women. In the Harley Owners' Group, a woman who rides as a passenger is a member of the group only through her association with a male rider who is a member, and then she receives only associate status. A woman who rides her own bike, however, may become a full member. These women are treated very differently from associate members. As Barbara Joans puts it: "Enter the woman biker and all gears shift. The men, so distant and publicly neglectful of women passengers, fall all over themselves to accord women riders respect. It is almost as if each of the men takes pride in female mastery over biker machinery."[25]

Both women riders and female associate members can join Ladies of Harley (LOH), an organization established by the Harley-Davidson company as an auxiliary organization to make women feel more a part of HOG, and hence more likely to stay involved with their men in riding. As Joans points out, however, in LOH, all women, whether passengers or riders, have full membership, and the organization has taken on a status that extends beyond its original conception as an auxiliary. Thus, as she observes, "While LOH is made up of two very different groups of women, they have the road in common. They are both bikers. They TALK BIKES."[26]

In the Gold Wing Road Riders Association (GWRRA), couples sometimes have both their names painted on the bike as a way of indicating joint ownership and equal participation in riding. At Gold Wing rallies, courses are offered for two-up riding (rider and passenger), and for co-riders themselves. Both types of courses typically emphasize the critical role of the co-rider in ensuring overall safety by keeping a constant watch for hazards and monitoring the decisions and well-being of the operator. The organizational structure of the GWRRA also reflects a couple-oriented character. Many officer positions, such as chapter director, codirector, or educator, are held not by individuals but by couples. The organization also sponsors an annual Couple of the Year contest to identify a husband-and-wife team who will serve as a public relations symbol for the organization during the coming year.[27]

Although the Gold Wing culture is more egalitarian than outlaw or pseudo-outlaw culture, it still incorporates some of the more general social stereotypes of men and women in American culture. For example, it is common to hear jokes and commentary about men wanting to spend more money on motorcycle parts than their wives would approve, or about women always wanting to stop and shop while traveling, or about men typically wanting to ride faster than the women on the back would like. Despite this, however, there is little sense of gender inequality among these couples. Most of the women we know who are part of Gold Wing couples are co-riders by choice. They have little interest in riding their own motorcycles; instead, they see their role, the woman on the back, as a partnership with their men. Women will often refer to "our bike" and be as involved in planning trips as the men. Men whose wives are not as enthusiastic about riding as they are often look with envy at men whose spouses are active partners in motorcycling life. Sometimes women who are widowed will even continue to attend GWRRA meetings and to participate in other GWRRA activities. For example, one GWRRA member whose husband had died was learning to ride a trike so that she could continue to ride to rallies.

Much has been written about and by women who ride their own motorcycles, but little about women who ride behind their husbands or partners, even though more women ride behind male partners than ride their own bikes. Just as these women are seen as second-class citizens within outlaw clubs and in such motorcycle organizations as HOG, so they seem also to be perceived in the literature on motorcycling. As Joans rightly points out, many of the women who ride their own motorcycles do not see themselves as "unfeminine," but rather as redefining the nature of femininity.[28] To see women who ride on the back of the bike as only fulfilling "traditional feminine roles," as Joans suggests, however, is to stereotype these women because they have chosen a particular relationship to motorcycle riding.[29] Many of the women we know, while they prefer to be passengers rather than riders, hardly fit the image of traditional women. Jill, for example, has repaired her own car, remodeled her own kitchen, refinished floors, and become an expert sailor. Nevertheless, she has made a deliberate decision not to devote money and attention to owning her own motorcycle. Besides, she enjoys the closeness of riding two-up and of sharing a motorcycle, and she is happy with joint trips that satisfy her desire for the open road without requiring she take on the responsibility of dealing with her own separate motorcycle.

In some sense, then, the scholarly and media focus on women who break the gender barriers to engage in what is generally conceived of as a masculine activity—riding a motorcycle—valorizes the masculine and makes invisible, or at least less visible, the women who participate in motorcycling, and who regard the bike upon which they ride as "ours," but who do not ride their own individual machines. This is important in the context of the Run for the Wall, because women on the Run ride in a variety of ways—behind their men, beside their men on their own bikes, solo on their own bikes, and as hitchhikers with various riders along the way. Yet whatever their relationship to the machine and to riding, all of them play significant roles in the Run through their support of their men and of the other veterans who make the journey.

FIGURE 25. Women play a crucial role in supporting their men at the Wall.

"MY FIGHT IS THE VIETNAM IN HIM"

While women may share with men many elements of the experience of motorcycle riding, they generally do not share what remains a primarily male experience, the experience of combat. Women have certainly endured the horrors of war throughout the centuries, both directly as civilians and indirectly through the loss of loved ones. But the experience of actual battle has generally been a male one.[30] This poses special difficulties for the woman who seeks to support the returned warrior still suffering from the traumas of war, for these traumas result from an experience she cannot share and, in most cases, cannot imagine.[31]

Sometimes a woman may not even understand that her husband or partner is suffering, let alone the nature of his pain. Our friend Linda, for example, told us that she had no idea her husband, Phil, had anything to "get over" when he returned from his tour in the navy. "We just loved him," Linda said of the welcome he received from family and friends in his hometown. With a new family to care for, and with Phil back from the war, she felt they were ready to "get on with their lives." Almost twenty-six years after Phil returned from duty in the waters off the coast of Vietnam, he and Linda visited the Vietnam memorial at Angel Fire, New Mexico. It was there that Phil suddenly found his memories of the war pressing in on him, and there that both he and Linda realized that the pain of the war and the memory of the hostile reception he received when he disembarked in San Diego remained to be dealt with.

In other cases, wives of returned veterans have found themselves having to deal with husbands suffering from more obvious war-related problems. In many cases, their partner's behavior seemed inexplicable and idiosyncratic, both to the woman and to the veteran himself, as neither of them linked this behavior to his experiences in Vietnam. Myra MacPherson describes how William Mahedy, a counselor to veterans, approached the issue.

> For years immediately after the war, wives would drag their husbands in, insisting they were crazy. William Mahedy would . . . look at the two of them, never having discussed anything with them, and say to the husband, "I bet you won't sit with your back to a door in a restaurant." And the wife would blurt out, "No, he won't." . . . "I bet he won't kick a can or walk on a piece of paper." The woman, her eyes widening would nod that he was again correct. "I bet you he will always take a different route to and from work." The woman by then demanded, "How do you know all this?" Mahedy recalls, . . . "I can just click them right off. She thinks he's bonkers and *he* thinks he's bonkers. And when he walks in some center and someone says, "welcome to the club, you're one of several thousand"—what relief![32]

For many women, "just loving" their returned warriors was all they could do, even when they knew it was not enough. In a number of cases the men assumed that they had put Vietnam behind them. Yet sometimes the women in their lives saw more clearly the symptoms that indicated they had not. As one veteran put it, "'I never thought the war bothered me much. But, my wife says it did.' . . . 'He got back in 1966, and we got married in 1967,' [his wife] recalls. 'It bothered him a lot—especially his sleeping for about a year and a half.'"[33] Consequently, a number of the men that we have met on the Run were initially urged to participate by their wives, girlfriends, or other women who cared about them and who saw the Run as an opportunity for catharsis and healing for their troubled men.

In addition to the women who are married to veterans, there are other women who have suffered from Vietnam through the loss of a loved one, whether father, son, brother, husband, or fiancé. The many letters left at the Wall by those who were bereaved testify to the continuing pain of the loss, and to the permanent holes left in the lives of many by relationships that were severed at the moment of their greatest youthful intensity. For many women, the man they lost to the Vietnam War was their first real love, their first husband, the father of their first child. These relationships remain forever untarnished in memory, and the pain of their loss never fully abates. In addition, for those whose loved ones are still missing, there is the ongoing pain of uncertainty. For these women there is no *place* to grieve, no grave at which to leave flowers or a letter.[34] Women bearing these emotional burdens sometimes join the Run, either riding with the pack on all or part of its journey, or meeting with it along the way so that they can talk to veterans and participate in ceremonies to remember the dead and the missing. Such activities may be especially important for women whose men are MIA because not only do they lack a ceremonial center such as a grave site where they can mourn their loss, they cannot even be sure whether their loved one is alive or dead.

The women who join the Run for the Wall, and particularly those who make the entire journey, are a far cry from the "biker babes" who decorate the pages of *Easy Rider* and *Biker* magazine. One seldom sees leather halter tops or extensive bared flesh, especially on all-the-way women. Instead, they are typically dressed in practical riding clothes: jeans, boots, leather jackets, scarves, and gloves. It is also hard to look glamorous after a long day's ride—one is more likely to be sweaty, wind blown, reddened by the sun, hair in a tangle from the wind (or smashed flat by a helmet—as expressed in pins on jackets or vests that say "Hairdo by Harley" or "Hairdo by Honda"). While men will sometimes ogle a scantily clad day rider, these are not the women who undertake the discomfort of a cross-country journey, and who earn the respect of the men who travel with them. While the roles of these women on the Run are most often complementary to those of men, this complementarity is a reflection of the maleness of warfare and not of an acceptance of stereotyped, "traditional" female roles by these women. Indeed, many of the all-the-way women would fit poorly into the life of a stay-at-home wife. That is why they are on the road with their men.

Phil and Linda, who ride together on the same motorcycle, have participated in the Run every year since 1996. During much of the rest of the year they serve as motorcycle missionaries, carrying their Christian message to churches around the country.[35] When we first met them, they were riding an older Honda Gold Wing. After an accident in D.C. following the 1996 Run, they bought a new Harley touring bike. Like many other Gold Wing couples we know, Phil and Linda operate as partners in their motorcycling activities. They typically make decisions as a team about where they will go, where they will stop, and what they will do, and to Linda, their Harley-Davidson Ultra Glide touring bike is "our motorcycle." They are also equally committed to the Run for the Wall, and they share in planning their participation in the Run just as they share in planning their motorcycle ministry.

Puma and Tigger are another couple who have gone together on the Run. When we first met Puma in 1998, he was riding by himself, on a midsized Yamaha motorcycle. Although Tigger did not accompany him on the trip, like many wives she encouraged him to go, and she later flew out to Washington, D.C., to join him for the Rolling Thunder parade.[36] During his first trip, Puma questioned us about our Gold Wing, and it was obvious that he was thinking about acquiring a bike more suitable for two people. Shortly after our return from the Run, he called us from Phoenix to ask if he and Tigger could ride up to Flagstaff for a visit. We thought something was up, and sure enough, when they showed up it was aboard their new candy-red Gold Wing. It was obvious that the bike was a commitment to their joint participation in the Run for the Wall, and the following year, 1999, they both rode all the way.

In neither of these cases are the women particularly interested in riding their own bikes. Yet, at the same time, Linda and Tigger are equal partners with their men. Additionally, both play key roles in supporting not only their husbands, but also other veterans in search of healing on their pilgrimage to the Wall. Both have become women to whom others turn when they are in need of someone to talk to or just a hug. In addition, the Run was a life-changing experience for Tigger. This was eloquently and insightfully expressed in an e-mail she sent us titled "A Lesson in Humility." Here are some excerpts from her account:

> I could see Jim, and the other guys, through new eyes. Is *this* what it was like to go through boot camp? Is *this* what it was like to be in a war fighting unit? Did they *really* have to obey orders trusting it was for their own good? Did they *really* have to rush the chow line, queue up at the head, elbow their way through a crush of people to be acknowledged or helped? It was apparent I had never served on active duty!
>
> These guys are survivors. Not just of "the war," but of the humiliating, dehumanizing process that prepared them to go to Vietnam 35 years ago. . . . I can't *imagine* what mental gymnastics they endured during training and in the field, just to survive. Then they returned home to friends and family who were as naive about the whole thing as I. . . . The men who returned only "looked" like the boys who left (well, the "lucky" ones still *looked* like the same guys). Inside they were changed. In too many ways to count, the subtle and not so subtle differences drove wedges between them and much of society. . . .
>
> Participating in the Run for the Wall gave me that moment of insight that was missing through our 20 years of marriage. *I* had to change *my* thinking in order to survive the Run, just as *he* had to change a lifetime ago. . . . The military changes people and war ingrains it further, like cinders ground into a fallen child's knee. Some scars are bigger and more visible than others, but the trauma behind them remains great in each child's mind.
>
> *Thank you, Lord, for helping me to be kind to Jim today. Help me to be kind tomorrow, and the day after, and the day after that. Amen.*

An example of a woman who rides her own bike without a male partner is Barbara. Like several other solo women, Barbara was introduced to the Run by her friend Smoke, a World War II veteran who regularly rides with the Run. It was not political interest that initially attracted Barbara to the Run, but the fact that she wanted to ride her motorcycle across the country. Smoke suggested to her that joining up with the group might be a good way to make the journey. Although a little nervous at first, Barbara found herself well accepted by the men on the trip, and she made a successful journey to Washington, D.C. By the time she arrived there, she not only had fulfilled her dream of a cross-country motorcycle trip, but also found herself committed to the Run's mission. After that, she became a Run regular and an active contributor to its efforts. For several years, Barbara made a RFTW theme quilt from t-shirts given to her by Run for the Wall riders. Raffle tickets for the quilt were sold along the way, the money used to defray Run expenses.

Yet another type of female participation on the Run was that of Deborah. Deborah, who had worked with Vietnam veterans in Tucson, rode up to the first overnight stop of the 1996 Run at Ash Fork, Arizona, with a biker friend who had come to help serve dinner to the group. She was so captivated by the Run that even though her friend had to turn back, she decided to go all the way to the Wall. She had not planned to make the trip, had packed no clothes, and had no vehicle to take her to D.C. So she began hitching rides on various motorcycles, shared rooms with people who had reservations, and was sustained on her way by gifts of toiletries, clothes, and other necessities of life on the road from other riders. Deborah impressed everyone she met with her decision to continue on the Run, and with the way she seemed so moved by the pilgrimage we were making. "I never realized what America was about before," she told us at one point in the trip. She was only on the Run that one year. Illness subsequently kept her from rejoining the group, and in 1999 she died. Yet her memory remains strong with all those who met her, both for her spur-of-the-moment journey and for the poem she read at Angel Fire during the memorial service for Vincent Trujillo. She composed the poem spontaneously as an ode to the Run and its participants, and to the Run's "healing thunder." (It is from her poem that we have taken the phrase "pilgrims for America.") When her death was announced on the RFTW bulletin board, it saddened and moved many who knew her, and the bulletin board was used to post virtual memorials to her. One of the more touching read: "I am both sad and elated to report that Deborah Fahnestock died yesterday. I am greatly saddened in that I/we have lost a good friend and supporter. I am elated in that she is no longer suffering. Lift a glass with me in her memory."

Another Run hitchhiker was Fyreckr, who came to the Run in memory of her first love and his best friend who were both lost when their planes were shot down over North Vietnam in 1969. Fyreckr had owned her own bike but was no longer able to ride it any distance due to a job-related injury that left her with little strength in her forearms. One day in a Harley shop she saw a poster for the Run for the Wall and, like so many other participants, "just knew I had to go." If you are really committed to the cause, she noted, once you go on the Run, "you're hooked." Fyreckr continued to participate in subsequent years by hitching with various riders across the country. In 1998, however, her hitchhiking days came to an end when she met another Run for the Wall rider, whom she married in Ontario, California, at the start of the 1999 Run.

These women and the others like them, whether on their own bikes, riding behind their partners, or hitchhiking rides, are equals of one another and of the men on the Run. They have paid their dues and demonstrated their commitment to the Run and its purposes by traveling across the country with the group. Once they have made the trip, they will be given as much respect as most of the men when they speak about the Run or when they take part in its other activities, including planning for future Runs. Any woman who has gone all the way with the Run, with or without her own bike, will typically be held in higher esteem than any male day rider, regardless of how desirable or prestigious his motorcycle. In this sense, the Run is an equal-opportunity event. If you do it, you are part of it—male or female. Normally important identity markers such as gender, race, or age quickly become secondary in the face of the more significant fact of completing this motorcycle pilgrimage to the Wall.

GENDER TALK

Although men and women may enjoy equal esteem on the Run, this does not mean that there are no differences in how they participate. For instance, while men and women on the Run socialize with each other, men will often connect with other men through certain kinds of male talk about motorcycles. This talk is often framed in ways that enable men to demonstrate their knowledge about motorcycles as machines, and their skill and experience as riders. It provides men who have just met with a basis for initiating conversation, and it also serves as a mechanism through which men can establish their credentials as bikers. This opening is important in part because men on the Run typically do not ask one another about their wartime service or experiences until they have established some other basis of contact. The Run attracts many people for whom the war is still a raw emotional wound. In recognition of this, it is more common for men to let others volunteer information about their wartime experience than to question them about it as a way to start a conversation. Thus, remarks such as "Nice ride" (that is, nice bike), "I like your scoot," or "Where did you get that ———?" (some aftermarket accessory), serve to start a conversation. The more accurately a man can identify the year and model of a bike, the more he is recognized as a knowledgeable member of the biker fraternity, and even more knowledgeable if he has an understanding of less visible matters such as engine modifications. Thus, "That's a really sweet-looking '95 Road King you've got there" serves the same purpose as "Nice ride" as a conversation opener and also lets the other rider know that you know your bikes. If a comment displays knowledge of mechanical esoterica, such as "That engine sounds like it's been breathed on" (modified) or "Did you put in a stroker kit?" the speaker announces that he understands the internals as well as the externals of motorcycles.

Another common point of connection and credentialing among men on the Run is riding skill. This is typically established by referring to various triumphs over road hazards. After a particularly bad stretch of road, for instance, someone might say, "Man, I haven't been on anything that rough since I crossed Cottonwood Pass." At this point, without being consciously aware of it, the listener knows he is supposed to extend an opening by asking, "Where's Cottonwood Pass?" This gives the first man a chance to say, "Oh, it's a graded dirt road over the Rocky Mountains near Aspen," thereby establishing that he's done some hard traveling on his bike, and not just on paved asphalt highways. Similarly, at the end of a long day's ride, someone might say, "Shit, I haven't been this tired since I had to ride from San Antonio to San Diego in one day to make my brother's wedding." Here the rider establishes not only his credentials as an "iron-butt" rider, but also his skill in knowing how to manage fifteen hundred miles in the saddle without crashing from exhaustion.

In some ways the references to journeys taken and hazards surmounted appear similar to name-dropping in other circles, attempts to one-up other participants in the conversation. In actuality, how-

ever, on the Run and in motorcycling circles generally, they are often less about acquiring status than about gaining acceptance and
determining the appropriate level of conversation. Whether experienced or novice, male riders want to put something forward to convince others that they belong to the fraternity of riders. At the same
time, if the initial exchange indicates that the other rider is a relative novice, either in terms of journeying or motorcycle mechanics,
more experienced riders will often look for ways to put the conversation on a more even footing. In our experience, at least, most motorcycle riders, much like most sailors we have known, typically avoid
being overly boastful about their accomplishments. They know that
the road—or the sea—can humiliate even the most experienced traveler with little warning. Thus, credentialing talk among male bikers
on the Run serves more to explore points of contact than to create
hierarchies. It is also in keeping with the Run's overall egalitarian
character.

While some women (especially those with their own motorcycles)
may be as or more knowledgeable and skilled as the male riders on
the Run, motorcycle talk is not the way that women on the Run usually connect with one another (although such talk may take place
among women as well). Women on the Run do not seem to have as
much need to prove themselves in terms of motorcycle savvy in encounters with women or with other men. Conversations among
women at rest stops are more likely to consist of observations about
the stretch of the trip just completed, questions about whether the
person has been on the Run before, discussion of riding gear and
clothes, complaints about the weather, and (sometimes) conversations
about their husbands or partners, and especially if the men are veterans, about their war-related problems as well. (Because the number of men on the Run is far greater than the number of women,
another frequent topic of comment among women at rest stops is
how nice it is to see men instead of women waiting in a long line
for the restroom.)

While women do not have to prove themselves with motorcycle
talk, they engage in another kind of proving by demonstrating their
willingness to endure the difficulties of the journey, and by being
committed to the Run itself. It is through this commitment that one
earns the accolade of all-the-way woman.

ALL-THE-WAY WOMEN

Every year that we have been on the Run, the first stop upon reaching Washington, D.C., has been the Iwo Jima memorial. Here group pictures are taken, including pictures of everyone who rode into D.C. with the Run, of those who went all the way, of those from particular branches of service, of all the participants who are firemen and policemen, and so on. Among these pictures is one of the all-the-way women, those who made the entire journey across the country with the Run. Unlike the other groups, when the women line up for their photos, there is a burst of applause from those—mostly men—who are watching. It is both an expression of appreciation for women who were willing to engage in a male form of endurance by riding across the country, and of thanks for their willingness to do so in support of their men. The support that women provide does not end when the Run arrives in D.C., however, for women are also needed at the Wall. Here they help look up names at the Wall and offer support and comfort to their own partners and to other men as they break down in front of the names of their dead comrades. In addition, many of these women must deal with their own tragedies when faced with that evocative expanse of polished black granite.

At the Wall at the end of the 1999 Run, Linda was helping various people from the Run look up the location of names on the Wall from one of the many directories provided there by the U.S. Park Service. When we joined her, she was talking to a woman who had come on the Run with her husband, a Vietnam veteran. The woman was trying to locate a name on the Wall. She knew the pronunciation but was uncertain of the spelling. Those of us standing around made various suggestions as to how the name might be spelled, but none of them proved to be the right one. She explained that the name she was looking for belonged to a man who would have been her brother-in-law had he survived the war. He had been engaged to her sister when she herself was only twelve, and she vividly remembered how he took her, his kid-sister-to-be, for a ride on his motorcycle. Shortly afterward he shipped out for Vietnam and later signed on for a second tour of duty. He was killed soon after he returned to the war. As she told her story, she began to cry, and Jill put her arms around her. "I know it's foolish to feel this way after all this time," the woman apologized, wiping her eyes. "No, not at all," Jill reassured her. After all, how many times had we witnessed the freshness of grief more than a quarter century after the war's end? Later, we reflected on how traumatic it must have been for her, as a child, to lose her big-brother-to-be, a man whom she obviously adored. With this loved one dead, and her own husband in need of support, she had carried a heavy burden to the Wall. She is but one example of the scars that women on the Run still bear from America's longest war.

When Ray first contacted John Anderson, the 1996 national co-ordinator, about joining the Run for the Wall, he asked if it mattered that we were not vets. "Anyone who supports the cause is welcome," John told him. "My wife is my biggest supporter," he added, and "she's not a vet." It is clear from our experiences that women, whether riders or passengers (or even riders in chase vehicles), are important, even essential, to the Run. For most women, the only role that they can play in helping a Vietnam veteran deal with the aftermath of the war is to provide emotional support; they cannot directly share the wartime experiences that these men have had. Yet, for many women, helping their men cope with PTSD, nightmares, unpredictable anger, or great sadness in front of the Wall is one of the most troubling and difficult experiences of their lives. As one t-shirt we saw put it:

> His Fight Was In Vietnam.
> My Fight is the Vietnam in Him.
> I Am a Vietnam Veterans Loved One.

The suffering of women as a result of the Vietnam War has not received as much attention as that of the men who fought in it. In addition to losing sons, husbands, lovers, and brothers, women have also endured the doubts and bitterness attendant upon the war itself, including the feeling that their men never received the recognition that should have been bestowed upon them for their service to their country. In some cases, bereaved women were even harassed: "I received my *first* harassment call on Saturday, the day after Dan's funeral," one mother who lost her son in Vietnam reported. The same woman was told several times that "it wasn't so bad to lose my son, *because it wasn't a declared war!*"[37]

Another group of women who suffered more directly from the war were the women who served there. Surprisingly, there is no clear information on just how many women fall into this category. The Vietnam Women's Project estimates that about 11,000 women served in Vietnam, about 90 percent as nurses. Hendrickson estimates somewhere between 7,500 and 11,000 women served as nurses. Van Devanter suggests that official statistics regarding the number of nurses serving in Vietnam are wildly inaccurate, and that many more served there than the Pentagon acknowledges. In light of these fluctuating accounts, Hendrickson observes in *The Living and the Dead*: "The ironic truth is that in the high-tech McNamarian body-count logarithm war, no one ever computed the exact number of nurses. Were they not thought important enough? . . . Somehow it is easier to find the nursing figures from World War II than from Vietnam."[38]

The women who served as combat nurses in Vietnam were exposed to the gruesome consequences of the war sometimes more intensely than the men who fought in it: "Nurses often suffered a more severe emotional mauling than soldiers who have respites in combat. . . . They saw waves of mutilated flesh from the battlefield, who in previous wars would never have been saved that long."[39] In addition, as one counselor put it, "The nurses, brought up to nurture and protect others, felt like failures because no matter what they did the GIs kept dying."[40] Many of these women, when they returned, received no better reception than that reported by many male veterans, and in some ways their reception was worse: "Ignored by the VA and rejected by the service organizations, they were also looked at askance by men who thought they were 'combat-boot' feminists or who speculated on how many times they got laid in that world filled with men."[41] In addition, many nurses found themselves stigmatized by both those on the political right (who felt women shouldn't be in the military) and those on the political left (because of their association with the war). It took considerable persistence before the postwar problems of these nurses were recognized and they began to receive treatment at veterans centers.[42] Finally, in 1993, the Vietnam Women's Memorial was erected on the Mall to make more visible the role that women played in the war.[43]

But what of the women who did not support their warriors? While many veterans returned home to loving families, wives, and fiancées, some of them returned to face rejection, not only from the wider society, but from women in their lives. For many on the Run, there is no better symbol of this rejection than Jane Fonda.

FIGURE 26. After a quarter century, Jane Fonda remains a target for Vietnam veterans.

NOT FONDA JANE: THE LEGACY OF "HANOI JANE"

When we first joined the Run for the Wall, we noticed patches on several of the riders' vests and jackets that said "Jane Fonda, American Traitor Bitch." Even more curious, some of these patches were worn upside down. Another anti-Fonda patch we have often seen reads "Vietnam Vets are not Fonda Jane." One participant who has been on the Run every year for the last ten years carries a bumper sticker on his motorcycle that reads "Jane Fonda is pro-choice; who's the baby killer N.O.W.?" a sentiment aimed at challenging the baby-killer label that many veterans feel Jane Fonda and other antiwar protesters unfairly pinned on them.

These patches took us by surprise. While we both could recall Jane Fonda's controversial visits to Hanoi, it was something that had faded to the back of our consciousness, submerged by the larger issues and controversies of the war and the antiwar movement. Not so for many veterans, however. For them, what they see as Jane Fonda's betrayal of both her country and the men who were serving in Vietnam remains a painful memory and a burning issue. This is apparent not only in anti-Fonda patches and bumper stickers, but also in comments on the RFTW bulletin board. Typical of the anti-Fonda sentiments that predominate among RFTW riders is this story posted on the bulletin board in February 2000:

> So I'm out on the scooter the other day and stopped at a bar in Scottsdale AZ, which is not exactly a hot bed of Vet hangouts. At any rate I'm sitting at the bar with my Bud in hand when a young yuppie asks why the anti Hanoi Jane patches on my vest. I give him a short run down on low-life Jane's trip to Hanoi, her statements encouraging desertion and the picture of her smiling, seated on an NVA AA Gun. By this time a few of his friends had began to listen in, and after a few "no sh—" and "is that true?" one young POLO clad youngster said, "let me buy you a beer man." Well not to go on and on, it was quite a stop (not that I'll be making it a regular watering hole), some of the kids' parents may have been at San Fran when I returned with their greeting of jeers and spit. What goes around comes around, with their reaction . . . there is hope, because if they [their parents] get the chance the @*(#&$^@(@)#$& will try and do it again.

The hostility toward Jane Fonda runs so deep that anti-Jane postings appear on the RFTW web site not only when there is some public event that involves Fonda herself, but whenever there is something in the news involving her soon to be ex-husband, Ted Turner, or her former husband, Tom Hayden. Even things only vaguely associated with Fonda can elicit a negative reaction, as when several people posted notices on the bulletin board saying that it was too bad that the Atlanta Braves, who had just won their division, were owned by Ted Turner, husband of the "traitor bitch."

In addition to the RFTW bulletin board, there are several Vietnam vet web sites that contain ongoing discussions about Fonda's behavior during the war. These often include debates over her actions, with opinions ranging from those who see her acts as treasonous, to those that regard it as youthful folly in the course of otherwise legitimate opposition to the war, to those who view it as an appropriate act of protest. Some of these postings are from people who are too young even to remember the war, indicating that Fonda's support for the North Vietnamese has become an established part of the story of the Vietnam War. Whenever some issue involving Jane Fonda is current, predictably one or more people will copy materials from these other web sites to the RFTW bulletin board. In 1999, for instance, Fonda was slated to receive the American Association of University Women's "Speaking Out Award." Shortly after the upcoming honor was announced, a column by *Boston Post* writer Jeff Jacoby that questioned the award and criticized Fonda for her wartime actions was posted on a general Vietnam veteran bulletin board and quickly copied to the RFTW bulletin board.[44]

Why, out of all the antiwar protests of the 1960s and 1970s, did Jane Fonda's visit to Hanoi leave a particular legacy of bitterness among veterans that remains to the present day? In order to understand this, we need to examine not only the specific events of her visit to Hanoi, but also the larger question of how cultural concepts of gender create an image of the ideal relationship between warriors and women.

When Jane Fonda visited Hanoi in July 1972, she already had a history of activism against the Vietnam War. Contemporary retellings of the story of Jane Fonda in Hanoi typically focus on two elements. One was the broadcast on Radio Hanoi in which she said to U.S. pilots engaged in the bombing raids in North and South Vietnam: "I don't know what your officers tell you . . . but your weapons are illegal and the men who are ordering you to use these weapons are war criminals according to international law. In the past, in Germany and Japan, men who committed these kinds of crimes were tried and executed." Today this speech is remembered as one in which Jane Fonda called *all* U.S. servicemen, not just those who ordered the bombings, "war criminals."[45]

The other common media image of Fonda's visit to Hanoi is of her seated at a North Vietnamese antiaircraft gun. This image is perhaps the greatest source of bitterness for many Vietnam veterans, for they see it as symbolic of Fonda's willingness to kill the soldiers of her own country. Because a number of American POWs, including many who remain missing, were captured or lost when their planes were shot down by antiaircraft fire, and because the Run's most public purpose is to support the POW/MIA cause, the image of Fonda manning an antiaircraft gun has become a powerful symbol not only of what many veterans on the Run feel as their betrayal by the antiwar movement in general, but also of their view that America has abandoned its POWs and MIAs.[46]

Two other accusations sometimes directed at Jane Fonda are that she added to the U.S. death toll in Vietnam by buoying the hopes of the Vietnamese, and that she betrayed POWs who secretly gave her slips of paper bearing their names, hoping she would inform their families of their whereabouts. According to anti-Fonda accounts, instead of passing on this information to their families, Fonda betrayed them to their captors, with the consequence that these POWs were subsequently subject to brutal beatings by their North Vietnamese jailers. This last accusation has been the source of some controversy among Vietnam veterans, in part because the story has been attributed to an American POW who denies that it happened that way. Whether true or not, this story of betrayal has achieved the status of legend among Vietnam veterans and is an important part of the anti-Fonda lore among those on the Run.[47]

Had Fonda's labeling of American soldiers as war criminals not been reinforced by public stereotypes of Vietnam veterans as baby killers, perhaps her actions might not have cut so deeply or have been so long remembered. As it was, the fact that she was a major celebrity, and that her highly publicized accusations were seen as embodying the sentiments of the wider world of antiwar protesters, intensifies the bitterness and anger that her name still evokes. That Fonda has since publicly apologized and stated that she only wanted to end the war quickly and bring U.S. soldiers home cuts little ice with most veterans. From their perspective, as one posting about Jane Fonda on the RFTW Bulletin Board proclaimed, "Sorry is not enough."

The bitterness over Jane Fonda's activities stems not simply from the antiwar content of her message, or from the fact that her activities were given so much publicity, but also from the fact that she was failing to fulfill her role as a woman in relation to America's warriors in Vietnam. While women have certainly fought to defend country, home, and family, there is no society, past or present, that has employed women equally in combat with men. And while currently the question of American women's appropriate role in the military is being debated, the issue of women in combat had not even been raised at the time of the Vietnam War. Hence, women's roles in the war were mainly the traditional ones of supporting the warriors, whether at home or near the front lines as nurses. At home, women were supposed to wait for their warrior's return. Herein lies the shame of the "Dear John" letter—the missive from the woman who, rather than waiting while her man is at risk, not only abandons him but also increases that risk by putting him in a state of depression or grief.[48] In the war zone, women supported the men directly in combat situations (as nurses or other support personnel) or worked to keep up

FIGURE 27. Just one of the many "traitor bitch" patches worn on the Run.

their morale, as did Connie Stevens, Gypsy Rose Lee, and other female performers who, along with male performers such as Bob Hope, put on shows to entertain the troops.[49]

As a show business figure and a female icon of the '60s,[50] Jane Fonda not only failed to fulfill such appropriate female roles but, by virtue of her highly publicized visits to North Vietnam, actively betrayed the men that she should have been supporting. No wonder, then, that the "Jane Fonda, American Traitor Bitch" patch is worn upside down. It symbolizes much that was upside down about the Vietnam War—including Fonda's overturning of her traditional female supportive role and her betrayal of the troops. In addition, Fonda has come to symbolize the antivet sentiment that many veterans feel shadowed their lives after they returned home. The fact that Jane Fonda has enjoyed a successful career since the Vietnam era (in contrast to the life course of many of the veterans on the Run), and the recent announcement by Barbara Walters that she would include Jane Fonda in her end-of-the-century feature, "100 Years of Great Women," has fanned once again the bitter flames of memory.

On the Run, Jane Fonda is seen as the antithesis of all-the-way women who support the veterans in their lives, because of what she did, as well as because of the women she has come to symbolize. At a personal level, Jane Fonda embodies the rejection from women that many veterans we know reported experiencing when they returned home from Vietnam. In the case of one Vietnam veteran on the Run, for example, his date warned him not to tell her friends he had been in Vietnam when they went to a party. Another Vietnam vet told us how his date simply got up and left him sitting at a table in a restaurant when he answered her question about what he had been doing the previous year by telling her he had been in the army in Vietnam. Another RFTW rider we know said: "When I got back from Nam, all I wanted to do was get a job, get my life in order, and find a girl. That was all I thought about when I was over there. But after I got back, anytime a girl found out I was a Vietnam vet, she'd have nothing to do with me. I thought, 'If I'm such an evil person, I'll just go back and be the worst son-of-a-bitch there ever was.'" So he reenlisted, this time joining the Navy Seals, an elite special-forces group expert at covert attacks under or from the water.

For such men, the acceptance and support of women on the Run is especially welcome, and Jane Fonda's betrayal is especially heinous. Little did Jane Fonda know in her days as an antiwar activist that she would come to stand for every women who ever turned a cold shoulder to a Vietnam veteran because he was a soldier in an unpopular war.[51] She also stands in contrast to the wives and partners of veterans who have chosen to go "all the way" with their men, both on the Run and in life.

7

"I'VE SAID MY PIECE"
Individualism and Community in a Folk Organization

On Veterans' Day 1999, the Run for the Wall Bulletin Board hummed with messages. From Washington, D.C., where a group of RFTW riders from different parts of the country had gathered for Veterans Day, Dragonrider wrote, "We all met and enjoyed being with 'family' at the Wall." And from New Mexico, LittleMac wrote:

> This morning, bright and early, the NM—RFTW folks from Albuquerque met for breakfast. After a great meal we rode to the Albuquerque Veterans' Park for the ceremonies. . . . Afterwards, we formed up side by side, with Dave in the missing man slot and paraded through town (having gathered more riders at the ceremony) and stopped at a VFW and the local Fleet Reserve (all of whom had the POW/MIA flag flying high.) The old timers welcomed us and saluted us. It is nice to see that us Vietnam Vets (and Vietnam Era Vets) are now being seen as "real" veterans.

Other postings were simple expressions of thanks and appreciation to American veterans, such as "To all the vets thank you for my freedom," "Happy Veterans Day to all who have served in Wartime and in Peacetime," and "Thank you for all you have given and continue to give." Still others sent longer messages of appreciation, including one from a schoolteacher who had ridden part of the way with the Run the previous May: "With Veteran's Day tomorrow I wanted to take a few minutes to write and thank you all, and it has turned into

FIGURE 28. Along the route, communities welcome the Run.

a family event! I hope you enjoy the kid's letters. It seems as if there are few heros left in this country for my kids to look up to. Sports figures, movie stars, and politicians are all out for whatever they can get for themselves." She followed this with letters from her children, one of which read: "Hi. I am in the 3rd grade. Thank you for saving our country so we could be free and go to any school that we want. And so I could wear any clothes that I want without getting hurt and going to jail. I hope you like this letter. Proud of YA!"

Another entry, titled "A Veterans Christmas," a variation of "The Night Before Christmas," told the tale of a veteran living "all alone in a one bedroom house made of plaster and stone," with "No tinsel, no presents, not even a tree," but who, nevertheless, is able to tell his saddened visitor, "Santa don't cry, this life is my choice; I fight for freedom, I don't ask for more, my life is my god's, my country, my corps. . . . Carry on Santa, it's Christmas day, and all is secure." The poem was so popular that a number of people had either posted it in its entirety on the RFTW bulletin board or listed other web sites where it could be found.

From reports of local RFTW gatherings, to expressions of thanks to U.S. veterans, to tales of forgotten warriors, these postings on Veterans Day are just one example of the ways in which the Run for the Wall continually reconstitutes itself as something more than a once-a-year motorcycle run. By creating images of the Run for the Wall as a family and of veterans as heroic Americans occupying a special, and not always appreciated, place in society, the RFTW bulletin board helps promote a sense of solidarity among those who visit or contribute to it. This sense of solidarity, as we will see, is a critical part of how the Run is able to function as a voluntary organization.

STRUCTURE AND IDEOLOGY: THE BASIS FOR ORGANIZATION

Almost as soon as the Run for the Wall web site and bulletin board were established in 1997, they became important parts of the Run's organizational framework. Run leaders use the web site to communicate information to the Run for the Wall family about upcoming events and other Run business. The bulletin board also serves as an information source, a forum for opinion and debate, and a way to maintain year-round solidarity among computer-using riders. Run participants also use the RFTW bulletin board to locate or obtain information about friends and comrades, to tell their own stories of how the Run affected their lives, or to comment on political issues of interest to Vietnam veterans. Sometimes those planning to ride with the Run for the first time come to the bulletin board seeking information, and they almost always receive both practical advice and encouragement from those who have already traveled with the Run. When an RFTW rider or supporter is ill, has had an accident, or is facing some other crisis, the news will often be posted on the board, including information about where to send assistance or get-well cards. Typically these postings generate many follow-ups in which members publicly express their sympathy and support for the brother or sister who is having difficulties. In one instance, a call was put out on the bulletin board notifying Run members that a longtime and well-known participant was in need of costly blood transfusions. Soon some of the members had donated blood on the person's behalf, and the board was filled with wishes for a speedy recovery. When someone who has been part of the Run for the Wall dies, that person will typically be memorialized on the bulletin board, making it a virtual replica of the way dead riders are memorialized in motorcycle culture more generally. At times the board may also serve as a community service vehicle. In 1998, for instance, when the town of Rainelle had difficulty raising money for its annual Christmas toy distribution, a call for help was posted on the RFTW bulletin board, and enough money was raised to provide not only toys for Rainelle's children, but also gifts for the town's shut-in seniors.[1]

The RFTW web site represents just one of the more recent developments in the Run's history as a folk organization. Folk organizations are grass-roots voluntary associations that develop spontaneously and nonhierarchically, and that tend to use semiformal institutional frameworks to organize their activities and ensure their continuation. Folk organizations differ from formal voluntary associations such as the March of Dimes or the League of Women Voters by being more spontaneous and do-it-yourself in character, and by the desire of their members to avoid creating formal structures of authority and responsibility.

Like any organization, the Run for the Wall involves an interaction between structure and ideology. The structure of an organization consists of all the ways work is divided among its members, the way information, orders, and materials are transmitted by the organization, and the mechanisms by which leaders are selected, new participants are incorporated, and rewards are distributed. The structure of an organization is not abstract. It resides in routine practices. Who does what? Who contacts whom? Who gets what? The answers to these questions are useful indicators of an organization's real structure. They reveal both its day-to-day character and the likely sources of its problems.

In contrast to its structure, the ideology of an organization consists of the beliefs and values that explain why the organization should exist, why it should be structured in the way it is, and how members should relate to one another. Organizational ideologies are never absolute but are typically subject to question and change. As a result, every organization experiences some degree of internal debate over its purpose and strategies. Unless an organization is on the verge of collapse, however, these debates typically take place within a framework of general agreement on principles and goals. For instance, while Run for the Wall members may sometimes argue over the best route from L.A. to Washington, they all agree that the goal is to bring the group safely to the Wall.

While we can speak of ideology and structure as two components of an organization, they are always intimately linked. It is never really possible to tell where one stops and the other begins. For instance, the way the Run for the Wall selects its leaders is a reflection of its beliefs that the organization should look more like a family than a business. At the same time, by using informal procedures for selecting its leaders, the Run reinforces the idea that it is supposed to be a close-knit group of people who trust one another like brothers and sisters rather than a gathering of business associates. Thus, we cannot understand the relationship between the beliefs (ideology) and the behaviors (structure) that define the character of any organization without first examining the character of each of these elements.

THE STRUCTURE OF VOLUNTARY ASSOCIATIONS

The Run for the Wall is just one example of a longstanding penchant among Americans to create and join private organizations that are outside the realms of business and government. This tendency was already an established part of life in Anglo America by 1835 when the French political theorist Alexis de Tocqueville observed: "In no country in the world has the principle of association been more successfully used or applied to a greater multitude of objects than in America. Besides the permanent associations which are established by law under the names of townships, cities, and counties, a vast number of others are formed and maintained by the agency of private individuals."[2] In many respects the kinds of organizations de Tocqueville was talking about represent the particular notion of freedom that was crafted by the political and religious dissidents who fled or were forced out of England, and who found themselves trying to forge a new social order in a new land. Despite the religious tyranny imposed in some of the early colonies, a belief in "freedom of association" rapidly established itself as one of the basic freedoms within the colonial consciousness. Since that time, the right to establish formal and informal associations without requiring governmental or religious approval or support has been a fundamental part of the American definition of freedom.

This American notion of freedom shapes the character of voluntary associations in the United States. That is, voluntary associations are groupings of people that "come together with others to create or participate for collective benefit."[3] These associations typically have a name, goals and procedures that are written down or otherwise formally stated, an administrative or governing body, and people who are considered to belong to the group.[4] The most important feature of voluntary associations, however, is that they are just that, *voluntary*. This means that people will join and remain with a voluntary association as long as it provides the collective benefit for which they joined. Moreover, the benefits for which people most often join voluntary associations are *expressive* in nature, such as the satisfaction of feeling that they are doing good for their community or enjoying a sense of belonging. Instrumental reasons such as making money or gaining political power are far less important in the decision to join or remain a member of a voluntary association.[5] When individuals feel that such organizations are not serving their expressive needs, or no longer accomplishing the goals for which they attached themselves to the organization in the first place, they see themselves as free to withdraw. This means that the membership of voluntary associations tends to be fluid, with people joining and leaving on a regular basis.

The voluntary, expressive, and fluid nature of voluntary associations is what makes them dynamic, attractive, and accessible to many people. These characteristics can also be the source of problems. Because these associations are voluntary, those in positions of leadership can do little to order or compel people to perform the work of the association. Instead, leaders in voluntary associations must constantly strive to ensure that members are deriving the satisfactions that led them to join the association in the first place if they hope to convince them to work on its behalf and to keep them from leaving. Yet, because many people are seeking expressive satisfactions, leaders in voluntary associations may have difficulty satisfying some of the members. It is almost impossible to ensure that all or even most of those who participate in a voluntary association are enjoying the expressive benefits they hoped it would provide them. Expressive benefits are largely internal emotional experiences, and as a result, they can vary substantially from one person to the next. A meeting that leaves some people with a strong sense of solidarity and belonging, for instance, may leave others feeling isolated because, in their view, the organization is being run by a small clique of insiders. When it comes to the Run for the Wall, there are some members who feel that they are doing good for the veteran and POW/MIA cause simply by being part of a high-profile cross-country parade. Others may feel that they are really doing good only if the Run stops at as many VA hospitals along the way as possible, or if it uses its visible presence in Washington as an opportunity to publicly present petitions or other demands to lawmakers.

By contrast, in organizations where instrumental rewards such as money or other forms of material gain are among the primary benefits of participating, there is typically greater agreement about what constitutes a benefit or reward for participation. While some workers in these organizations may be less satisfied with the size of their salaries than others, for instance, they generally all agree on the value of money. In contrast, as Margaret Harris notes, voluntary associations face special problems of organization and leadership: "They [the members] do not feel obliged to join in the first place, they feel free to participate or not as it suits them, and they assume that they should be able to contribute in whatever way, to whatever extent and for whatever period, they wish. They do not generally expect to be told what to do and how to do it in 'their' organization, and they expect their relationships with other members of the organization to be informal and fulfilling."[6]

The organizational consequence is that voluntary associations typically cannot have the top-down hierarchy found in businesses and governmental institutions. Rather, voluntary associations such as the Run for the Wall must rely on networks of friendship and feelings of affinity to ensure that the necessary work of the association gets done. At the same time, the more informal the association, the more disorganized it will seem, often leading to dissatisfaction among at least some of these members, who feel that things should be run more efficiently. Attempts to solve problems of disorganization by creating more formal structures, however, will typically generate resistance from other members, who see this as violating the basic spirit of a non-hierarchical folk organization.

Despite the tensions inherent in the structure of voluntary associations, such organizations remain an important and growing part of America's social landscape.[7] What binds these fragile structures into effective organizations is a sense of purpose and community shared among the members that is powerful enough to override the tensions that result from ambiguities surrounding matters of leadership and reward.

INDIVIDUAL AND COMMUNITY: THE IDEOLOGY OF
VOLUNTARY ASSOCIATIONS

The story of how the Run for the Wall relies on ideals about individual and community to create a folk organization is a particularly
American story. Indeed, as Hervé Varenne, a French anthropologist
who studied a small Midwestern community in the United States, observed, "Voluntary and non-institutionalized associations are paradig-
matic of the American experience."[8] In order to understand the beliefs
that keep the Run together, we need to explore how American ideas
about democracy, equality, individual freedom, community, family,
and brotherhood are conceptualized and deployed by participants in
the Run, and how they enable the Run for the Wall to function as a
folk organization.

As in most aspects of life in the United States, the Run's belief
system incorporates the seemingly contradictory values of individual
freedom and community. Yet, as Varenne has suggested, drawing on
his perspective as an anthropologist and a foreigner, neither individualism nor community is primary in American culture, even though
the people he studied felt otherwise. For them, "individualism gen-
erates community . . . individualism is natural, community problem-
atical. *Society has to be built.* . . . Society was created by a joining
together of individuals for the greater good of each of them. And the
institutions of society . . . were created in the same manner for the
same purpose." He goes on to note: "The internal organization of
American individualism shapes, and is shaped by, the internal organization of the American notion of community. The opposition is
dialectical and generative. Each term may appear to deny the other,
but, in fact, implies it."[9]

In other words, the freedom of the individual and the obligations
that come with community membership exist in a relationship in
which each defines and determines the other. In this view, communities exist only because individuals *freely* choose to create them, and
individuals find the best expression of their freedom by belonging
to and accepting the rules of these communities. This is particularly
true in American society because personal identity is something that
people must *construct*: It is not given to them at birth. As Faye
Ginsberg observes, "The American social system stresses the importance of individual identity, yet lacks or diminishes regular forms of
person-defining ascription that characterize other cultures, such as a

FIGURE 29. Some riders return to the Run year after year.

kin group or caste. . . . Consequently, a critical task for social actors . . . is to constitute a social identity."[10]

A social identity, however, is difficult to construct alone. Thus, as we have pointed out in previous chapters, for many Americans the route to constructing identity is joining with others who share a similar identity. Whether it is through participation in a particular church, political party, or pastime (including motorcycling), or by energetically embracing some ethnicity or occupation as a key element of one's self, Americans typically take an active role in creating their identities. Ginsberg, again: "What is important to note here is that the social forms that focus on making or remaking the self in new terms require association with like-minded others. It is this process of self-definition through social action . . . that helps foster the proliferation of social experiments and voluntary associations . . . that so impressed de Tocqueville in 1831 and many others since then."[11]

The observations by Varenne and Ginsberg about individualism and community in the United States are also well illustrated by the process of identity building through submission to the group that is typical of biker clubs. As Wolf notes in *The Rebels*, while the outlaw bikers he studied regarded themselves as independent, self-reliant individualists operating outside, and in defiance of, conventional society, nonetheless they banded together with other bikers in highly organized clubs governed by sets of fairly rigid formal and informal rules that were enforced by other members. This seeming contradiction was noted by the reader of a biker magazine who recently wrote: "Many bike clubs with constitutions predicated on the freedoms of individuals maintain a policy of Harley exclusivity. Freedom I ask you? No, bondage to a dogma."[12] For many Americans, what this writer is complaining about is not really a contradiction at all. For instance, bikers who join clubs that require members to ride a certain kind of bike, wear only certain kinds of insignia, and meet a number of other obligations actually do so to reenforce and support what they see as their individual freedom by obtaining group support for their particular life choices. As Wolf notes, "A club offers a social framework of biker activities and a sense of community that provide the biker with positive feedback about his developing identity and support his personal philosophy of biking as an acceptable alternative lifestyle." Or, in the words of one biker quoted by Wolfe, "The club gives me the freedom to be the kind of biker I want to be."[13] While outlaw biker clubs are an extreme and deviant form of community (at least by the standards of conventional society), the principles that underlie their organization are similar to those of other forms of American voluntary associations—including the Run for the Wall.

As Varenne noted, the American view of community is that it is built by individuals who come together for a common purpose. "In native terms, 'individuals' create 'communities' by congregating with other individuals whom they decide to consider similar to themselves."[14] Such communities, like the biker clubs, serve the needs of the individuals who are involved in them. The voluntary association of *free* individuals is thus based on both their private interests and a sense of community that comes from sharing these interests with others. As Varenne puts it, quoting John Dewey, "Men live in communities by virtue of the things which they have in common. . . . What they have in common in order to form a community or society are aims, beliefs, aspirations, knowledge, a common understanding, like-mindedness as the sociologists say."[15]

Both sociological and popular notions typically view communities as groups of people situated in and bounded by some distinct physical space. From this perspective communities are contained within the physical space defined by such things as neighborhoods, towns, churches, schools, and so on. This image of community, however, no longer reflects the full reality of life in the United States. While physical communities remain, many Americans now find their most important communities by associating with people who share their interests or recreational passions, but who may be scattered throughout the country or even the world. With the increasing spread of electronic communications via the internet and the World Wide Web, communities can develop even in the abstract universe of cyberspace. As sociologist Thomas Bender notes, "A preoccupation with territory . . . ultimately confuses our understanding of community. A community involves a limited number of people in a somewhat restricted *social* space or network held together by shared understandings and a sense of obligation."[16] This sense of community as a social rather than a physical space characterizes not only the Run for the Wall, but also other motorcycle groups such as the Gold Wing Road Riders Association with which we have been involved, as well as nonmotorcycle groups such as the senior full-time RVers studied by Dorothy and David Counts.

Such ideas of community reflect life in the contemporary United States, where identity increasingly hinges less on work or place of residence and more on nonwork activities, such as riding a motorcycle or pursuing some other hobby or voluntary activity. These ideas, however, also have roots in older American experiences and social formations. A mobile population, a history of having to continually incorporate new immigrant groups, the value placed on openness and friendliness, the frontier experience, notions of equality, and an emphasis on individual freedom of choice have long contributed to ideas of communities as voluntary and fluid associations.

Counts and Counts suggest that there may be a negative side to the construction of fluid communities based on shared interests. While these communities may bring together those who are very similar, they may also isolate themselves from those who have different interests, ideas, or values. This can be particularly true for lifestyle enclaves of people who construct personal relationships based on leisure and consumption.[17] Lifestyle communities, whether age-restricted RV parks for senior citizens or motorcycle clubs, are typically more homogeneous with respect to age, interests, and values than are spatial communities.

As an interest-based community, the majority of whose members live far removed from one another, the Run for the Wall is typical of this new type of community. Like other nonspatial communities, the Run for the Wall brings together a specific segment of American society—those who ride motorcycles and who in some way care about veterans' issues and POWs and MIAs. At the same time, however, we have found that, contrary to what the Counts say about RVers, on all other social dimensions the Run promotes inclusion, not exclusion. Rather than seeking to keep the group exclusive, participants encourage new people to join.[18] Individual participants will often reach out to suffering veteran brothers, urging them to ride in the Run and to seek healing for their psychic wounds. Run members are always open to attracting new participants. For instance, when Cookie Monster was asked if he ever had any problems wearing his vest with its RFTW patch around riders wearing the colors of outlaw motorcycle clubs, he said, "Hell, as soon as they bring it up I give them an earful about what the Run and my patch stand for. After that they want to buy me a beer and start talking about joining the Run."

The Run brings together people representing a wide variety of backgrounds, experiences, and views based on their shared concern for healing the wounds of the Vietnam War. From veterans on disability to well-to-do business people, from fire fighters to college professors, from in-country combat vets to nonveterans, the Run welcomes them all. The one caveat is that participants must behave respectfully toward the Run's dual mission of obtaining a full accounting of all U.S. POWs and MIAs and helping those who still suffer from the war's impact on their lives. While some might see this shared concern for the effects of the Vietnam War as representative of a narrow and primarily conservative slice of the U.S. political spectrum, our own experience as nonveterans with left-of-center political values suggests differently. As a pilgrimage, the Run places its participants in a state where they are often emotionally open and vulnerable. In doing this, it enables them to see the real human beings and the real human sorrows that lie behind the narrow social, economic, and political labels that allow us to imagine that somehow only those who are like us and who agree with us are good people. In this sense, the Run creates a community among those who are different on a number of dimensions by creating a space where these differences matter far less than they do in everyday social life.

THE RUN AS AN ORGANIZATION

How does the Run blend its structural arrangements and its belief system into an ongoing organization? Addressing this question reveals how some of the fundamental features, including certain kinds of contradictions and conflicts that are an inherent part of voluntary associations in America, manifest themselves on the Run for the Wall.

The Run for the Wall is a group of like-minded individuals who come together once a year for a collective endeavor focused on a common purpose. The Run began with a collection of motorcycle-riding veterans who responded to an announcement of a cross-country motorcycle run to the Wall. Every year since then, new riders join the Run, often in response to a spontaneous "I've got to go" reaction they feel when they first hear about it. This spontaneity in large part is what gives the Run its folk quality. There is nothing to hold members to the Run for the Wall except the sense that they are called to make the journey, once or perhaps many times. Thus, while the Run has a degree of organizational structure, this structure exists primarily to make the spontaneous happen.

While the Run is a common endeavor, it is also a journey whose nature is different for each individual who makes it. It is also different each time one makes it. These differences from one person to another, and from one time to another, can become a source of unhappiness with, and conflict over, the Run and can even lead some participants to withdraw. But these tensions and conflicts are more than personal. They also reflect organizational and structural characteristics of voluntary organizations in general, as well as some of the specific features of the Run itself.

Since 1996, when we first joined the Run, we have seen it grow considerably and have watched as it has suffered through some of the organizational problems that growth typically brings to organizations. During the Run's formative years, leadership was informally passed among those who had participated in some of the earliest runs, and the national coordinator, in consultation with a few other RFTW friends, decided on the itinerary and other arrangements. This system continued until the late 1990s, when the Run inaugurated a somewhat more formal organizational hierarchy.

Since its inception, the Run has had few formal rules. The closest the Run comes to having formal guidelines are the rules of the road that are handed out with an itinerary sheet when participants sign in. These rules are a mixture of road procedures drawn from the wider culture of group motorcycle riding and special rules for riding the Run, such as the role of road guards, and the procedures for gassing up at stops. These rules are emphasized and elaborated by the Run's leader at the daily morning predeparture meeting, and spoken additions or amendments may be made to the road rules as problems or difficulties arise en route. For example, almost every year we have been on the Run, that year's leader has emphasized the need to keep a tight formation in the line. In 1997, however, there was a particularly troubling problem with a rider who moved in and out of the pack as it was going down the road, making everyone slow down when he cut in, or forcing one side of the two-column line to move up when he vacated his spot. In response to complaints about the hazard posed by this one rider, Deekin, that year's leader, admonished the riders to stay in place while the group was moving so as not to create confusion or hazard in the line. "Pick a spot and stay with it until the next stop," he said. Even though the offending rider left the next day, the rule of "pick a spot and stay with it" has been reiterated at rider briefings ever since. Another example of a rule created in response to a problem resulted from a few riders drinking alcohol while on the Run in 1998. The following year a policy was announced that drinking during the course of the day's ride would not be allowed. Deekin, who was again the national coordinator in 1999, emphasized that this rule was both to insure safety and to avoid riders being given tickets for DUIs (as had happened the previous year), which would cast a bad light on the Run as just another bunch of wild bikers and thus tarnish its image as an event with a serious mission. Anyone who chose not to abide by this rule would be asked to leave the Run. The prohibition, however, did not extend to drinking once the group had stopped, because this was seen as an appropriate matter of individual choice. Thus, the problem of alcohol on the Run was handled in a way that was clearly consistent with American culture by drawing a sharp line between community good while on the road and individual freedom once the day's riding was done.[19]

Each of these cases is an example of how the Run's rules of the road are an evolving body of knowledge that is passed on informally from one year to the next. Many of these rules have never been written down but become part of the group's oral tradition (although the rule against alcohol consumption while riding did make it onto the sheet given to riders when they sign in). Basing rules on specific past problems, rather than on a set of guidelines that are formulated and written according to some general theory of how the Run should operate, is a very American thing to do. As inheritors of the English system of common law, Americans are familiar with the idea that the outcome of specific cases can determine the content of rules. In the United States, the result of specific court appeals based on constitutional issues, such as the right to equality of education or the right to abortion, can change the law of the land. This differs notably from the practice in most European countries, where the outcomes of specific appeals do not change the general law.[20] Although the knowledge of specific cases in the Run's past is mostly contained in an oral tradition, this use of specific problems as a basis for general rules is another example of how the Run deploys underlying elements of American culture as it deals with organizational problems.

Another important consequence of the Run's reliance on informal patterns of organization is that its boundaries tend to be permeable and indefinite. The Run is open to whoever supports the cause, veteran or not. There are no requirements for participation other than showing up, preferably on a motorcycle, and being (mostly) able to pay your own way across the country and back. There is also no single place for joining the Run and no required distance that one must ride. As we have noted earlier, people can and do join up anywhere from the initial starting point in Los Angeles all the way to the last stop in Virginia before the Run rides into D.C. Participants are asked to sign in when they join the Run so the organization can have an official count of riders, and so that all who participate will receive the Run's periodic newsletter. While many long-distance riders do sign in, every year there are an unknown number of others, particularly short-distance riders, who do not. As a result, these riders are not listed anywhere as RFTW participants, yet—to some extent at least—their participation automatically makes them part of the RFTW family. Those who have signed in are obligated to nothing more than agreeing to the Run's policy of "no attitudes" and following the rules of the road. Finally, there is no formal mechanism for resigning from the Run. Since no one is officially a member, there is no need for anyone to formally quit. People who no longer wish to be part of the Run simply do not show up the next year.

The Run's boundaries are also indefinite because its total participant base includes not only those who make all or part of the actual motorcycle trip, but also many supporters (both individuals and groups) along the route who organize events, provide hospitality, greet the bikers, and in various other ways connect themselves to the riders and the event. These nonriding contributors typically do not sign in anywhere; they just show up with their local veterans organization or motorcycle club to help serve food, organize ceremonies, or even wash motorcycles, as in Huntington, West Virginia. In some cases these community contributors identify strongly with the Run and its goals and will stay in touch with the Run from one year to the next, becoming ongoing members of the association as much as those who ride in the Run. Consequently, there is no way of knowing how many people are part of what is often called the Run for the Wall family.

The legal character of the Run also plays a part in the indefinite boundaries of the Run's membership. For many years the Run was simply a coming together of like-minded riders. As a result of growth and the need to raise money for its expanding operations, the Run was chartered as a nonprofit association in 1998, enabling supporters to make tax-deductible contributions. Unlike many voluntary nonprofits, however, the Run does not have official members. In legal terminology, the Run is not a "membership organization." While people *belong* to the Run for the Wall family, they are not *members* in the way that someone might be a member of a bowling league or a neighborhood association. Those who are part of the Run for the Wall neither pay dues to the organization nor vote as a body on matters such as where the Run will travel or stop, what its policy will be, or who will be its leaders. The organization's leaders make arrange-

ments for a once-a-year event, issue calls for participants, and over-
see the Run itself. Anyone who participates in the Run belongs to
the family, but like a family, it is rarely clear exactly how decisions
get made. Participants who interact with the Run's leaders may have
informal opportunities to influence plans and policies, but there are
no formal votes through which Run participants can speak decisively
as a body.

The lack of a formal membership structure, and the subsequent
informality of decision making and leadership selection, has led some
RFTW riders to suggest that the group should be reconstituted as a
membership organization with formal voting rights for its members.
Becoming a membership organization, however, would have some
undesirable legal consequences. Under its current status, the Run is
not legally liable for damage that its riders might do to themselves
or others while traveling with the Run to D.C. As Deekin explained
to us, if the Run became a membership organization, it would face
the problem of having to purchase enough liability insurance to protect itself from any lawsuits that might arise as the result of taking
several hundred motorcycles across the country. In the current liti-
gious climate, the costs would be substantial. This, in turn, would
require the Run to institute a mandatory dues structure. For many
current riders, a formal dues system would be objectionable, not only
because of the cost, but also because it would signify an end to the
Run's character as a folk organization. The value many Run members place on informal organization is evidenced by the critical way
some RFTW participants speak about Rolling Thunder, *Incorporated,*
the organization that oversees the annual Rolling Thunder parade in
Washington, D.C. While most RFTW riders support and appreciate
Rolling Thunder, the fact that it bears the *Inc.* label associated with
businesses and has established dues-paying chapters around the country is seen by some Run for the Wall participants as an indicator that
its leaders have lost sight of the original POW/MIA mission and that
it has become, as one RFTW rider put it, "just another business out
for itself."

The question of whether the Run should or should not become
a membership organization touches upon another important characteristic of the way the Run is organized—its process of leadership
selection. Without a voting body, it is difficult to be certain whether
the people who are selected for leadership positions represent the will

of the majority. Nor is it entirely clear to whom the Run's leaders must answer. This sometimes creates problems on both sides of the leadership/membership line. Membership organizations typically have the advantage of formalized voting systems for selecting leaders; in more informal associations such as the Run for the Wall, leadership selection is often a fluid interpersonal process. The disadvantage of an informal selection process is that it can lead to the perception among some Run for the Wall riders that the route to leadership is through supporting—or as some would say, "sucking up to"—the current leaders.

Informal organizations are fertile ground for the idea that things are being run by a small clique of insiders. We ourselves were portrayed by some riders as part of an insider group when we began riding near the front of the pack with R.C. in 1997. At first we thought this was a strange idea: We rode up front simply because a friend asked us to ride next to him. On reflection, however, it became apparent that what seemed to us a very tenuous insider status was a good example of how American-style, do-it-yourself organizations draw participants into taking responsibility for their operations.

The debate among some members over whether the Run should become a membership organization is a good example of how the desire for a predictable organizational structure, formally answerable to its participants, and the desire to maintain an informal, non-hierarchical association can create tension in a folk organization such as the Run for the Wall. If the Run did become a membership organization, it would gain a greater degree of organizational predictability. At the same time, it would lose some of the do-it-yourself qualities that make it attractive to many who participate. Nor is it clear that formal leadership selection is always the best choice. Formal elections in voluntary associations, for instance, can produce leaders who are popular, but who have had relatively little experience in running the organization. Informal processes of leadership selection, while vulnerable to real or perceived problems of favoritism, tend to select people who are not only known to existing leaders, but who have also paid their dues by their involvement in the organization, and in doing so have acquired a working knowledge of it. Neither leadership selection mechanism is necessarily preferable for voluntary associations; however, the Run's informal processes of making decisions and selecting leaders gives it a mildly anarchist quality that reflects the desire of many of its members to avoid formal hierarchy as much as possible.

The Run's looseness of membership and organization, and the conflicts that have arisen during its brief history, can make the Run seem questionable as an ongoing proposition. Ironically, however, the Run's permeable and flexible membership boundaries, its way of making and communicating rules through a kind of oral case law, and its informal mechanisms for selecting leaders, are all evidence that the Run enjoys one of the key characteristics of an organization— the ability to reproduce itself regardless of the comings and goings of specific individuals. When we have raised the issue of how long the Run will continue, participants typically reply that it will continue "as long as there are veterans," or "until the last POW comes home and the last MIA is accounted for." In this sense, the Run for the Wall is clearly greater than the sum of its individual members.

So far, we have discussed the organization and operation of the Run at a general sociological level. How the Run's organizational informality and its adaptation of the American ideals of individual and community operate on the ground is captured in the following description of a particular Run for the Wall event, the October 1997 Western reunion in Payson, Arizona.

PRACTICING INDIVIDUALISM AND COMMUNITY

Our first experience with a Run for The Wall reunion was Columbus Day weekend, 1997, in Payson, Arizona, about a three-hour ride from our home in Flagstaff. The dates for the reunion had been posted on the RFTW web site and confirmed for us by Mountain Man, but we had no information on exactly where the event was to be held or how to get there. A local biker friend involved with the Run gave us the name and telephone number of the state RFTW coordinator, and we contacted him. However, he also didn't know what was happening and suggested we call George and Linda, at whose house in Payson the reunion was being held. We reached Linda and finally managed to get the information we needed about the days of the reunion and the directions to their house. Later, when we discussed our difficulties with R.C., he said he himself had only learned of the reunion a day or so beforehand, as he does not have a computer and didn't even know the reunion was that weekend, illustrating some of the problems of relying on electronic communication for RFTW information dissemination. (There is an RFTW newsletter, but some untimely computer problems had kept it from being mailed out until the Friday before the reunion weekend.) Several participants later commented on the dedication of those who showed up for the reunion, given the difficulty many of them had in getting information about it.

People began gathering in Payson on Saturday, but because it was very windy and cold in Flagstaff, with intermittent snow showers, and because we would have to travel over mountain roads to reach Payson, we decided to wait until Sunday to ride to the reunion. We could have gone in our four-wheel-drive "cage," but it didn't seem right to go to this gathering without the bike, especially because we were newcomers to the Run for the Wall, attending our first reunion. Sunday dawned cold but clear, and we were on our way.

We arrived at George and Linda's home to find the cul-de-sac where it is situated filled with motorcycles. People were gathered on the front steps of the house, talking, laughing, and drinking beer and soda. At first we felt a little awkward, as there was almost no one there we knew. But then we entered the house and found many of the friends we had made on the Run, some local, others from as far away as Illinois, California, and New Mexico. We shared long, strong, emotional embraces with them—not the light, obligatory hugs that have become commonplace social exchange. Several of our friends, we were sad to find, had fared badly since we had last seen them on the Run. One had been in a motorcycle accident (the second since we first met him) and wore a brace on his leg, another's wife had died, one had just lost his job of twenty-one years, and another was suffering from back problems.

Later in the afternoon there was a full barbecue with chicken, pork, and sausages, accompanied by a variety of cold salads, followed by pie and coffee for dessert. A collection was taken to reimburse George and Linda for the food, with each giving what he or she could, a typical American collective effort that left the amount of participation up to individual choice.

Leadership, Followership, and Speaking Out

After we had eaten, Skipper and Redlite began the meeting. There were several items for discussion, some of which proved contentious. The most troublesome was a change in the RFTW route for 1998. Skipper had decided to relocate the departure point to Long Beach instead of Ontario, California, which had been the Run's starting point for a number of years. This choice led to considerable debate, with the key issue being safety. Ontario is located on the far eastern edge of Los Angeles, allowing both arrivals and departures to take place with minimal exposure to L.A. freeway traffic. Some riders expressed concern that leaving from Long Beach would expose the Run to a long ride in heavy traffic at the Run's most difficult point, when the group would be new and not yet used to riding together. Skipper supported his preference for Long Beach by saying that the Run would receive more publicity and help in Long Beach than it ever had in Ontario because so many veterans lived there. He also addressed concerns about safety by saying that the California Highway Patrol would escort us until we were free of the heaviest traffic. Others countered by saying that promised police escorts only showed up about 60 percent of the time. At one point, someone asked if any of this discussion would lead to a change in the starting place, and Skipper said no, it had already been arranged that the Run would leave from Long Beach. Once it became clear that the Run's starting point was fixed, some of the group expressed their support for this idea, while others who did not want to ride in Long Beach traffic said they would join the Run farther on. And some took a military approach to the matter, agreeing with one rider who said, "Skipper is the leader, and if he says we are leaving from Long Beach, I will follow him."

Another issue that arose was the matter of finances. This is a typical source of friction in voluntary associations, and the Run for the Wall is no exception. Questions were raised about where the Run's money comes from (donations, as well as the sale of t-shirts and patches), and where it goes (the newsletter, the family dinner in D.C., gas for chase vehicles, and so on). There was some discussion about whether the budget should be in the Run's newsletter, with some of those present noting that it would be useful for members to have this information when asking potential contributors to donate money to the Run. Still others expressed their concerns that the Run should not be too focused on money matters or on asking for contributions and emphasized that we shouldn't lose sight of what the Run was all about—the POW/MIA issue and personal healing. Linda, the RFTW treasurer, was particularly eloquent about the need not to lose perspective on what the Run is about. Placing her hand over her heart she said, "The Run happens inside."

There was also a discussion of the design for t-shirts and patches. Skipper had planned to have an emblem printed on both the front and back of the t-shirt. Several people noted, however, that this unnecessarily increased costs because no one sees the back of a t-shirt when riders are wearing vests or jackets, as they typically do on the Run. This was followed by a discussion about the All the Way patch and who should be allowed to wear it. Should it be restricted to those who started out in California, or just to those who went all the way to D.C., whatever their starting point? After some discussion, Redlite asked for a show of hands, which revealed that the majority favored a more restrictive use of the patch. This was the closest the meeting came to a vote, and the head count was phrased as simply getting a sense of how people felt, not as an actual deciding vote.

Issues regarding leadership and succession also came up in the discussion at the reunion in Payson. There seemed to be an undercurrent of concern about the way national coordinators were selected. Most of this concern arose not from objections to the selection of any particular leader, but more from uncertainty as to exactly *how* people were selected to lead the Run. Someone suggested that it was important there be some continuity in the top slot, and that whoever held that position should remain in it for several years. These concerns reflected, in part, the fact that until John Anderson stepped down as national coordinator in 1996, Run leaders often held that position for several years. Since then, however, the position of national coordinator had begun to change hands on a yearly basis. Others pointed out that while there certainly should be continuity, it didn't necessarily have to be in the form of a national coordinator who held that position for several years, as there were always others, including past leaders, who would be active in the Run and could provide a degree of continuity and institutional memory.

There was also discussion about the route for the 1998 Run, particularly questions about where the Run would stop and where it would not. This last item, as we have learned, is always a matter of some contention when the Run for the Wall's route is discussed, because there are more organizations and communities along the way that would like to host the Run for the Wall than the Run is able to accommodate. In addition, different people on the Run will often feel committed to stopping at different places.

In addition to the old-timers attending the reunion, there were several people who were planning to join the Run for the first time the following year. One of these was Nancy, a photographer for *Easy Rider* and *Biker* magazine. She had come to the reunion to do a feature story on the Run for the Wall for *Biker* and planned to go all the way with the Run the following May. People at the reunion were pleased with the idea of the publicity that the Run would receive with the story (although, as we noted earlier, not everyone was happy to have the Run featured in a magazine that promoted the image of bikers as outlaws). Whatever people felt about *Biker*, however, Nancy herself was welcomed by the group. At the same time, as a "newbie" she was subject to a certain amount of good-natured ribbing. One RFTW regular, for instance, convinced her that he was a professional wrestler and male model, although in fact he was a fireman. (The following summer, Nancy would earn her stripes by riding all the way with the group, sometimes mounted backward on a motorcycle in order to take photos of the group. Her story on the Run later appeared as a separate thirty-page insert in *Biker*.)[21]

The meeting began to break up sometime after dark. People continued to mill around for awhile, talking, saying goodbye, and making promises to keep in touch. We finally took our leave, a lengthy process that involved hugging everyone and saying long goodbyes. Like many of the others there, we found it hard to leave and were sad to say farewell to our Run for the Wall family. We finally arrived at the Payson Holiday Inn around 8:30 and collapsed. We had just been through an experience almost as intense as the Run itself. Seeing and talking to people with whom we had shared the emotional experience of the Run, encountering the tensions of the meeting, worrying about the next year's Run and the future of the Run itself, left us tired and yet oddly exhilarated. Instead of sleeping, we spent the next several hours talking with one another about what we had just experienced.

The Reunion as an American Event

In many ways the reunion had seemed to be a unique event. And yet there was nothing really special about it. Gatherings like this happen all the time, all over America. The purposes may differ, yet the processes are essentially the same. People run their own meetings, they arrive at decisions, and they implement these decisions. Although the reunion did not follow *Robert's Rules of Order* and seemed informal and democratic, it followed a set of unspoken guidelines and was shaped by rituals and structures that would be recognized by any American who has attended a meeting in almost any voluntary association or business anywhere in the United States. Democratic processes and the equality of all individuals present were assumed. Formal rules of procedure were deliberately eschewed—as Skipper stated at one point, "We don't take votes." Nevertheless, agreement was reached on issues such as the design of the t-shirts and the wearing of patches. People spoke up—loudly and angrily at times—and even interrupted each other. Yet at no point did the meeting disintegrate into chaos. The right of every person there to speak was acknowledged and respected, as was the obligation to do so. As one person who had strongly objected to the decision to leave from Long Beach instead of Ontario said: "It's okay. I've said my piece." Thus, while there were features of the reunion that were unique to the Run for the Wall, the overall structure of the meeting was clearly American and reflected important American cultural beliefs about equality, democracy, and the appropriate relationship between individual and community.

THE RUN FOR THE WALL AS FAMILY

Aside from the more formal business of the meeting just described, reunions serve other purposes for those who attend. While they inevitably involve only a small percentage of all those who participate in the Run, they play a critical role in creating the solidarity among a core group that is essential to voluntary associations. In a community that is scattered across the country, and that is united by an event that takes place only once a year, reunions keep people in touch with friends and allow them to catch up on news and reaffirm their commitment to the cause. In addition, reunions are also an opportunity to recreate some of the camaraderie that prevails on the Run, a camaraderie that is often lacking in participants' everyday life.

The emotions expressed on the Run or at reunions when people talk with one another about such things as troubled homecomings and life difficulties are those of close intimate relations. This is why images of kinship play an important role in RFTW rhetoric. There are frequent references to the Run for the Wall family, and to participants in the Run as brothers and sisters. Such usage expresses the idea of community in a familiar idiom by no means unique to the Run for the Wall. In their study of senior full-time RVer's, for example, Dorothy and David Counts found that RVers use the metaphor of family to express the sense of community they feel with one another. This imagery is rooted in American ideas of kinship. In this view, as Varenne points out, kinship is not limited to ascribed or biological ties. Instead, because the relative is viewed as an *individual*, not just part of a group, one may *choose* (to some extent, at least) whether or not to interact with people or groups who are relatives by blood or marriage depending on one's personal likes and dislikes. In addition, Americans will often treat people with whom they have no formal family ties as if they are relatives. "Some will not even say that their group is 'like a family,' but that it *is* a family, because family is a way of relating."[22]

But what does being a family mean in such contexts? Counts and Counts see the metaphor of family as a way of expressing community. "RVers frequently use the metaphor of family to describe their feeling of community. To describe the family feeling they use such words as 'friendship,' 'love,' 'trust,' and 'caring,' and recount times when other RVers helped and supported them in a crisis."[23] Being friendly, open, and accepting are other characteristics expected of those who are part of a family. There is a similar idea of family among many of the participants in the Run for the Wall, for whom ideas of love and brotherhood imply equality, trust, and mutual support, qualities that one should find in a family but that not all veterans experienced from their actual families upon their return from Vietnam.

According to Varenne, the concept of love in American culture is essential to these kinds of metaphoric extensions of kinship. While love is certainly not felt by each RFTW participant toward every other participant, the concept of love plays an important role in the RFTW ideology, just as it does in many of the friendships among its participants. Thus, the emotional hugs exchanged by RFTW participants express the love given to a suffering veteran, or the thanks for a supporter's commitment to the cause. They are also a mark of family, similar to the hugs the Counts noted among RVers. As one senior put it: "After all, one usually hugs new relatives, even when meeting for the first time. We believed that we were part of a 'family.'"[24]

Although participants frequently invoke metaphors of kinship and love when talking about the Run for the Wall family, these ideals are by no means always realized. Interpersonal conflicts and intergroup distinctions are as likely to emerge among those who participate in the Run for the Wall as in any other organization. Distinctions between vets and nonvets, or between longtime participants and newcomers, or between those who want more versus less organizational formality can sometimes lead to difficulties that threaten idealized images of the Run as a family and community. At the same time, like families, the Run has repeatedly demonstrated itself to be capable of enduring internal conflict and dissension without dissolving. And, perhaps like families, for better or for worse, those who have ridden the Run for the Wall together share a bond that is hard to escape.

Individualism, Freedom, and Community on the Run

The inherent tension in the Run between individualism and individual freedom on the one hand, and structure and authority on the other, manifests itself in various ways. We have heard Run leaders criticized for being too authoritarian and for not being authoritarian enough. Sometimes the same person is criticized for both. It is important that leaders keep the group safe, structure arrivals and departures on time, and deal firmly with individuals who cannot or will not ride in a harmonious way with the group. Yet someone who is too heavy-handed or authoritarian may be resented by those who feel they should be free to ride their bikes as they wish.

For some, even the limited regimentation of the Run for the Wall is a bit too reminiscent of the military. As one RFTW rider noted when we were waiting in a long line of bikes to gas up at a station with too few pumps: "Hell, I've waited in enough lines and taken enough orders to last me for a lifetime." However, for others, we suspect, there is a certain attraction, or at least familiarity, in the quasi-military flavor of the Run. Sometimes the common military experience is played upon in a semijoking manner. For example, when the Run leader is trying to get the group's attention, someone may yell "Ten-*shun!*" and people will nudge each other and repeat the order to get everyone to come to attention. At the same time, there is ambivalence about imposing military order. "At ease," someone might call out when the leader is trying to get the group's attention, adding, "We don't stand at attention anymore."[25]

There are other tensions between participants and leaders as well, some related to personal issues and past problems, some related to the individual personalities. A wide range of individuals comprises the Run, some active in motorcycle groups, loners who have never ridden with a group before (and certainly never one this large), veterans who bring a variety of personal and political issues to the event, and others (like ourselves) who find themselves becoming supportive of many of the Run's goals after participating. Indeed, it sometimes amazes us that the Run takes place at all, let alone that it brings several hundred motorcycles safely to its destination in Washington, D.C., every year. That it does so is a testimony to the way in which individuals can come together to create and sustain community in the American context. Yet while the open and fluid character of the Run for the Wall is one of its strengths, it also creates problems. When an organization is highly informal, it sometimes becomes difficult for individuals to agree upon what interests it should serve or how it should serve them. This is manifest in the ways in which the Run has changed its organization in the last two years, in the consequences of these changes, and in various individuals we know who are constantly negotiating their own relationship to the Run.

GROWTH, LEADERSHIP, AND DECISION MAKING

The kinds of tensions and problems that can arise in a folk-style voluntary association were illustrated by the discussions that took place at the reunion in Payson. Many of the issues discussed at the reunion reflected, sometimes implicitly and sometimes explicitly, the fact that the Run had grown well beyond a small operation that could be managed by a group of friends. Next to decline, growth is probably the most stressful thing that can happen to an organization. This is even more the case when the organization is a loosely knit voluntary association without the clearly developed growth plan that might be found in businesses or highly formalized voluntary associations such as the Sierra Club or the Christian Coalition. For some of those whose memory of the Run reaches back to its earlier years, it has become too big, too anonymous, and too bureaucratized. For many newer participants with no point of comparison, the size of the Run is impressive and part of its attraction.

The Run leadership—informal though it is—has not been unresponsive to the organization's growth problems. In 1997 the Run formalized its system of state coordinators, and in 1998 it established a board of directors. Like most organizational restructuring, however, this led to some confusion over lines of authority. In the past, the national coordinator oversaw all of the necessary prerun arrangements, from deciding on the route, to booking blocks of motel rooms at the Run's various stopping points, to making sure there would be new t-shirts for the upcoming Run. He also served as the operations leader as the Run traveled across the country. This meant being the Run's primary spokesperson in communities and at media events along the way, and handling all manner of problems that might arise along the route—ensuring that police escorts appeared where they were needed when they were needed, settling disputes between riders, dealing with riders who were reluctant to follow the Run's rules of the road, and so on.

When the system of state coordinators was formalized, the idea was that these state-level activists would help plan the best route through their state, arrange for escorts as needed, and raise money or other donations of support from local businesses. While this system removed some of the burden from the national coordinator, it was not without its problems. In some cases, state coordinators felt that their efforts were overlooked or unappreciated by the national leadership, while other coordinators felt that some state leaders had overstepped their authority. The creation of an RFTW Board of Directors led to some similar tensions and hard feelings. The question arose, Who was in charge? Who should have final say over where the Run would start and what route it would follow? Who was responsible for deciding such things as the final design of the Run's t-shirt? Who should speak for the group while it was on the road, the national coordinator, a member of the board, or the coordinator for the state in which the event was taking place? These ambiguities led to occasional conflicts and hard feelings among people in different positions in the RFTW organization, some of which spilled into the wider membership as people chose to support one side or the other.

While we recognize the importance of these issues for those involved in them, it is fairly clear from an organizational perspective that tensions over how and by whom the Run should be managed were the result of the kinds of structural problems that are inevitable when an informal folk organization moves closer to becoming a bureaucratized and formally structured voluntary association. When new positions were created, they often lacked detailed job descriptions outlining their duties, prerogatives, and limits. Nor were these new positions initially arranged into organizational flow charts delineating lines of responsibility. We are not suggesting that the Run for the Wall should have implemented these strategies, which are more typical of formal organizations. Taking its lead from these kinds of bureaucratized institutions may be contrary to the Run's best qualities as a folk organization. At the same time, sidestepping bureaucratic detail in favor of informality will mean that the path toward change will always be a bit bumpy. The Run for the Wall's struggle with growth and change is an interesting study in the contradictions that face any folk organization that is successful enough to expand to a point at which it can no longer be what it once was—an informal network of friends.

In 1999 the RFTW Board of Directors took another major step toward creating a more formal hierarchy for the Run. Specifically, it established a formal, three-year path to the position of national coordinator that involved serving first as road guard captain, and then as assistant national coordinator. The winter 2000 issue of the RFTW newsletter explained the new system in a call for a captain of the road guards for the 2001 Run:

> The RFTW Board of Directors is now accepting applications for Road Guard Captain for 2001. The individual appointed must be willing to serve for at least three years—as Road Guard Captain in 2001, Assistant National Coordinator in 2002, and as National Coordinator in 2003. Qualified applicants must be experienced riders who meet the criteria for Road Guards . . . and must be committed to riding "All the Way" with the RFTW for at least the next three years. . . . Past experience as a Road Guard is helpful, but is not necessary.

At the time it established this system, the board also selected two other riders, Milo and Sidecar, to serve respectively as the road guard captain and assistant national coordinator for 2000, putting them on the path toward becoming national coordinator. This system is a good example of the way that the process of bureaucratization in voluntary associations is often the formalizing of existing practice. In recent years, most national coordinators have had extensive experience with the Run, both serving as road guards and heading up the road guards. Not only that, but at least on the road, road guard captains have often served as informal advisors to the national coordinator, in much the same manner that the new assistant coordinator might. By formalizing these practices, however, the new system has the advantage of making it clear to all of the Run participants who is in line for eventually becoming the national coordinator. In this way, the Run for the Wall has grown more similar to many professional organizations that have third and second vice presidents who move up to president. The one major difference, however, is that despite its changes, the Run is still not a formal membership association, and thus the people selected to eventually move into the national coordinator slot will be chosen by the Board of Directors rather than elected through a vote of the membership. At the same time, this system represents a degree of democratization insofar as the selection of people to enter the path to national coordinator will be made by a board rather than by the current national coordinator. Some of the Run for the Wall regulars we know feel this is an important step in the right direction because it ensures predictability, continuity, and a national coordinator with a backlog of accumulated experience with making the Run happen. Others feel that the selection process still represents the buddy system of the past, because every year the road guard captain and eventual national coordinator will be selected by a board that is appointed rather than elected. In any case, the change to the new system is evidence that what was once a small, quasi-anarchist organization of friends and comrades who passed the leadership from one rider to another has begun to develop the rudimentary framework of a formal organizational structure.

Another important change resulting from the growth of the Run for the Wall is the planning for an RFTW southern route in 2001. This route would leave from Ontario, California, at the same time as the main or central-route group but would head southeast toward Phoenix on the first day, instead of east toward Kingman, Arizona. From there the southern route would cross Texas, Louisiana, Mississippi, Alabama, Tennessee, and Virginia, joining up with the central body at Toms Brook, Virginia, the Run's last gas and lunch stop before riding into Washington, D.C. In May of 2000, twenty riders undertook a southern route reconnaissance run to work out possible problems with distances, gas stops, and planned overnight stops, and to make contact with veteran support groups and communities along the way. Based on their success, the Run for the Wall board authorized a full-fledged Run for the Wall southern route for 2001.

Creation of a southern route for the Run for the Wall is a good example of how organizational growth not only requires adaptation, but can also provide opportunities to advance goals other than accommodating that growth. The prominent factor behind the development of a southern route for the Run is that the main body is approaching the practical limits of safe travel. Deekin explained it to us this way: "When you start getting much more than two hundred motorcycles at any one time, you are approaching the physical limits of how many vehicles you can safely get on, and particularly off, a highway. Once the line exceeds the length of an off-ramp, you've got trouble." He went on to say that entering highways poses similar problems in terms of merging several hundred motorcycles into high-speed traffic lanes. Considering that the Run for the Wall typically must enter and exit major interstate highways sixty or seventy times on its trip across the country, the question of safe merges and exits is no small matter.

While the Run's growing size clearly played a major role in gaining board approval for a southern route, it was not the only factor. For some time, various RFTW riders who are especially committed to getting out the Run's message have talked about the need for the Run to reach out to parts of the country that are not touched by the Run's route through the central portion of the United States. In addition to, and sometimes linked with, this concern is the interest among some riders who are not part of the older, more established leadership group to play leadership roles in the Run. These riders recognized that creating a southern route would increase the number of slots for road guards, on-the-road leaders, and off-the-road organizers and would enable them to be on the ground floor of establishing the route. Adding a new route provides an opportunity to address these concerns and advance these interests. It is unlikely, however, that the first two concerns—distributing the message more widely and creating more leadership roles—would have been sufficiently convincing to the leadership to open another route without the pressure of growth.

FIGURE 30. A concern for the future, not just for the past, is part of the Run as well.

Inaugurating a Run for the Wall southern route represents one of the most significant changes the Run has undergone in its twelve-year history. At this point it is unclear whether the southern route will divide the current number of riders into two smaller groups, or whether it will attract a whole new body of riders. What is clear is that the Run for the Wall is currently somewhere between its past as an informal folk organization and a possible future as a hierarchically organized and bureaucratically managed national voluntary association. Whether resistance to change will keep the Run nearer to its folk roots, or whether the demands of growth will propel it more deeply into the realm of organizational formality, remains to be seen. In either event, the Run is likely to continue into the foreseeable future, and it will continue to change itself, just as it changes those who ride with it.

8

FORGETTING AND REMEMBERING
The Pathway toward Healing

In 1999 we again went all the way to Washington, D.C., with the Run. Our experience that year was both different from, yet similar to, the 1998 Run described in chapter 2. The things that made it different were matters of geography, weather, timing, and organization. In 1999 we left from Ontario rather than Long Beach. Instead of cold and snow, we enjoyed almost perfect weather all the way across the country. Instead of stopping at Angel Fire at the end of the second day, we backtracked from the overnight stop at Cimarron to visit the Angel Fire memorial on the morning of the third day. The Run made fewer stops in 1999, so we arrived at each day's destination earlier, giving us more time to relax and socialize with other participants. And unlike the other years when we went all the way to Washington, D.C., we did not stay for Rolling Thunder but made a quick turnaround and were back on the road for a rapid four-and-a-half-day return journey to Flagstaff.

The things that remained the same occurred at the level of senses, emotions, and memory. As always, the Run was a powerful sensual experience composed of endless hours on a motorcycle surrounded by the sights, sounds, and scents of a large group of bikes traveling down the road in formation. From our first encounters in Ontario the afternoon before the Run began to our last goodbyes on Sunday morning in Washington, D.C., the 1999 Run was filled with the deep

feelings of caring, friendship, and camaraderie that come from sharing a cross-country pilgrimage with others. We talked with friends
we see only once or twice a year about happy things and sad things,
pleasant things and hard things, with an ease that is often absent in
conversations with people we see every week in Flagstaff. Most of all,
however, we once again experienced both the pain and the release
that come from remembering the human tragedy, both past and
present, of the Vietnam War.[1]

Our goal here has been to tell the story of how a diverse collection of bikers has created a pilgrimage to help them construct personal and political narratives of the Vietnam War that will help them
come to terms with its memory and its pain. Much of what we have
written has been in the vein of sociological and anthropological analysis constructed by observant participants. Yet perhaps the most telling thing about how politics, ritual, and pilgrimage come together
to create new understandings is the impact the Run has had on us.

We have learned from our years on the Run that it is through
remembering what happened both during and after the Vietnam War
that we can begin to come to terms with what that war did to our
generation and to the Vietnamese. For us, part of this remembering
has meant coming to know and understand those of our generation
who fought in a war that the nation would have liked to forget.

Several weeks after we returned home from the 1999 Run for the
Wall, we found ourselves sitting in our living room one evening talking with Phil and Linda, the Run for the Wall regulars and Christian
motorcycle missionaries we have come to know and care about
through our years on the Run. Phil and Linda were among those in
our cohort of FNGs our first year on the Run who subsequently became part of our social world. Yet we are so different from one another. They spent decades pastoring Assembly of God congregations
and are now motorcycle missionaries. We are university professors
with no regular religious practice or church affiliation. They supported
America's war efforts in Vietnam, and Phil himself is a combat veteran. We opposed sending American soldiers into Vietnam, and Ray
never wore a uniform. Along these and many other dimensions that
are supposed to keep people apart, we differ. And yet we come together around our desire to remember the war and what it did, and
to heal its wounds in ourselves and others. Without the Run, we
would have never met them and others like them whom we now

number among our friends, and without the Run we would not have learned to care as much about how Americans who fought the Vietnam War continue to struggle to find meaning in that experience.

Peter Ehrenhaus and Richard Morris suggest that the contemporary American experience is in many ways a continuation of the war, which in its repercussions continues to be felt, through symbolic processes that form collective memory.[2] It could be argued that the POW/MIA issue is primarily about permanently replacing the memory of the suffering caused by the United States with the memory of the suffering endured by U.S. soldiers and their families, as some have suggested.[3] While this motivation may play some role in animating the POW/MIA movement in general, our experience with the Run for the Wall and its commitment to that movement suggests a different view. That is, remembering that Americans also suffered and continue to suffer, physically and emotionally, from the Vietnam War is not a door to forgetting but a pathway to remembering and feeling the full tragedy of that war. Only if we can feel the fullness of this tragedy can we truly grieve for *all* the human lives, both American and Vietnamese, that were destroyed or damaged by it. Additionally, it is only through knowing veterans whose lives had been altered by the Vietnam War that we have come to appreciate how much our own lives, and those of so many of our generation, have also been shaped by that war. None of us is isolated from its effects. You cannot come to adulthood in a country torn by dissension over a confused war without being torn and confused yourself. Like many veterans we have met, we thought we had gotten on with our lives once the war was over. Our involvement in the Run has shown us the many ways the legacy of the war continues to affect the lives of Americans, ourselves included.

Because this book is about an American pilgrimage, we have written little about the ways Vietnamese men and women suffered, and continue to suffer, from the war.[4] Yet whenever we see the Wall or think of it, as we do almost constantly when we are on the Run, we are aware that each name inscribed there is multiplied many times over in Vietnam.[5] For every American who died in Vietnam, at least twenty Vietnamese lost their lives, and for every American who remains missing in action, there are more than fifty Vietnamese bodies that were never returned to be buried in the villages of their ancestors. It is hard for us not to feel a deep sadness in the face of so much human loss. As one commentator observed, so much youth-ful energy was spent in Vietnam that put to any other purpose would have "lit up Southeast Asia for a hundred years."[6]

All memory is selective. We create our present by constructing stories about the past. But some memories are more selective than others. Any attempt to remember the Vietnam War that excludes ei-ther the suffering of the Vietnamese people, *or* the suffering of the American people, is an attempt to craft a story about the present by forgetting important parts of the past. In recent years, some Ameri-cans have sought to create a new narrative about the Vietnam War as a good, or at least a better, war that could have been won if only the military had not been sabotaged by a vacillating government and an unpatriotic antiwar movement. There have been equally as many attempts to discount Vietnam veteran and POW/MIA movements as little more than attempts to rehabilitate U.S. militarism. Both perspec-tives are based on forgetting—forgetting that the United States ap-plied massive military force to have its way in a small, underdeveloped nation looking for a path out of colonialism, and forgetting that most of the Americans who answered the call to serve in that war were young men who believed they were doing right as they had been taught to understand it.

American culture allows little space for tragedy. It is a culture grounded in the belief that all outcomes result from choices made by individuals exercising free will. In such a culture every offense must have a villain, and behind every tragedy there must be a guilty party that renders it not a tragedy but a crime—or perhaps a sin. And just as our everyday culture makes it difficult for us to label some great sad event a tragedy (unless caused by nature), the culture of social science often makes it almost impossible for analysts to recognize that terrible consequences can flow from mistakes.[7] And so for both or-dinary Americans and social analysts alike, it becomes difficult to re-member the U.S. handling of its political concerns in Vietnam as a mistake that had tragic consequences for the people of both nations. Yet only when we cease to look for villains, whether they be cold-hearted Vietnamese communists, heartless, baby-killing U.S. soldiers, cynical politicians, or cowardly draft dodgers, can we begin to heal the wounds of the Vietnam War. Only when we have the courage as a nation to face the hard truth that this was a war that need not have happened, between people who need not have been enemies, brought about by people on all sides who deeply believed that they were in the right, can we open ourselves to truly remembering instead of forgetting.

On Veterans Day in 1996, Phan Thi Kim Phuc, the woman whose photograph as a naked nine-year-old child running toward the camera screaming in agony became one of the most searing images of the Vietnam War, spoke at the Vietnam Veterans Memorial. Her words told eloquently of the need to remember the past in order to create the future: "Even if I could talk face to face with the pilot who dropped the bombs, I would tell him, We cannot change history, but we should try to do good things for the present and for the future to promote peace."[8]

Remembering is not about living in the past, it is about building the future. Only if we remember the war can we care enough to create a more peaceful future. But we cannot create a more peaceful future if we do not first try to do good things for the present, and where the Vietnam War is concerned, that means continuing to work to heal the physical and psychic wounds of all those—American and Vietnamese—who still suffer from that conflict. The Wall stands just a short distance from the memorial to President Lincoln, whose words are as meaningful today as they were more than a century ago: "Let us bind up the nation's wounds; to care for him who shall have borne the battle, and for his widow and his orphan—to do all which may achieve and cherish a just and lasting peace among ourselves, and with all nations."

Notes

1. INTRODUCTION

1. The tendency to disparage Japanese motorcycles and those who ride them is most wide-spread among those belonging to so-called outlaw motorcycle clubs. For explorations of the symbolic importance of the made-in-America Harley for outlaw bikers, see Yves Lavigne, *Hell's Angels: Taking Care of Business* (Toronto: Ballantine, 1987); Hunter Thompson, *The Hell's Angels: A Strange and Terrible Saga* (New York: Ballantine, 1967); Daniel R. Wolf, *The Rebels: A Brotherhood of Outlaw Bikers* (Toronto: University of Toronto Press, 1991). In contrast to the outlaw ideal, many contemporary Harley-Davidson riders are middle-class re-turnees to motorcycling who once owned and prized Japanese motorcycles as younger men. On this point see Peter Egan, "The Same Guy," *Cycle World*, October 1996, 14.
2. While some Vietnam veterans never had anyone welcome them home, many returned from the Vietnam War to warm and loving welcomes from families and friends. Regardless of the type of welcome they received personally, however, most Vietnam veterans we have met feel that they were never welcomed home by their country.
3. Michael "Mad Mike" Sargent, "Hell Train," in Laura Palmer, *Shrapnel in the Heart: Letters and Remembrances from the Vietnam Veterans Memorial* (New York: Norton, 1987), 52.
4. Jerry Lembcke, *The Spitting Image: Myth, Memory, and the Legacy of Vietnam* (New York: New York University Press, 1998).
5. Lawrence A. Tritle, *From Melos to My Lai: War and Survival* (New York: Routledge, 2000), 197.
6. David A. Woodrith, reported in Bob Greene, *Homecoming* (New York: Putnam, 1989), 94.
7. For details see Richard Stacewicz, *New Winter Soldiers: An Oral History of the Vietnam Veterans Against the War* (New York: Twayne, 1997), 16; Stanley Karnow, *Vietnam: A History* (New York: Viking, 1983), chap. 1; George C. Herring, *America's Longest War: The United States and Vietnam, 1950–1975* (New York: Knopf, 1986), chaps. 7 and 8.
8. This goal was set forth in a 1954 National Security Council recommendation and remained the guiding principle for the duration of U.S. involvement in Vietnam. For details see Herring, *America's Longest War*, 44–45.
9. Data compiled from Run for the Wall electronic bulletin board (www.rftw.org). Terry Porter, the Run for the Wall national coordinator for 1998, estimates that two hundred people went all the way. As of 1999, Lone Wolf, the newsletter editor, had a subscription list of 870 people who signed in while riding on the Run, but this does not include some number of short-time riders who did not sign in, bringing the actual number of participants closer to 1,000.
10. See *www.rollingthunder1.com*.

11. The Rolling Thunder constitution states that "Rolling Thunder, Inc. Major Function Is to Publicize the Pow–mia Issue: to Educate the Public That Many American Prisoners of War Were Left Behind after All past Wars: to Help Correct the past and to Protect Future Veterans from Being Left Behind Should They Become Prisoners of War–missing in Action. Second, We Are Committed to Helping Disabled Veterans from All WARS. See www.geocities.com/ Pentagon/ 5975/miss.htm.

12. In her Miss America platform statement, Heather French said, "As the daughter of a disabled Vietnam veteran, I pledge my heart, my hands and my voice to helping homeless veterans fight the battles they face on our nation's streets. So they don't face these battles alone, I urge all Americans to lend their support to these often forgotten men and women." See www.missamerica.org/missamerica/index.html#where.

13. As Rolling Thunder, Inc., began to develop a national organization with its own sponsored rides to Washington, D.C., the place of the Run for the Wall contingent within the Rolling Thunder parade has become less certain.

14. For treatments of the personal and social consequences of the Vietnam War for veterans, see, among others: J. D. Bremner, et al., "Chronic PTSD in Vietnam Combat Veterans," *American Journal of Psychiatry* 153, 3 (1996): 369–400; Caroline D. Harnly, *Agent Orange and Vietnam: An Annotated Bibliography* (Metuchen, N.J.: Scarecrow, 1988); Lembcke, *The Spitting Image*; Robert Jay Lifton, *Home from the War: Learning from Vietnam Veterans* (Boston: Beacon, 1992); Myra MacPherson, *Long Time Passing: Vietnam and the Haunted Generation* (New York: Doubleday, 1989); Murray Polner, *No Victory Parades* (New York: Holt, Rinehart and Winston, 1971); Wilbur Scott, *The Politics of Readjustment: Vietnam Veterans Since the War* (New York: Aldine de Gruyter, 1993); Paul Solotaroff, *The House of Purple Hearts: Stories of Vietnam Veterans Who Find Their Way Back* (New York: HarperCollins, 1995); Stacewicz, *Winter Soldiers*; Paul Star, *The Discarded Army: Veterans After Vietnam* (New York: Charterhouse, 1973); Allan Young, *The Harmony of Illusions: Inventing Post-Traumatic Stress Disorder* (Princeton, N.J.: Princeton University Press, 1995).

15. Victor Turner, *Dramas, Fields, and Metaphors: Symbolic Action in Human Society* (Ithaca, N.Y.: Cornell University Press, 1974); Victor Turner and Edith Turner, *Image and Pilgrimage in Christian Culture* (New York: Columbia University Press, 1978).

16. See, for example, Alan Morinis (ed.), *Sacred Journeys: The Anthropology of Pilgrimage* (Albuquerque, N.M.: Greenwood, 1992); M. N. Pearson, *Pious Passengers: The Hajj in Earlier Times* (London: Hurst, 1994); Jill Dubisch, *In a Different Place: Pilgrimage, Gender, and Politics at a Greek Island Shrine* (Princeton, N.J.: Princeton University Press, 1995).

17. Kristin Hass, *Carried to the Wall: American Memory and the Vietnam Veterans Memorial* (Berkeley: University of California Press, 1998), 8.

18. For treatments of the impact of the Wall on its visitors, see in particular ibid.; Palmer, *Shrapnel in the Heart*; Jan C. Scruggs and Joel Swerdlow, *To Heal a Nation: The Vietnam Veterans Memorial* (New York: Harper and Row, 1985).

19. As late as 1990, 57 percent of Americans still felt that U.S. intervention had been a mistake (P. Witteman and M. Duffy, "Vietnam:15 Years Later," *Time*, April 30, 1990, 18–22). Moreover, the belief that the Cold War logic that led to American entrapment in Vietnam was misguided created a new sense of isolationism and opposition to U.S. military involvement in world trouble spots. See in particular Oli R. Holsti and James N. Rosenau, *American Leadership in World Affairs: Vietnam and the Breakdown of Consensus* (Boston: Allan and Unwin, 1984); Earl C. Ravenal, *Never Again: Learning from America's Foreign Policy Failures* (Philadelphia: University of Pennsylvania Press, 1978).

20. Lydia Fish, *The Last Firebase: A Guide to the Vietnam Veteran Memorial* (Shippensberg, Pa.: White Mane, 1987), 3.

21. Hass, *Carried to the Wall*, 1, 3.

22. See, for example, Daphne Berdahl, "Voices at the Wall: Discourses of Self, History, and National Identity at the Vietnam Veterans Memorial," *History and Memory* 6, 2 (Fall/Winter 1994): 88–124; Grant F. Scott, "Meditations in Black: The Vietnam Veterans Memorial," *Journal of American Culture* 13, 3 (1990): 37–47.

23. For an exception, see Charles G. Watson, et al., "Effects of a Vietnam Memorial Pilgrimage on Veterans with Post Traumatic Stress Disorder," *Journal of Nervous and Mental Disease* 183, 5 (1995): 315–319. This article concludes that such a pilgrimage leads to short-term, but not lasting, improvement in veterans with PTSD. However, the pilgrimage in this case was a one-time journey, not repeated, and it lacked the ritual elements that characterize the Run for the Wall.

24. The many benefits that Vietnam veterans were eligible to receive, such as GI Bill funding for education and housing, Veterans Administration (VA) health services, and in some instances, federal and state civil service credits for years in the military, were initially established as a way for the nation to reward the veterans of World War II for their service. By the time of the Vietnam War, however, these benefits had become a taken-for-granted part of the military service package and had lost any sense of constituting a special "thank you" from the nation. While dollar-for-dollar, Vietnam-era veterans may have received more benefits for their service than those who served in World War II, these benefits had ceased to feel like a symbolic statement of gratitude from the country.

25. On the sensual nature of fieldwork, see Judith Okely, "Vicarious and Sensory Knowledge of Chronology and Change: Ageing in Rural France," in *Social Experience and Anthropological Knowledge*, ed. Kirsten Hastrup and Peter Hervick (London: Routledge, 1994), 45–64; C. Nadia Seremetakis, ed., *The Senses Still: Perception and Memory as Material Culture in Modernity* (Boulder, Colo.: Westview, 1994); Paul Stoller, *Sensuous Scholarship* (Philadelphia: University of Pennsylvania Press, 1997).

26. There has been considerable recent literature in both anthropology and sociology about the process of doing ethnographic research and about the roles of reflexivity, autobiography, and the analyst's reactions in this process. For just a few examples of this literature, see Hastrup and Hervik, *Social Experience and Anthropological Knowledge*; Ruth Behar, *The Vulnerable Observer: Anthropology That Breaks Your Heart* (Boston: Beacon, 1999); Judith Okely and Helen Calloway, eds., *Anthropology and Autobiography* (London: Routledge, 1992); Renato Rosaldo, *Culture and Truth: The Remaking of Social Analysis* (Boston: Beacon, 1989); Jay Ruby, ed., *A Crack in the Mirror: Reflexive Perspectives in Anthropology* (Philadelphia: University of Pennsylvania Press, 1989). On doing fieldwork in a politically charged context, see Raymond Michalowski, "Ethnography and Anxiety: Fieldwork in the Vortex of U.S. Cuban Relations," in *Reflexivity and Voice*, ed. Rosanna Hertz, (Thousand Oaks, Calif.: Sage, 1997), 45–69.

27. Although we speak of these approaches together here, they are not exactly the same. For a good discussion of performance and practice approaches and their differences and similarities, see Catherine Bell, *Ritual: Perspectives and Dimensions* (New York: Oxford University Press, 1997). For an example of a performance approach to pilgrimage, see Simon Coleman and John Elsner, "Performing Pilgrimage: Walsingham and the Ritual Construction of Irony," in *Ritual, Myth, Performance*, ed. Felicia Hughes-Freeland (London: Routledge, 1998), 46–65.

28. Bell, *Ritual*, 73.

---

2.   CHRONICLE OF A CROSS-COUNTRY PILGRIMAGE

1. When we first joined the Run in 1996, we were told that only those who traveled from that year's starting point in Ontario could receive All the Way patches. Since we joined the Run in Flagstaff that year, we assumed we were not eligible. In 1999, however, the Run's national coordinator offered a different definition of "all the way." He said, "'All the way' means all the way to the Wall. I don't care where you start from, if you make it to the Wall, you have gone all the way." This shifting definition is one example of the flexible nature of rules in a folk organization (see chapter 7).

2. The FNG designation as it was used in Vietnam carried a certain tension because the inexperienced arrival posed a danger to his comrades under conditions of combat. There is sometimes a similar edge to the term in the context of the Run for the Wall, as those inexperienced in riding with such a large group can also pose a danger to other riders. In order to soften this edge, and to make new riders understand that they are indeed welcome, FNG is sometimes smilingly translated as "Fun New Guy" and the FNG button referred to as "a badge of honor."

3. For both hard-core and outlaw bikers the term "colors" applies only to the back patches of established motorcycle clubs with formal, and usually rigorous, rules for prospecting (being a club initiate). In 1997, when the Run for the Wall created and sold an official RFTW back patch for the first time, some members of established clubs, including the Hell's Angels, expressed concern that the Run was trying to pass itself off as a motorcycle club without meeting any of the requirements set forth for motorcycle clubs by the various state confederations of clubs.

4. During the World War II Pacific campaign, Navajo soldiers were used to translate coded messages into their native tongue, a language so distinct from both English and Japanese, and so difficult to decipher, that it proved impenetrable to the enemy.

5. On November 18, 1997, President Clinton signed the Defense Authorization Bill into law. As part of this legislation the U.S. Postal Service, plus other selected government agencies, were required to fly the POW/MIA flag on six designated days each year: Armed Forces Day, Memorial Day, Flag Day, Independence Day, National POW/MIA Recognition Day, and Veterans Day, November 11.

6. On May 7, 1998, Secretary of Defense William S. Cohen ordered that the remains be removed from the Tomb of the Unknowns in Arlington National Cemetery for examination and identification. The remains removed on May 15, 1998, were later identified as those of Lieut. Michael J. Blassie and reburied under that name near Blassie's childhood home in Missouri on July 11, 1998. See Randy Kennedy, "Remains of Vietnam Serviceman Ordered Exhumed from Tomb of Unknowns," *New York Times,* May 8, 1998, sec. A; Randy Kennedy, "From Tomb of Unknown to Grave of Lieut. Blassie," *New York Times,* July 12, 1998, sec. 1.

7. The 50/50 is found at other biker gatherings as well. On the Run, it seems to have become customary for the winner of the 50/50 to donate the money back to the Run.

8. Although the Run has used road guards for a number of years, many of the tasks they perform are not legal. In most states, only designated officers of the law can legally stop traffic or interfere with the normal flow of vehicles. Despite the questionable legality of their duties, Run for the Wall road guards have historically enjoyed wide tolerance in many of the police jurisdictions where they have performed their duties because they can play an important role in helping local law enforcers ensure that the long line of bikes moves safely through local streets and off and on roadways. Despite this, beginning in 1999, the Run for the Wall substantially limited the road guard functions to keep their activities within legal limits.

9. The Black Hills Classic, otherwise known as the Sturgis Rallies and Races, is the oldest continuously running motorcycle rally in the United States. Since the 1960s, it has also been the single largest gathering of outlaw motorcycle clubs, and even though the influx of new yuppie bikers has changed the tone somewhat, Sturgis is still renowned for outrageous and rowdy biker behavior.

10. The repatriation of the remains of those killed in battle overseas has generally been a greater concern for Americans than for Europeans. See Tony Walter, "War Grave Pilgrimage," in *Pilgrimage in Popular Culture,* ed. Ian Reader and Tony Walter (Basingstoke, Eng.:Macmillan, 1993), 75.

11. This particular effort to make sure newcomers are identified may be less necessary since the institution of the FNG buttons.

12. Eric Lipton, "'Rolling Thunder' Comforts Vietnam Veterans: Annual Rolling Thunder Rally Fueled by Memories, Questions," *Washington Post,* May 25, 1998, sec. D.

---

3.   "POLITICS OF REMEMBERING AN UNEASY WAR

1. Phil McCombs, "Leaving Vietnam Behind," *Washington Post,* May 8, 2000, national weekly edition, 6–8.

2. Lewis Sorley, *A Better War: The Unexamined Victories and Final Tragedy of America's Last Years in Vietnam* (New York: Harcourt Brace, 1999); "Remembering Vietnam," *Washington Post,* May 8, 2000, national weekly edition, 24.

3. Covert U.S. involvement in the war in Vietnam extends as far back as 1946, when the United States sought to assist the French military efforts against the indigenous communist liberation movement headed by Ho Chi Minh. For detailed accounts of this period of U.S. involvement in Vietnam, see, in particular, Karnow, *Vietnam,* chaps. 3, 4, and 5; Herring, *America's Longest War,* chap. 1; Donald Lancaster, *The Emancipation of French Indochina* (London: Oxford University Press, 1961); Ronald E. Irving, *The First Indochina War: French and American Policy* (London: Croom Helm, 1975).

4. *New York Times Magazine,* May 26, 1996, 54.

5. We take the view that culture is always contested terrain, and that it is historically inaccurate to view American culture before the 1960s as characterized by untroubled agreement on values, morals, and manners. At the same time, we suggest that the social epoch that is characterized as the sixties framed the debate over the appropriate content of American culture in ways that shaped the country's culture wars for the balance of the century. On this point, see, in particular, James William Gibson, *Warrior Dreams* (New York: Hill and Wang, 1994); Todd Gitlin, *The Sixties: Years of Hope, Days of Rage* (New York: Bantam, 1987).

6. Hass, *Carried to the Wall,* 1.

7. For an example of this kind of revisionist history of World War II, see Daniel Guérin, *Fascism and Big Business*, trans. Frances and Mason Merrill (New York: Pathfinder, 1973).

8. Even 130 years after the surrender of the Confederacy, the Civil War remains a point of contention and dispute for many Southerners. When we began teaching in North Carolina in the 1970s, for instance, students informed us that the term "Civil War" was a Yankee creation that hid the fact, in their eyes, that the Union was a foreign power that had invaded and subjugated the free and sovereign Confederates States of America. In their minds, a more accurate term for the conflict is "The War Between the States." It is a noteworthy irony that the Run for the Wall arrives in Washington, D.C., each year in time for the Memorial Day weekend, the day of national observance originally created in remembrance of that other war over which Americans do not agree.

9. Long before the antiwar protests of the mid-1960s and early 1970s, there were many over-thirty Americans, both inside and outside government—including military figures—who counseled against U.S. military involvement in Vietnam. This particular slice of political history, however, has been obscured by the more vivid and visual nature of student antiwar protests.

10. For an excellent discussion of how the government's failure to produce convincing arguments in support of U.S. military involvement in Vietnam created a war at home that became an increasing impediment to pursuing the war abroad, see Loren Baritz, *Backfire: A History of How American Culture Led Us into Vietnam and Made Us Fight the Way We Did* (New York: Morrow, 1985).

11. See, for instance, Philip Caputo, *A Rumor of War* (New York: Holt, Rinehart and Winston, 1977); Michael Herr, *Dispatches* (New York: Avon Books, 1978); Peter Goldman and Tony Fuller, eds., *Charlie Company: What Vietnam Did to Us* (New York: Morrow, 1983); Martin Greenberg and Augustus Norton, eds., *Touring Nam: Vietnam War Stories* (New York: Quill/Morrow, 1985); David Donovan, *Once a Warrior King: Memories of an Officer in Vietnam* (New York: McGraw Hill, 1985); Bill Peters, *First Force Recon Company: Sunrise at Midnight* (New York: Ivy Books, 1999).

12. Robert Jay Lifton, "The Postwar War," *Journal of Social Issues* 31, 4 (1975): 181–195.

13. Christian G. Appy, *Working Class War: American Combat Soldiers and Vietnam* (Chapel Hill: University of North Carolina Press, 1993), 3–4.

14. Edward A. Hagan, "The POW/MIA Issue: A Case of Cultural Impotence," *Connecticut Review* 15, 2 (1993): 63.

15. Herbert Blumer, *Symbolic Interactionism: Perspective and Method* (Englewood Cliffs, N.J.: Prentice-Hall, 1969).

16. See Howard Becker, *Outsiders* (New York: Free Press, 1964); C. Wright Mills, *Power, Politics, and People: The Collected Essays of C. Wright Mills*, ed. Irving Louis Horowitz (New York: Oxford University Press, 1963).

17. In recent years a debate has developed over whether or not antiwar protesters frequently "spat on" U.S. soldiers returning from Vietnam. In *Homecoming*, journalist Bob Greene provides firsthand accounts of Vietnam veterans who say they were spat upon when they returned home. On the other hand, Jerry Lembcke, in *The Spitting Image*, argues that there is no credible evidence that such events ever really happened. While we disagree with Lembcke that the lack of media coverage means we can discount the many stories of being spat upon as false memories, we agree with him that the image of protesters spitting on U.S. soldiers is more than a recounting of past events. The image of the spat-upon soldier is part of the struggle to create a national memory of the Vietnam War. The spat-upon soldier symbolizes the Vietnam soldier as a good warrior who has been dishonored by others; in doing so, it helps shift the blame for the Vietnam War from those who fought it to those who did not support it. See Greene, *Homecoming*, and Lembke, *The Spitting Image*.

18. Curtis E. LeMay (with MacKinlay Kantor), *Mission with LeMay* (Garden City, N.Y.: Doubleday, 1965), 42.

19. In *A Better War*, a widely read revisionist history of the Vietnam War, Lewis Sorely argues that by 1970, "The fighting wasn't over, but the war was won." Sorely agrees with historian George Herring that by 1972, "the U.S. position in South Vietnam was stronger . . . than at any previous point in the war," but these solid military accomplishments were undermined by politics on the home front. Sorely's goal, as a third-generation West Point graduate, is to exonerate the U.S. military of the charge of having lost the war. His argument that the real blame for the U.S. loss in Vietnam rests with those who opposed the war is very similar to that of many of the veterans on the Run for the Wall, who feel that the military lost the war

because "we were not allowed to win." Also see George C. Herring, "The Nixon Strategy in Vietnam," in *Vietnam as History: Ten Years After the Paris Peace Accords,* ed. Peter Braestrup (Washington, D.C.: University Press of America, 1984), 57.

20. For strongly contrasting viewpoints on the POW/MIA issue, see Monika Jensen-Stevenson and William Stevenson, *Kiss the Boys Goodbye: How the United States Betrayed Its Own POWs in Vietnam* (Toronto: McClelland and Stuart, 1990), and H. Bruce Franklin, *M.I.A. or Mythmaking in America* (New Brunswick, N.J.: Rutgers University Press, 1993).

21. See Barbara Tuchman, *The March of Folly: From Troy to Vietnam* (New York: Ballantine, 1984), 234–239, for an account of President Franklin Roosevelt's initial strong objection and later capitulation to demands by French president DeGaulle that the United States aid France in regaining control of its former Vietnamese colony.

22. Graham Greene's *The Quiet American* (New York: Viking, 1956) was first serialized in the *Picture Post* of London in December 1955. It was published in the United States in March 1956. *The Ugly American* (New York: Norton, 1958) was first serialized in the *Saturday Evening Post* in 1958 and published in book form that same year.

23. John Helman, *American Myth and the Legacy of Vietnam* (New York: Columbia University Press, 1986), 4.

24. For an analysis of the role of revitalization movements in American culture, see Harold K. Bush, Jr., *American Declarations: Rebellion and Repentance in American Cultural History* (Urbana: University of Illinois Press, 1999); for a more general theoretical discussion, see two works by Anthony F. C. Wallace: *Religion: An Anthropological View* (New York: Random House, 1966), and *Culture and Personality,* 2d ed. (New York: Random House, 1970), 188–199.

25. J. Fred MacDonald's *Television and the Red Menace: The Video Road to Vietnam* (New York: Praeger, 1985), provides an excellent analysis of how images of Nazi evil were readily transformed into images of Communist evil in the post–World War II context of McCarthyism, and how the role played by the mass media in communicating this idea helped create a cultural acceptance of America's need to fight in Vietnam as essential for its claim to being the moral as well as military and economic leader of the free world.

26. Greene, *The Quiet American,* 158.

27. Karnow, *Vietnam,* 236.

28. "U.S. Inherits Another Headache: France Turns Over Indo-China Job to Americans," *U.S. News and World Report,* December 10, 1954, 24–26; Karnow, *Vietnam,* 220.

29. Frances Fitzgerald, *Fire in the Lake: The Vietnamese and the Americans in Vietnam* (New York: Vintage, 1972), 104–105.

30. Le Ly Haslip (with Jay Wurts), *When Heaven and Earth Changed Places: A Vietnamese Woman's Journey from War to Peace* (New York: Plume/Penguin. 1989), xv.

31. Howell Raines, *My Soul Is Rested* (New York: Penguin, 1983); Van Gosse, *Where the Boys Are: Cuba, Cold War America, and the Making of a New Left* (New York: Verso, 1993).

32. Mitchell K. Hall, *Because of Their Faith: CalCAV and Religious Opposition to the Vietnam War* (New York: Columbia University Press, 1990).

33. See G. Louis Heath, ed., *Mutiny Does Not Happen Lightly: The Literature of the American Resistance to the Vietnam War* (Metuchen, N.J.: Scarecrow, 1976).

34. The Port Huron Statement, the founding charter of SDS, emphasized solidarity between students and workers, and between white and black Americans, as a means to form a left-of-center political party whose primary goals would be the creation of racial and economic justice in America. Todd Gitlin, *The Whole World Is Watching: Mass Media in the Making and Unmaking of the New Left* (Berkeley: University of California Press, 1980).

35. Daniel Cohn-Bendit, *Obsolete Communism: The Left-Wing Alternative,* trans. Arnold Pomerans (New York: McGraw-Hill, 1968).

36. Tom Hayden, *Reunion: A Memoir* (New York: Random House, 1988).

37. Murray Edelman, introduction to *Cultural Legacies of Vietnam: Uses of the Past in the Present,* ed. Richard Morris and Peter Ehrenhaus (Norwood, N.J.: Ablex, 1990), 1.

38. For discussions of the impact of the Vietnam War on U.S. culture, see Walter Capps, *The Unfinished War: Vietnam and the American Conscience* (Boston: Beacon, 1982); Morris and Ehrenhaus, *Cultural Legacies of Vietnam;* Tai Sung An, *America After Vietnam: From Anguish to Healing* (Brookfield, Vt.: Ashgate, 1997); Jeffery Walsh, ed., *Vietnam Images: War and Representation* (London: Macmillan, 1989).

39. Morris and Ehrenhaus, *Cultural Legacies of Vietnam.*

40. The Vietnam-era military contained a large proportion of citizen-soldiers. The demographics of draft policy meant that working-class—and particularly minority working-class—youth

were less likely to benefit from student deferments. It should be noted, however, that most officers and air force pilots were college educated and often middle class by birth. See Appy, *Working Class War*. On minorities in Vietnam see, in particular, Charley Trujillo, *Soldados: Chicanos in Viet Nam* (San Jose, Calif.: Chusama House, 1990); James E. Westheider, *Fighting on Two Fronts: African Americans and the Vietnam War* (New York: New York University Press, 1997); Juan Ramirez, *A Patriot After All: The Story of a Chicano Vietnam Vet* (Albuquerque: University of New Mexico Press, 2000). While motivations sometimes differed, opposition to the war or to specific military policies emerged within the fighting corps itself among working-class, minority, and college-educated soldiers. For general discussions of antiwar sentiments within the military and among Vietnam veterans, see James R. Hayes, "The Dialectics of Resistance: An Analysis of the GI Movement," *Journal of Social Issues* 31, 4 (1975): 125–137; Ron Kovic, *Born on the Fourth of July* (New York: McGraw-Hill, 1976); Robert Buzanco, *Masters of War: Military Dissent and Politics in the Vietnam Era* (Cambridge University Press, 1996); Richard R. Moser, *New Winter Soldiers: GI and Veteran Dissent During the Vietnam Era* (New Brunswick, N.J.: Rutgers University Press, 1996); Stacewicz, *Winter Soldiers*; Lembcke, *The Spitting Image*, 37–77.

41. Lawrence M. Baskir and William A. Strauss, *Reconciliation After Vietnam: A Program of Relief for Vietnam-Era Draft and Military Offenders* (Notre Dame, Ind.: University of Notre Dame Press, 1977).

42. Jamila Bookwala, Irene Frieze, and Nancy Grote, "The Long-Term Effects of Military Service on Quality of Life: The Vietnam Experience," *Journal of Applied Social Psychology* 24, 6 (March 1994): 529–546.

43. Neil Sheehan, et al., *The Pentagon Papers* (New York: Bantam, 1971), 237–241.

44. Quoted in Paul Hendrickson, *The Living and the Dead: Robert McNamara and Five Lives of a Lost War* (New York: Vintage, 1996), 232.

45. Noel Malcolm, *Kosovo: A Short History* (New York: New York University Press, 1998).

46. Mark Sauter and Jim Sanders, *The Men We Left Behind: Henry Kissinger, the Politics of Deceit, and the Tragic Fate of POWs After the Vietnam War* (Washington, D.C.: National Press Books, 1993).

47. Sheehan, et. al, *The Pentagon Papers*, 556–604.

48. Hazel Erskine, "The Polls: Is War a Mistake?" *Public Opinion Quarterly* 34, 1 (spring 1970):134–150.

49. Ray Bonds, ed., *The Vietnam War: An Illustrated History of the Conflict in Southeast Asia* (New York: Smithmark, 1996), 145.

50. Hall, *Because of Their Faith*; Heath, *Mutiny Does Not Happen Lightly*.

51. Nancy Zaroulis and Gerald Sullivan, *Who Spoke Up? American Protest Against the War in Vietnam, 1963–1975* (Garden City, N.Y.: Doubleday, 1984).

52. Jensen-Stevenson and Stevenson, *Kiss the Boys Goodbye*, 2.

53. Chimp Robertson, *POW/MIA: America's Missing Men, the Men We Left Behind* (Lancaster, Pa.: Starburst, 1995), 22.

54. Franklin, *MIA or Mythmaking in America*, 7.

55. Herring, *America's Longest War*, 259.

56. J. Edgar Hoover, *Masters of Deceit* (New York: Holt, 1958); see also MacDonald, *Television and the Red Menace*, for an excellent analysis of the use of mass media to construct negative public sentiment toward communism and communists.

57. Robertson, *POW/MIA*, 184.

58. Franklin, *M.I.A. or Mythmakiing in America*, 27.

59. Library of Congress, *Missing in Action Database*, http://lcweb2.loc.gov/pow/ powdbhis.html.

60. "House Panel Declares No American Is Still Indochina War Prisoner," *New York Times*, December 16, 1976, sec. 1.

61. Recent reports of U.S. soldiers still living or held captive in North Korea help fuel the idea that it is reasonable to expect that Vietnam-era POWs, who, in many cases, would be almost a decade younger than those who fought in Korea, may still remain alive in Southeast Asia. See Phillip Shenon, "North Korea May Still Hold P.O.W.'s, Inquiry Suggests," *New York Times*, June 15, 1996; "Pentagon Says It Has No Proof of U.S. Captives in North Korea," *New York Times*, June 18, 1996; "U.S. Knew in 1953 North Koreans Held American P.O.W.'s," *New York Times*, September 17, 1996.

62. See Paul D. Mather, *M.I.A.: Accounting for the Missing in Southeast Asia* (Washington, D.C.: National Defense University Press), for details about the U.S. and joint U.S.-Vietnamese efforts to account for missing U.S. servicemen.

63. M. H. Siegel, "Missing in Action Could Be Declared Dead, Court Rules." *New York Times*, November 24, 1977, sec. 1.
64. One of the more poignant examples of how the Wall and other Vietnam veterans memorials have become a central site of remembrance for families is that Father's Day has become a day of particularly heavy visitation, with some memorials such as Angel Fire in New Mexico holding special Father's Day programs for all who lost fathers or grandfathers in the Vietnam War.
65. Frank Snepp, *Decent Interval: An Insider's Account of Saigon's Indecent End Told by the CIA's Chief Strategy Analyst in Vietnam* (New York: Random House, 1977).
66. Johnathan Schell, *The Real War: The Classic Reporting on the Vietnam War* (New York: Pantheon, 1987).
67. Franklin, *M.I.A. or Mythmaking*, 75–77.
68. The League's purpose can be found at www.pow–miafamilies.org/leaguebackgrnd.html.
69. William Chambliss, *On the Take: From Petty Thieves to Politicians*. (Bloomington: Indiana University Press, 1985).
70. See, in particular, Jensen-Stevenson and Stevenson, *Kiss the Boys Goodbye*, chaps. 9 and 10.
71. Gary Webb, *The Dark Alliance: The CIA, the Contras, and the Crack Cocaine Explosion* (New York: Seven Stories, 1998).
72. At its farthest fringes, some versions of the POW/MIA cover-up theory begin to overlap with conspiracy theories about black helicopters and secret plans to impose a U.N. government on the United States. More typically, however, the alleged cover-up is seen as the work of small groups inside the government who are trying to protect their own interests rather than promote some governmentwide project.
73. Philip Agee, *On the Run* (Secaucus, N.J.: Stuart, 1987); James Bamford, *The Puzzle Palace: A Report on America's Most Secret Agency* (Boston: Houghton Mifflin, 1982).
74. See George J. Veith, *Code-Name Bright Light: The Untold Story of U.S. POW Rescue Efforts During the Vietnam War* (New York: Dell, 1998), chap. 2, for a description of specific black operations.
75. Johnathan Shay, *Achilles in Vietnam: Combat Trauma and the Undoing of Character* (New York: Atheneum, 1994).
76. See www.asde.ntet/~pownet/statistics/htm (page 4).

---

4.   VETERANS, BIKERS, AND AMERICAN POPULAR CULTURE

1. As we discuss in chapter 5, in which we characterize the Run for the Wall as a "secular pilgrimage," we do not mean that it is devoid of religious practices, but rather that it is not organized around a religious belief system.
2. The four men who founded the Harley-Davidson motorcycle company in 1903 envisioned their machines as solid, everyday transportation for U.S. workers. More than seventy years would pass before the management of the Harley-Davidson company would accept that their machines were attractive primarily not to workaday citizens, but to people seeking a way to symbolize their disaffection with mainstream society.
3. Andrew Dudley, *The Image in Dispute: Art and Cinema in the Age of Photography* (Austin: University of Texas Press, 1997); John Rothenstein, *Nineteenth-Century Painting: A Study in Conflict* (Freeport, N.Y.: Books for Libraries Press, 1996).
4. As a result of higher taxes on automobiles, higher gasoline prices, and more congested urban centers, motorcycles and motor scooters have played a more central role in Europe and Britain as basic transportation than in the United States.
5. Stuart Ewen, *Captains of Consciousness: Advertising and the Social Roots of the Consumer Culture* (New York: McGraw-Hill, 1976).
6. The emergence of "extreme" sports in recent years, such as parachuting off bridges, antennas, towers, and high land formations (BASE jumping), may represent ways of challenging the dominant cultural values of security, safety, and predictability. Such activities, however, also serve to reinforce the value American culture assigns to ruggedness, individualism, and competition.
7. Motorcycling also has its own "extreme" version in the form of the Iron Butt Rally, an eleven-day, eleven-thousand-mile road rally in which riders earn bonus points for making side trips and still completing the entire journey in the allotted time.
8. For data regarding motorcycles registered in the United States, see U.S. Department of Commerce, Bureau of Transportation, *Transportation Statistics*, appendix A (Washington, D.C.: National Bureau of Transportation, 2000).

9. The four largest U.S.-based motorcycle riders associations registered a total of 935,000 members as of January 2000. These are the Harley Owners Group (HOG) with 500,000 members, the American Motorcycle Association (AMA) with 240,000, the Honda Riders Club (HRC) with 125,000, and the Gold Wing Road Riders Association (GWRRA) with 70,000. The figure of 935,000 association members, however, overestimates the actual number of individuals belonging to such organizations because many hold overlapping memberships, especially between AMA and HOG, and HRC and GWRRA, and because the figures reported by these organizations represent their *worldwide* membership, not just U.S. motorcyclists. For membership data, see Harley Owners Group (hog.com/about /about_ index.asp), American Motorcycle Association (ama-cycle.org/whatis/), Honda Riders Club (honda-motorcycle.com/hrca/), and Gold Wing Road Riders Association (gwrra.org/ welcome.html).

10. For a detailed discussion of motorcycle imagery in American popular culture, see, in particular, Frank Rickenbaugh Arnold, *Ordinary Motorcycle Thrills: A Circulation of Motorcycle Meanings in American Film and Popular Culture* (Ph.D. diss., University of Southern California, 1997).

11. Melissa Holbrook Pierson, *The Perfect Vehicle: What Is It About Motorcycles* (New York: Norton, 1997), 66.

12. Clement Salvadori, "The Cultural Icon," *Rider*, June 1998, 36.

13. Johannes Lange, *Crime and Destiny* (New York: Charles Boni, 1930), 238.

14. District of Columbia police inspector Milton Smith, 1947. Quoted in Chris Kallfelz, "Government Update," *American Motorcyclist,* August 1998, 23.

15. Max Weber, *The Protestant Ethic and the Spirit of Capitalism*, trans. Talcott Parsons (London: Unwin, 1985).

16. For a particularly succinct description of this process in U.S. culture, see Edward Luttwak, *Turbo Capitalism: Winners and Losers in the Global Economy* (New York: HarperCollins, 1999), 17–25.

17. Charles Loring Brace, *The Dangerous Classes of New York, and Twenty Years' Work Among Them* (New York: Wynkoop and Hallenbeck, 1880).

18. Brock Yates, *Outlaw Machine: Harley-Davidson and the Search for the American Soul* (New York: Little, Brown, 1999), 13.

19. Pierson, *The Perfect Vehicle*, 20.

20. Thompson, *Hell's Angels*.

21. See Robert Merton, "Social Structure and Anomie," *American Sociological Review* 3 (October 1938): 672–682; and Richard Cloward and Lloyd E. Ohlin, *Delinquency and Opportunity A Theory of Delinquent Gangs* (New York: Free Press, 1966), for discussions of retreatism and retreatist subcultures.

22. Randal Montgomery, "The Outlaw Motorcycle Subculture," *Canadian Journal of Criminology* 18 (1976): 332–342; James Quinn, "Sex Roles and Hedonism Among Members of 'Outlaw' Motorcycle Clubs," *Deviant Behavior* 8 (1987): 58–64; Wolf, *The Rebels*; Hunter S. Thompson, *The Proud Highway: Saga of a Desperate Southern Gentleman* (New York: Villard, 1997), 497–538.

23. Theodore Rozak, *The Making of a Counterculture* (Garden City, N.Y.: Anchor, 1969).

24. Yates, *Outlaw Machine*, 15.

25. The outlaw motorcycle club is typically portrayed as a group of *white* men, even though there were also black motorcycle clubs that formed in the years after World War II. The idea that the outlaw biker is a white man (or woman) may have entered American cultural consciousness because the highest-profile outlaw organizations such as Hell's Angels, the Outlaws, and the Pagans were overtly racist, prohibiting black members.

26. For descriptions of the Battle of Hollister and its mass-media aftermath, see Arnold, *Ordinary Motorcycle Thrills*, 94–121; Yates, *Outlaw Machine*, 15–22; Pierson, *The Perfect Machine*, 67–74.

27. *Hollister Free Lance*, July 3–16, 1947. Partial reprints by Jerry Smith in *American Rider*, November 1994, 46–50.

28. "4000 Touring Cyclists Wreak Havoc in Hollister," *San Francisco Chronicle*, July 6, 1947.

29. "Cyclists' Holiday," *Life*, July 21, 1947, 31.

30. Smith, *American Rider*, 48.

31. From nineteenth-century movements to place delinquent youth on farms, to the creation of the Boy Scouts and Girl Scouts to ensure that urban youth would develop a love for the outdoors, to contemporary outward-bound programs, Americans have a long history of turning to the nation's rural roots to solve social problems, particularly those involving disaffected youth. For details, see David E. Shi, *The Simple Life: Plain Living and High Think-*

ing in American Culture (New York: Oxford University Press, 1985); Barry Krisberg and James Austin, eds., *The Children of Ishmael: Critical Perspectives on Juvenile Justice* (Palo Alto, Calif.: Mayfield, 1978).

32. Evan Hunter, *The Blackboard Jungle,* (New York: Simon and Schuster, 1954); Jack Kerouac, *On the Road* (New York: Viking Press, 1957).

33. Pierson, *The Perfect Vehicle,* 68.

34. In many ways the spread of outlaw motorcycle style from the West Coast throughout the country parallels the spread of hippie style. The early hippies—or late "beats"—of San Francisco typically wore clothes such as navy-issue bell-bottom denims that could be purchased cheaply at army-navy stores. As these counterculture rebels became the objects of news stories and films, the bell-bottom pants and other symbols of hippie style spread rapidly around the country.

35. Stuart Ewen and Elizabeth Ewen, *Channels of Desire: Mass Images and the Shaping of American Consciousness* (Minneapolis: University of Minnesota Press, 1992); Neil Postman, *Amusing Ourselves to Death: Public Discourse in the Age of Show Business* (New York: Viking, 1985).

36. Fredric Jameson, *The Political Unconscious: Narrative as a Socially Symbolic Act* (Ithaca, N.Y.: Cornell University Press, 1981).

37. Glenn Jeansonne, "The Automobile and American Morality," *Journal of Popular Culture,* summer 1974, 125–131; John L. Wright, "Croonin' About Cruisin'," in *The Popular Culture Reader,* ed. Christopher D. Geist and Jack Nachbar (Bowling Green, Ohio: Bowling Green University Press, 1983), 102–110.

38. "'69 Honda CB750: Happy 30th to the Motorcycle that Changed the World," *Motorcyclist,* December 1999, 68–69.

39. This numeric decline resulted not only from an actual decrease in the number of Harley-Davidsons sold annually, but also from the fact that nearly all of the substantial growth in the motorcycle market at the time was in under-1000cc machines, an area in which Harley-Davidson offered few products. See Yates, *Outlaw Machine,* 101–115.

40. Walt Whitman, "Song of the Open Road," in *Leaves of Grass and Selected Prose,* ed. Scully Bradley (New York: Rinehart, 1949), 124.

41. Victory Motorcycle Corporation, 1998; Mitch Boehm, "A Good Pitch," *Motorcyclist,* July 998, 13.

42. Kawasaki Motorcycle Corporation, 1999.

43. Frederick Jackson Turner, *The Frontier in American History* (New York: Holt, 1921); Richard Slotkin, *Gunfighter Nation: The Myth of the Frontier in Twentieth-Century America* (New York: Atheneum 1992).

44. Dorothy Ayers Counts and David R. Counts, *Over the Next Hill: An Ethnography of RVing.* (Peterborough, Ontario: Broadview, 1997), 39.

45. Isaiah Berlin, *Two Concepts of Liberty* (Oxford: Clarendon, 1958); C. B. Macpherson, *The Political Theory of Possessive Individualism: Hobbes to Locke* (New York: Oxford University Press, 1964).

46. Samuel Bowles and Herbert Gintis, *Democracy and Capitalism: Property, Community, and the Contradictions of Modern Social Thought* (New York: Basic Books, 1986); Michael Parenti, *Democracy for the Few* (New York: St. Martin's, 1988).

47. Philip E. Slater, *The Pursuit of Loneliness: American Culture at the Breaking Point,* 3d ed. (Boston: Beacon, 1990). The desire for a life not constrained by relationships that Slater describes may represent a particularly *male* vision of freedom. Some social analysts, particularly women, have suggested that because women in American society often place a greater value on familial and friendship relationships than do men, they may be less inclined toward pursuing freedom through solitude than men are.

48. Melissa Holbrook Pierson, "Precious Dangers: The Lessons of the Motorcycle," *Harper's Magazine,* May 1995, 72; Clement Salvadori, "The Rhythm of the Road," *Rider,* September 1996, 22.

49. Garri Garripoli and friends, *Tao of the Ride: Motorcycles and the Mechanics of the Soul* (Deerfield Beach, Fla.: Health Communications, 1999), 81.

50. Ewen, *Captains of Consciousness,* chap. 3.

51. Jim Rogers, *Investment Biker: Around the World with Jim Rogers* (Holbrook, Mass.: Adams Media Corporation, 1995); Ed Culberson, *Obsessions Die Hard: Motorcycling the Pan American Highway,* reprint (North Conway, N.H.: Whitehorse, 1996); Ted Simon, *Jupiter's Travels: Four Years Around the World on a Triumph,* reprint (Covelo, Calif.: Jupitalia Productions, 1996).

52. Garripoli and friends, *Tao of the Ride*, 30.
53. Wolf, *The Rebels*, 37.
54. Darwin Holstrom, "How Much Is Enough?" *Motorcyclist*, June 1998, 16.
55. There are a variety of such jokes that circulate in biker culture, often told by riders of one brand about another brand. Thus Honda Gold Wing riders tell Harley jokes, while Harley riders make jokes about Gold Wings (often focusing on their size and excessive aftermarket ornamentation).
56. Quoted in Yates, *Outlaw Machine*, 161.
57. Wolf, *The Rebels*, 48.
58. Dean MacCannell, *The Tourist: A New Theory of the Leisure Class* (New York: Schocken Books, 1989), 22.
59. Wolf, *The Rebels*, 31.
60. "Hogs in the Spotlight," *Motorcyclist*, June 1998, 36.
61. Although many recent devotees of biker culture think that the attraction to Harley-Davidsons dates back to the influence of *The Wild Ones*, those versed in motorcycle or biker trivia know that Marlon Brando's mount was a Triumph, not a Harley.
62. For examples of motorcycle club charters that mandate members ride Harley-Davidson motorcycles, see Wolf, *The Rebels*, 351; Livigne, *The Hell's Angels*, 174–178.
63. Quoted in Alec Wilkinson, "An American Attitude," *New Yorker*, July 1995, 68.
64. Clement Salvadori, "On Touring," *Rider*, June 1998, 36.
65. Saskia Sassen, *Globalization and Its Discontents* (New York: Free Press, 1998).
66. National Opinion Research Center, *General Social Survey (GSS)* (Ann Arbor, Mich.: National Opinion Research Center, 1998).
67. Mitch Bohem, "Company of the Century," *Motorcyclist*, December 1999, 12.
68. Harley owners are not the only ones who express their individuality through customizing. Honda Gold Wing owners, for example, often add a plethora of items to their stock motor-cycles, from touring conveniences to elaborate air brush designs to extensive chrome acces-sories that are the butt of dozens of jokes among Gold Wing owners. They do not, however, engage in the extensive mechanical work on their bikes that has characterized Harley rid-ers, especially outlaw and working-class bikers. Yet such additions to the motorcycle repre-sent the same process of creating individuality. BMW owners, on the other hand, scorn such elaborate additions to their bikes, preferring instead the spare utilitarianism that is its own form of elegance and the distinguishing mark of the BMW rider.
69. Calculated from *Cycle World*, "Motorcycling on the Rise," November 1999, 28.
70. In 1948, in response to Hollister, the president of the American Motorcycle Association declared that outlaw bikers were no more than 1 percent of motorcyclists in the United States. Like colonial patriots who turned the insult "Yankee Doodle" into a term of pride, outlaw bikers soon took the "one-percenter" label as a badge of honor, often having "1%" tattooed somewhere on their body.
71. Stephen Lyng and James Bracey, "Squaring of the One-Percenter," in *Cultural Criminology*, ed. Jeff Ferrell (Boston: Northeastern University Press, 1998), 235–276; Richard Stern, "The Graying of the Wild Ones," *Forbes*, January 1992, 40–41.
72. John W. Schouten and James H. McAlexander, "Subcultures of Consumption: An Ethnogra-phy of the New Bikers," *Journal of Consumer Research* 22, no. 1 (June 1995), 43–62.
73. For elaboration on the relationship between conservatism and the philosophy of individual freedom, see Milton Friedman, *Capitalism and Freedom* (Chicago: University of Chicago Press, 1982); John Kekes, *A Case for Conservatism* (Ithaca, N.Y.: Cornell University Press, 1998).
74. This does not mean that all RFTW participants choose to ride without helmets. We know several people on the Run who think that those who don't wear helmets are foolish. One friend, for example, who has had several accidents, always rides with a helmet and full leathers, even in the hottest weather. And we ourselves never ride without helmets, a prac-tice that has earned us the nickname the "Helmet People."
75. Mark Buckner, "Still the Same," *Motorcycle Consumer News* (June 2000), 36.
76. For discussions of the impact of populism on past and present American culture see: Jeffrey Bell, *Populism and Elitism: Politics in the Age of Equality* (Lanham, Md.: Regnery Gateway, 1992); Paul Gottfried, *After Liberalism: Mass Democracy in the Managerial State* (Princeton, N.J.: Princeton University Press, 1999); Michael Kazin, *The Populist Persuasion: An American History* (Ithaca, N.Y.: Cornell University Press, 1998).

77. For a critique of these images of American life, see Stephanie Coontz, *The Way We Never Were* (New York: Basic Books, 1992).
78. Richard O. Boyer and Herbert M. Morais, *Labor's Untold Story* (New York: Cameron Associates, 1955).
79. Wolf, *The Rebels*, 97.
80. Harley-Davidson Corporation, 1997.
81. Calculated from data provided in Baskir and Strauss, *Reconciliation after Vietnam*. See also U.S. Defense Department statistics available at http://members.aol.com/kwjaccard/statistil.htm.
82. For detailed discussions of the isolation and alienation of Vietnam veterans from mainstream life after their return from war, see, in particular, Charles R. Figley and Seymour Leventman, eds., *Strangers at Home: Vietnam Veterans since the War* (New York: Praeger, 1980); Lifton, *Home from the War*.
83. Sonny Barger, quoted in Thompson, *Hell's Angels*, 253.
84. Many Vietnam War veterans report that they found themselves unwelcome in mainstream veteran organizations in the years immediately following the war. For more details, see chapter 5.
85. Louis de Bernières, *Corelli's Mandolin* (London: Vintage, 1994), 38.
86. Throughout this chapter we have spoken of veterans and bikers and their respective subcultures. We want to make it clear, however, that we are speaking about a small segment of the larger populations of both Vietnam veterans and motorcycle riders. Not all bikers are veterans, and not all veterans are bikers. Nor does every motorcycling veteran (even those on the Run for the Wall) necessarily espouse the sentiments regarding patriotism, freedom, and individuality in exactly the way we have discussed here. Nonetheless, the ways in which biker and veteran subcultures interact on the Run for the Wall are an important part of its ability to attract participants, and to have an impact on all who encounter it.

5. THE POWER OF RITUAL

1. Task Force Omega describes itself as an organization of POW/MIA family members, Vietnam veterans, and concerned citizens that has "concentrated its efforts on the return of the POWs abandoned in Vietnam, Laos, and Cambodia after the Vietnam War" (*www.geocities.com/Pentagon* TFO.html).
2. Although in popular thought, ritual is usually associated with religion, even religious rituals may have a political dimension, and politics itself is a highly ritualized domain. See David I. Kertzer, *Ritual, Politics, and Power* (New Haven, Conn.: Yale University Press, 1988).
3. See William Arens, "Professional Football: An American Symbol and Ritual," in *The American Dimension*, ed. Susan P. Montague and W. Arens (Sherman Oaks, Calif.: Alfred Publishing, 1981), 1–10; also Susan P. Montague and Robert Morais, "Football Games and Rock Concerts" in the same volume.
4. On the invention of new rituals see Ronald L. Grimes, *Deeply into the Bone: Re-inventing Rites of Passage*, Berkeley: University of California Press, 2000.
5. Even in so-called traditional societies, rituals are subject to change, attrition, and alteration.
6. Clifford Geertz, *The Interpretation of Cultures* (New York: Basic Books, 1973), 89.
7. Victor Turner, *The Forest of Symbols: Aspects of Ndembu Ritual* (Ithaca, N.Y.: Cornell University Press, 1967).
8. For general discussions of ritual see Bell, *Ritual*; Ronald Grimes, *Beginnings in Ritual Studies*, rev. ed. (Columbia: University of South Carolina Press, 1995).
9. C. Nadia Seremetakis, ed., *The Senses Still: Perception and Memory as Material Culture in Modernity* (Boulder, Colo.: Westview, 1994), 9 (emphasis added).
10. Riders also wear a variety of objects not related to Vietnam: club patches, pins from rallies attended, and so on. See chapter 4 on biker style.
11. Richard Morris, "The Vietnam Veterans Memorial and the Myth of Superiority," in *Cultural Legacies of Vietnam: Uses of the Past in the Present*, ed. Richard Morris and Peter Ehrenhaus (Norwood, N.J.: Ablex, 1990).
12. Ibid., 200.
13. This process is similar to that found at many major religious pilgrimage shrines, where the history of miraculous events associated with the shrine and the accumulation of material offerings that represent such events help create the larger, public meaning of the shrine

and add to its power and renown. See Turner and Turner, *Image and Pilgrimage in Christian Culture*; see also Dubisch, *In a Different Place*.

14. There is not space here for us to discuss the wide range of objects left at the Vietnam Memorial. For a discussion, see Hass, *Carried to the Wall*; also Berdahl, "Voices at the Wall"; Laura Palmer, *Shrapnel in the Heart: Letters and Remembrances from the Vietnam Memorial* (New York: Random House, 1987). The practice of taking home objects that partake of the sacredness of a pilgrimage site is found at many religious shrines; see, for example, Dubisch, *In a Different Place*.

15. Morris, "The Vietnam Veterans Memorial," 201.

16. As, for example, in ancient Greece.

17. It is this desire for meaning, rather than simple morbid fascination, that draws people to such places as the sites of the Kent State shootings or the Oklahoma City bombing; Richard West Sellers and Tony Walter, "From Custer to Kent State: Heroes, Martyrs, and the Evolution of Popular Shrines in the USA," in *Pilgrimage in Popular Culture*, ed. Ian Reader and Tony Walter (New York: Macmillan, 1993), 196.

18. There is an extensive sociological, psychological, and popular literature on American attitudes and practices regarding death; as a starting point see Jessica Mitford, *The American Way of Death Revisited*, rev. ed. (New York : Knopf, 1998).

19. The phrase "getting on with my life" is heard often on the Run to describe what some of the participants thought that they had done, or tried to do, or should have done, upon returning from Vietnam.

20. See C. R. Hallpike, "Social Hair," *Man* 4 (1969): 256–264.

21. Wolf, *The Rebels*, 113. Mainstream rituals, it could be argued, are also never exactly the same in their details and execution from one occasion to the next.

22. Some suggest that pilgrimage is a universal pattern of human experience, an archetype in the Jungian sense; see Jean Dalby Clift and Wallace B. Clift, *The Archetype of Pilgrimage: Outer Action with Inner Meaning* (New York: Paulist Press, 1996).

23. At a 1999 motorcycle rally in Tucson, for example, part of the ceremonies was a reading of the names of the biker dead.

24. For a discussion of the particularly gruesome effects of the weaponry used in Vietnam, especially as compared to the weaponry of ancient times, see Shay, *Achilles in Vietnam*.

25. Shay points out that handling and washing dead loved ones can be restorative and help with the grieving process, whereas handling the bodies of dead strangers can be traumatizing; ibid., 65–66.

26. Ibid., 63.

27. Lifton, *Home from the War*.

28. Shay, *Achilles in Vietnam*, 6.

29. Sellers and Walter, "From Custer to Kent State," 189. See also Hass, *Carried to the Wall*.

30. Walter, "War Grave Pilgrimage," 75.

31. Ibid., 70

32. Ibid., 71.

33. Examples of this are the resting places of saints, such as the tombs of St. Nektarios and St. Rafail in Greece, or the tombs of Muslim saints in the Middle East visited by local women; see Fatima Mernissi, "Women, Saints, and Sanctuaries," *Signs* 3, 2 (1977): 101–112.

34. One variation of this image shows the vet with his motorcycle; it has been reproduced in various versions on a number of t-shirts we have seen on the Run.

35. Morris, "The Vietnam Veterans Memorial," 213.

36. Ibid., 218.

37. Ibid., 213

38. Quoted in Mary Battiata, "Remembrance on a Train: From Seattle and the Plains, Vietnam Veterans Make Pilgrimage to a Reunion at 'The Wall,'" *Washington Post*, November 10, 1984.

39. Sellers and Walter, "From Custer to Kent State," 189.

40. At the same time, while we speak of healing and multiple meanings, we are by no means suggesting that the Vietnam Veterans Memorial has necessarily brought about a reconciliation over the conflicts that Vietnam represented—and continues to represent—in American culture. Rather, what we are concerned with here is the memorial's power as a symbol and its focus for rituals such as the Run for the Wall that seek healing for the various wounds of the war. For a discussion of some of these issues, and of the conflict between the romantic and the heroic traditions of memorialization in American culture, see Morris, "The Vietnam Veterans Memorial."

41. Berdahl, "Voices at the Wall," 117.
42. For a critique of "Forget the War, Remember the Warrior," see Peter Ehrenhaus and Richard Morris, epilogue to "Forms of Remembering, Forms of Forgetting," in Morris and Ehrenhaus, *Cultural Legacies of Vietnam.*
43. Some pilgrimage sites (such as Mecca) have an ancient history; some (such as Medjegorge in the former Yugoslavia) are fairly recent in origin. Some are religious sites; others arise out of secular concerns and events. Some center around sacred personages such as saints and prophets; others, around such popular figures as Elvis Presley, whose shrine at Graceland has become an object of pilgrimage for many. Miraculous happenings can establish a particular locale as a pilgrimage site, but so can tragedy and death. (The site of the Oklahoma City bombing, for example, has now become a place to which people travel and leave offerings.) And even visits to such arenas of popular culture as Disneyland have been analyzed as pilgrimages. What such places have in common is that they are believed to have some power that is out of the ordinary, that they are places where the pilgrim can find personal and/or collective meaning and transcend everyday experience. For a discussion of such forms of secular, popular pilgrimage, see Reader and Walter, *Pilgrimage in Popular Culture.*
44. Walter, "War Grave Pilgrimage," 84.
45. Ibid., 72
46. Pilgrimage before death may be part of a cultural pattern of such journeys; see, for example, Christopher Justice, *Dying the Good Death: The Pilgrimage to Die in India's Holy City* (Albany: SUNY Press, 1997). It may also be undertaken to some place of particular significance to an individual, such as the Vietnam Veterans Memorial. An example is the case of the veteran who had terminal cancer who wanted to visit the Wall before he died ("Vietnam Veteran Delayed Trip Until His Dying Days," *Quincy, Mass., Patriot Ledger,* April 1, 1996).
47. On tourism as the characteristic pilgrimage of the present day see Zygmunt Bauman, "From Pilgrim to Tourist," in *Questions of Cultural Identity,* ed. Stuart Hall and Paul DuGay (London: Sage, 1996).
48. Not all day riders act this way, but even those who are well behaved may not appreciate such features of the Run as the importance of riding in formation and observing the Run's rules of the road. In addition to complaints about such riders endangering others, in recent years there has been some concern about those who join the Run only for the free food and gas along the way. While the introduction of wristbands for those who sign in has helped distinguish participants from drop-ins, it has not completely solved the problem.
49. Walter, "War Grave Pilgrimage," 84
50. Dubisch, *In a Different Place,* 42–43.
51. For an account of one such journey organized by a VA medical center, see Lisa Grunwald, "Facing the Wall," *Life,* November 1992, 24.
52. In 1984, for example, a group of veterans traveled by train to the Wall. Calling their journey the Reunion by Rail, these "pilgrims in camouflage" spoke to each other, and to a *Washington Post* reporter, about their feelings: "Oh yes, I'm afraid of the Wall"; "I'm hoping after I go to the wall I'll get the grieving out of the way, do it the way it should be done"; "We used to wear camouflage to disappear, we were ashamed. . . . No more." "Welcome home, brother!" the organizer of the trip said to each new veteran who boarded the train, a ritual greeting that has continued to be part of a pilgrimage to the Wall. Battiata, "Remembrance on a Train."
53. Turner and Turner, *Image and Pilgrimage in Christian Culture.*
54. Within some religious traditions there may also be the idea of an inner spiritual pilgrimage.
55. Riding a motorcycle is not the only way to set oneself apart in a pilgrimage to the Wall. One veteran, for example, recently made the journey in a horse-drawn covered wagon; Deirdre Shesgreen, "Veteran Finishes Pilgrimage to the Vietnam Memorial: St. Louisan Makes Trip in a Covered Wagon," *St. Louis Post-Dispatch,* June 23, 1999.
56. There is also a certain expectation of danger from other people on the road, a combination of the hostility many bikers expect from the general public and the mobilization for danger that is part of the legacy of Vietnam.
57. Robbie E. Davis-Floyd, *Birth as an American Rite of Passage* (Berkeley: University of California Press, 1992).
58. In a now classic article, "Lower Class Culture as a Generating Milieu of Gang Delinquency" (*Journal of Social Issues* 14 [1958]: 5–19), Walter B. Miller anticipates later explorations of "toughness" as part of the construction of "masculinities" among American men. See also James Messerschmidt, *Masculinities and Crime* (Lanham, Md.: Rowman and Littlefield, 1997).

59. This does not mean that people do not complain. There may be much moaning and groaning at the end of a hard day's ride, but it generally takes place within a framework of understanding that, despite the complaints, we are willing and able to go through with the journey.

60. Hardship in pilgrimage may also serve a symbolic function by replicating past hardships of significant figures. This may be the suffering of Christ (replicated as the Christian pilgrim to Jerusalem follows the Stations of the Cross) or of individual saints, or of a people's ancestors, in the case of the Mormons who seek to recreate the westward journey of their pioneer forebears through the wilderness.

61. On the physiology of ritual, see Davis-Floyd, *Birth as an American Rite of Passage*; also Eugene G. D'Aquili, et al., *The Spectrum of Ritual: A Biogenetic Structural Analysis* (New York: Columbia University Press, 1979).

62. Trujillo, *Soldados*; Westheider, *Fighting on Two Fronts*.

63. Walter, "War Grave Pilgrimage," 80–81. Such feelings may be intensified when at home there is opposition to, or indifference about, the war.

64. Ian Reader, *Pilgrimage in Popular Culture*, 225.

65. John Eade and Michael Sallnow, introduction to *Contesting the Sacred: The Anthropology of Christian Pilgrimage*, ed. John Eade and Michael Sallnow (New York: Routledge, 1991).

66. Reader, *Pilgrimage in Popular Culture*, 239.

67. Ibid., 240.

68. See, for example, Eade and Sallnow, *Contesting the Sacred*.

69. Chapter 7 addresses issues surrounding the organization of the Run in more detail.

70. As we point out in chapter 7, however, these conflicts and problems cannot be reduced to interpersonal differences but are part of the process of growth in a voluntary organization.

71. Eade and Sallnow, *Contesting the Sacred*, 15.

72. The ritual of the "Welcome home" was prominent at the dedication of the Vietnam Veterans Memorial and has continued as an important part of rituals of reunion and reconciliation since then (see Berdahl, "Voices at the Wall"). A biker veteran friend has told us that the greeting was first used by the Rainbow People to welcome returned Vietnam veterans.

73. Reader, *Pilgrimage in Popular Culture*, 230–231.

74. On the idea of the return, see Gwen Kennedy Neville, *Kinship and Pilgrimage: Rituals of Reunion in American Protestant Culture* (New York: Oxford University Press, 1987).

75. Wolf, *The Rebels*, 50.

76. For a good discussion of curing versus healing, see Loring Danforth, *Firewalking and Religious Healing: The Anastenaria of Greece and the American Firewalking Movement* (Princeton, N.J.: Princeton University Press, 1989), chap. 2. For an overview of anthropological work on the subject, see Allan Young, "The Anthropologies of Illness and Sickness," *Annual Review of Anthropology* 11 (1982): 257–285.

77. Danforth, *Firewalking and Religious Healing*, 52.

78. This is changing somewhat as the biomedical system is coming to pay more attention to the psychological and emotional dimensions of sickness and to the process of healing.

79. One might also experience healing even in the absence of a cure, as in the case of a veteran who is not cured of PTSD but who finds relief and emotional support from contact with other members of the Run for the Wall.

80. Walter, "War Grave Pilgrimage," 82.

81. In one case study, for example, a group of Vietnam veterans suffering from PTSD was taken from a VA medical center together by bus to the Wall. While, according to the various psychological tests administered to these vets before and after the visit, there was some improvement in their condition, this improvement was apparently not lasting. The difference between this example and the Run for the Wall is that the Run provides a ritual framework for the encounter with the Wall, repeated visits for those who wish to make the trip on a regular basis, and a support community between visits. Watson et al., "Effects of a Vietnam Memorial Pilgrimage."

82. And in many cases, participants would not even have been able to make the journey to the Wall if it was not for the impetus and the support provided by the Run.

83. Danforth, *Firewalking and Religious Healing*, 57; from Thomas J. Csordas, "The Rhetoric of Transformation in Ritual Healing," *Culture, Medicine, and Psychiatry*, 7, 4: 333–375.

84. Examples of such ritual support groups include the firewalkers of Greece and the Zar of North Africa—see Danforth, *Firewalking and Religious Healing*; Pamela Constantinides, "'Ill at Ease and Sick at Heart': Symbolic Behavior in a Sudanese Healing Cult," in *Symbols and Sentiments: Cross Cultural Studies in Symbolism*, ed. I. Lewis (London: Academic Press, 1977).

85. An extreme example of the marginalized veteran is the one who "comes out of the woods" to join the Run, an image often evoked by participants. Although a few of the vets on the Run fit this image literally, others have reported being almost as socially isolated before they joined the Run.

86. See Danforth, *Firewalking and Religious Healing.*

87. Ibid., 7.

88. This is not to suggest that the behavior in such groups does not have ritual or symbolic elements; see, for example, John Braithwaite, "Cultural Communication Among Vietnam Veterans," in Morris and Ehrenhaus, *Cultural Legacies of Vietnam.*

89. Reader, "Conclusions," in Reader and Walter, *Pilgrimage in Popular Culture,* 237.

90. For excellent firsthand accounts of how soldiers coped with the day-to-day reality of the Vietnam War, see Goldman and Fuller, *Charlie Company;* Greenberg and Norton, *Touring Nam.*

91. See Shay, *Achilles in Vietnam.*

92. This motivation was encouraged by some officers. "Don't get sad, get even!" one soldier was told by his company commander as he held the body of a dead friend. Shay, *Achilles in Vietnam,* 63.

93. Battiata, "From Seattle and the Plains."

94. Shay, *Achilles in Vietnam,* 31.

95. For discussions of the "self-traumatized" vet—that is, the veteran whose traumas resulted from acts he himself committed during war—see Robert Laufer et al., "Symptom Patterns Associated with Post-Traumatic Stress Disorder Among Vietnam Veterans Exposed to War Trauma," *American Journal of Psychiatry* 142 (1985): 1304–1311; Sarah Haley, "When the Patient Reports Atrocities: Specific Considerations of the Vietnam Veteran," *Archives of General Psychiatry* 30 (1974): 191–196.; Alan Fontana et al., "War Zone Traumas and Post-Traumatic Stress Disorder Symptomatology," *Journal of Nervous and Mental Disease* 180 (1992): 748–755. See also Lifton, *Home from the War.* Belief in the constancy of self is not found in all cultures. Shay discusses the concept of "moral luck" in the *Iliad,* in which events can cause individuals to commit acts against their character. See also Dorrine Kondo, *Crafting Selves: Power, Gender, and Discourses of Identity in a Japanese Workplace* (Chicago: University of Chicago Press, 1990), for a discussion of the Japanese conception of multiple selves.

96. Allan Young, *The Harmony of Illusions: Inventing Post-Traumatic Stress Disorder* (Princeton, N.J.: Princeton University Press, 1995), 244

97. There is a considerable literature on PTSD. For bibliographies see Charlotte Kenton, "Post-traumatic Stress Disorder: January 1982 Through June 1984, 105 Citations" (Bethesda, Md.: U. S. Dept. of Health and Human Services, Public Health Service, National Institutes of Health, 1984); D. Cheryn Picquet and Reba A. Best, *Post-traumatic Stress Disorder, Rape Trauma, Delayed Stress, and Related Conditions: A Bibliography* (Jefferson, N.C.: McFarland, 1986). Also Shay, *Achilles in Vietnam;* Young, *The Harmony of Illusions.*

98. See Young, *The Harmony of Illusions,* 107–108; Shay, *Achilles in Vietnam.*

99. Young, *The Harmony of Illusions,* 108.

100. Ibid.

101. Ibid., 109. Arguments against the idea of shell shock and similar conditions are nothing new. After World War I, for example, some viewed veterans who claimed such disorders as malingerers who were simply trying to obtain government compensation. See also Eric T. Dean, Jr., *Shook over Hell: Post-Traumatic Stress, Vietnam, and the Civil War* (Cambridge: Harvard University Press, 1997).

102. Young, *The Harmony of Illusions,* 114

103. Pierre Janet, *Psychological Healing* (New York: Macmillan, 1925), 662.

104. Braithwaite, "Cultural Communication Among Vietnam Veterans," 164–165. See also Young, *The Harmony of Illusions,* 169–175, on PTSD narratives.

105. Ernst Van Alphen, "Symptoms of Discursivity: Experience, Memory, and Trauma," in *Acts of Memory: Cultural Recall in the Present,* ed. Mieke Bal, Jonathan Crewe, and Leo Spitzer (Hanover: University of New England Press, 1999), 26.

106. Leslie Allen, "Offerings at the Wall," *American Heritage,* February/March 1995, 94. As Allen points out, the very arrangement of names on the Wall is a "broken narrative," which was Maya Ling's intent.

107. Isak Dinesen, *Out of Africa* (New York: Modern Library, 1952), ii.

108. Robin Wagner Pacifici and Barry Schwartz, "The Vietnam Veterans Memorial: Commemorating a Difficult Past, *American Journal of Sociology* 97, 2: 417.

109. Danforth, *Firewalking and Religious Healing*, 57.
110. Kovic's *Born on the Fourth of July* has an eloquent account of his own disillusionment. Suffering and almost dying in an inadequately equipped VA hospital, he realized that a government that could spend millions on a war overseas had no funding to treat veterans once they returned.
111. The involvement of individuals and communities along the route in pilgrimage is a generally neglected area in pilgrimage studies.

---

6. GENDER ON THE RUN

1. In the summer of 1997 the American Motorcycle Association sponsored "Women in Motorcycling," the first conference ever held on the subject. Among other things, conference participants detailed the long history of women riders and women's motorcycle organizations in the United States. See "A Common Road: Celebrating Women and Motorcycling," *American Motorcyclist*, November 1997, 28–30. See also American Motorcycle Association, *Proceedings: Women and Motorcycling National Conference* (Westerville, Ohio: American Motorcycle Association, 1998).
2. One indication of the centrality of female nudity to the appeal of outlaw biker magazines is that they are usually shelved with more general interest "skin mags" such as *Playboy* and *Penthouse*. In an effort to use cheesecake to sell motorcycle magazines, one publisher, Paisano Press, produces magazines with different versions of the same layouts. One is a hard-core version in which the models are completely nude, while the other offers a more sanitized family version with models wearing the bathing suit equivalent of G-strings and pasties to cover their nipples and pubic region.
3. For discussions about the treatment of women as unwelcome in some motorcycle communities, see Barbara Joans, "Women Who Ride: The Bitch on the Back Is Dead," manuscript in the authors' files.
4. Although we have met several women on the Run who are either active or retired military, we have not met any women who served in Vietnam. Given the small size of the Run's female contingent, especially those who go all the way to D.C., it is likely that we would have encountered such women if they were present.
5. Joans, "Women Who Ride," 2.
6. On the rise of the culture of momism and the relegation of women to domestic roles, see, in particular, Barbara Ehrenreich, *Hearts of Men* (Garden City, N.Y.: Anchor, 1983).
7. On biker chick movies, see Ann Ferrar, *Hear Me Roar: Women, Motorcycles, and the Rapture of the Road* (New York, Crown, 1996), chap. 4; see also Arnold, *Ordinary Motorcycle Thrills*.
8. Joans, "Women Who Ride," 92.
9. For instance, in 1995 we took part with several thousand motorcycles in a parade through the town of Lake George, New York, as part of the annual Americade rally there. By far the loudest applause and calls of approval from the crowd were directed at the woman ahead of us riding her well-maintained, vintage *pink* Harley-Davidson.
10. We met one such man while riding to a Gold Wing rally in Montana. He and his wife, both with their own Gold Wings, were camped next to us just outside Yellowstone. He had been looking for a long time for a woman with her own motorcycle, he told us, and when he found one, he married her.
11. As a testimony to the changing roles of women in motorcycling, a new patch has appeared: "If you can read this, she's riding her own motorcycle."
12. "Run for the Wall: Honoring Those Never Forgotten," *Easy Rider*, December 1977, 42–45; "Run for the Wall: The Road to Rolling Thunder," *Biker Magazine Supplement*, January 1999, 1–30.
13. Wolf, *The Rebels*, 144–162; Quinn, "Sex Roles and Hedonism."
14. Similar ideas about the weakening or distracting nature of women are found elsewhere in American culture. For example, athletes are segregated from their wives and girlfriends the night before a game, and recruits in boot camp surrender pictures of their girlfriends during their training period. These practices bear a strong similarity to the gender segregation found, for example, in certain New Guinea societies where women are believed to be so polluting and dangerous to men that men and women do not even live together.
15. Wolf, *The Rebels*, 162.
16. Ibid., 159.

17. The Motorcycle Industry Council reports that one out of every twelve motorcycle riders is a woman. See www.motorcycles.org/mediacenter3.html.
18. Pierson, *The Perfect Vehicle*, 168.
19. For a discussion of some of these women, and a general history of women in motorcycling, see Ferrar, *Hear Me Roar* and "A Common Road."
20. Pierson, *The Perfect Vehicle*, 8.
21. Ferrar, *Hear Me Roar*, xi.
22. Pierson, *The Perfect Vehicle*, 16.
23. Joans, "Women Who Ride," 90. Ferrar, in her chapter on choosing a first motorcycle, has a section on lowering the bike. It is not only women riders who share information. Women who ride as passengers also discuss various aspects of riding, though their conversations tend to focus on ways to make riding more comfortable through gear and clothing rather than on the mechanics of bikes.
24. Ferrar, *Hear Me Roar*, xi–xii
25. Joans, *Women who Ride*, 93.
26. Ibid., 94
27. When Jill and Barbara Joans were comparing their respective motorcycle cultures (Gold Wing vs. Harley), Jill mentioned this concept of the co-rider. Barbara reported later that when she told the men in her riding group about this, they just laughed.
28. Joans, "Women Who Ride."
29. Joans, "Dikes on Bikes Meet Ladies of Harley," in *Beyond the Lavender Lexicon: Authenticity, Imagination, and Appropriation in Lesbian and Gay Languages,* ed. William L. Leap (New York: Gordon and Breach, 1996), 87–106.
30. While women were not directly involved in combat, around eleven thousand women served in Vietnam, most of whom were nurses. See Dan Freedman and Jacqueline Navarra Rhoads, *Nurses in Vietnam: The Forgotten Veterans* (Austin: Texas Monthly Press, 1987); Hendrickson, *The Living and the Dead*, 241–288; Kathyrn Marshall, *In the Combat Zone: An Oral History of American Women in Vietnam* (Boston: Little, Brown, 1987); Lynda Van Devanter, *Home Before Morning: The True Story of an Army Nurse in Vietnam* (New York: Warner, 1983); Keith Walker, *A Piece of My Heart: Stories of Twenty-Six American Women Who Served in Vietnam* (Novato, Calif.: Presidio, 1986); Elizabeth Norman, *Women at War: The Story of Fifty Military Nurses Who Served in Vietnam* (Philadelphia: University of Pennsylvania Press, 1990); Winnie Smith, *American Daughter Gone to War: On the Front Lines with an Army Nurse in Vietnam* (New York: Morrow, 1992).
31. The one situation in which men and women may share equally in combat is in resistance movements. Such movements may represent a time of special freedom and power for women, especially in societies with traditionally restrictive female roles. Many Greek women who served in the resistance during World War II, for example, look back with a certain nostalgia on the freedom and the equality with men they enjoyed during that time; see Janet Hart, *New Voices in the Nation: Women and the Greek Resistance, 1941–1964* (Ithaca, N.Y.: Cornell University Press, 1996).
32. MacPherson, *Long Time Passing*, 271.
33. Harry Spiller, *Scars of Vietnam: Personal Accounts by Veterans and Their Families* (Jefferson, N.C.: McFarland, 1994), 156.
34. Edna Hunter, "Families of Prisoners of War Held in Vietnam: A Seven-Year Study," *Evaluation and Program Planning* 9, 3 (1986): 243–251.
35. There are several associations of Christian bikers, of which the most prominent is probably the Christian Motorcyclists Association (CMA), whose motto is "Riding for the Son."
36. It is not uncommon for RFTW participants' wives to join them at the end of the Run and perhaps do some touring before heading home. In some cases, wives cannot get away from work or other obligations to make the entire trip; in other cases, they do not care to undertake the long, grueling journey. There is also the reverse phenomenon of wives flying home after making the Run.
37. MacPherson, *Long Time Passing*, 414. Grief was not confined to mothers, of course. Fathers grieved also and sometimes felt guilty if they had urged their sons to go to war.
38. Hendrickson, *The Living and the Dead*, 403. See also the Vietnam Women's Project at www.VirtualWall.org/women.htm; Van Devanter, *Home Before Morning.*
39. MacPherson, *Long Time Passing*, 447. See also Elizabeth Norman, "Post-traumatic Stress Disorder in Military Nurses Who Served in Vietnam During the War Years, 1965–1973," *Military Medicine* 153 (1988): 238–242; Elizabeth Paul, "Wounded Healers: A Summary of the Vietnam Nurse Veteran Project," *Military Medicine* 150 (1985): 571–576.

40. MacPherson, *Long Time Passing*, 449.
41. Ibid.
42. Ibid., 449–450. At the same time, MacPherson notes, like some male veterans, these women may feel "a terrible nostalgia for the most intensely emotional time of their lives" (449). These varied reactions by women who served as nurses are not unique to the Vietnam War. For accounts of nurses' experiences in other wars see Carol Acton, "'I Alone Am Left to Tell the Tale . . . ': Memoirs by Women on Active Service," paper presented at the Memory of Catastrophe Conference, Southampton, England, April 2000.
43. See Hass, *Carried to the Wall*, 18–20. While there are eight women's names on the Wall itself, between 1959 and 1975 sixty-seven American women connected with U.S. efforts in Vietnam died or were killed there.
44. Jeff Jacoby, "When Jane Spoke Out," *Boston Globe*, June 16, 1999.
45. For details of Jane Fonda's antiwar activities both in and out of Vietnam, see http://teamhouse.tni.net/janebio.htm.
46. As recently as June 2000, Fonda reiterated that she regrets posing for that picture more than anything else she did during that period. "Hanoi Jane Regrets '72 Photo," *Arizona Republic*, June 22, 2000, E2.
47. "Hanoi Jane Rumors Blend Fact and Fiction." As an example of the veteran virtual information network, this story first appeared at http://urbanlegends.about.com/library/weekly/aa110399.htm on November 3, 1999. Two days later it appeared on the Vietnam vet web site, AllPOWIAI@aol.com, and on November 9, 1999, it was posted to the RFTW web site along with an explanation from the person who posted it: "Doesn't mean I defend her—I don't! It's just better to know the facts so you can recognize a lie when you see it. No matter how well-meaning, a lie is still a lie."
48. In some cases, such abandonment may have been seen as the norm. One veteran reports being told by his commanding officer to break off any relationships he had before he went overseas, as any woman he left behind would not be waiting for him when he got back. Spiller, *Scars of Vietnam*.
49. While women did not perform combat duties in Vietnam, their role as nurse was a critical one, and in 1993 the U.S. government recognized their contributions by dedicating the women's memorial. There in bronze, a field nurse cradles a gravely wounded solider, another huddles over medical equipment on the ground, while a third stands, forever anxiously scanning the sky for a chopper that can fly the wounded to safety. Estimates are that more than 50 percent of the women who served in Vietnam were so extensively and routinely exposed to the human horror of warfare that they exhibit symptoms of PTSD. On this last point see Jenny Schnaier, "Women Vietnam Veterans and Their Mental Health Adjustment," in *Trauma and Its Wake*, ed. Charles Figley (New York: Brunner and Mazel, 1986).
50. While Fonda in more recent years is remembered more for her political activities, her role as an exercise guru, and her marriage to Ted Turner, she gained early fame as a sex kitten in the sci-fi film *Barbarella*.
51. When Vietnam veterans recount the troubles they had with women after returning from the war, it is hard to know how many of these problems that are now remembered as a direct consequence of their service in the war may have been part of the normal difficulty many people experience in finding lovers and partners.

---

7.   INDIVIDUALISM AND COMMUNITY

1. At the same time, the Bulletin Board is not a place to appeal for charity of a more personal nature. Shortly after the RFTW web site was established, a veteran posted a message saying he was down on his luck and needed some help. Later we heard several people say this was an inappropriate appeal for the Bulletin Board. While the person was not an RFTW participant, it seemed not so much this fact that was the basis for criticism as the blatant appeal for personal charity.
2. Alexis de Toqueville, *Democracy in America* (New York: Vintage, 1945), 198.
3. James Bishop and Paul Hoggett, *Organizing Around Enthusiasms* (London: Comdecia, 1986), 3.
4. D. Billis, *Organizing Public and Voluntary Agencies* (London: Routledge, 1993).
5. See D. Knoke, "Commitment and Detachment in Voluntary Associations," *American Sociological Review* 46 (1981): 141–158; D. Knoke and C. Wright-Isak, "Individual Motives and

Organizational Incentive Systems," *Research in the Sociology of Organizations* 1 (1982): 209–254.

6. Margaret Harris, "A Special Case of Voluntary Associations? Towards a Theory of Congregational Organization," *British Journal of Sociology* 49, 4 (1998): 602–618.

7. In 1995 Harvard political scientist Robert Putnam created a storm of controversy when he presented a paper titled "Bowling Alone: America's Declining Social Capital," at the American Political Science Association meeting in September 1985 (see also Robert Putnam, *Bowling Alone: The Collapse and Revival of American Community* [New York: Simon and Schuster, 2000]). In his essay Putnam declared that civic life in America was all but dead, destroyed in large part by increasing public passivity created by the expansion of television and other mass media. Since then, a number of critics, particularly Everett Carl Ladd, executive director of the Roper Center for Public Opinion Research at the University of Connecticut, have challenged Putnam's conclusions, claiming instead, in Ladd's words, that "an explosion of voluntary groups, activities and charitable donations is transforming our towns and cities." Ladd's conclusion is consistent with what a number of sociologists have noted in recent years—that civic action, voluntary associations, and social movements have not disappeared, but rather have taken new forms. As older forms of civic participation—unions, fraternal groups such as Lions, Elks, Moose, and Kiwanis clubs, and established veteran organizations such as the American Legion and the Veterans of Foreign Wars—have declined in membership, new forms of social participation and social action have taken their place. These range from local groups concerned with environmental protection or women's rights, to global action groups such as Green Peace and Amnesty International, to the national action groups like the Run for the Wall. See, in particular, Harry Boyte, *The Backyard Revolution: Understanding the New Citizens' Movement* (Philadelphia: Temple University Press, 1980); Enrique Laraña, Hank Johnston, and Joseph R. Gusfield, eds., *New Social Movements: From Ideology to Identity* (Philadelphia: Temple University Press, 1994); Donatella della Porta, Hanspeter Kriesi, and Dieter Rucht, *Social Movements in a Globalizing World* (New York: St. Martin's, 1999). On the matter of "bowling alone" see Richard Morin, "Unconventional Wisdom: New Facts and Hot Stats from the Social Sciences," *Washington Post*, May 2, 1999, final edition, B-5; Thomas B. Edsall, "TV Tattered Nation's Social Fabric, Political Scientist Contends," *Washington Post*, September 3, 1995, sec. A; David S. Broder, "Beyond 'Bowling Alone'; Are We Really a Nation of 'Civic Slugs'?" *Washington Post*, December 17, 1997, sec. A.

8. Hervé Varenne, *Americans Together: Structured Diversity in a Midwestern Town* (New York: Teachers' College Press, 1978), 154.

9. Ibid., 69–70.

10. Faye D. Ginsberg, *Contested Lives: The Abortion Debate in an American Community* (Berkeley: University of California Press, 1989), 220–221.

11. Varenne, *Americans Together,* 200.

12. Paul A. Roy, "Calling Biker Billy," *Cruising Rider,* Spring 2000, 10.

13. Wolfe, *The Rebels,* 59.

14. Varenne, *Americans Together,* 157.

15. Ibid.

16. Thomas Bender, quoted in Counts and Counts, *Over the Next Hill,* 168.

17. Counts and Counts, *Over the Next Hill.*

18. When we first joined the Run, we heard that some of the old-timers were unhappy with the Run's expanding membership. This information came in the form of rumors that some riders felt the Run should continue the way it began, as a group of Vietnam combat veterans, rather than as a ride that was open to those who had not served in combat, and even to those who had never served in the military. While there may be some individual RFTW participants who hold these sentiments, we never encountered any evidence of these attitudes directly. Moreover, the Run's official position is that it is open to anyone who supports its cause.

19. The Run for the Wall is anything but the wild party some FNGs and biker groups along the way expect it to be. While some riders do party hearty on their way to Washington, D.C., many of those we have met along the way are in recovery from alcohol and drug problems or, like ourselves, are generally too worn out after a long day's ride to stay up late drinking and carousing. In addition, for some, the serious nature of the Run and their struggles with their own memories and problems lead them to reserve the parties for their homeward journey.

20. Erika Fairchild, *Comparative Criminal Justice Systems* (Belmont, Calif.: Wadsworth, 1993).

21. "Run for the Wall: The Road to Rolling Thunder."
22. Varenne, *Americans Together*, 189.
23. Counts and Counts, *Over the Next Hill*, 174.
24. Ibid., 173.
25. At a broader level, this ambivalence is seen in the tension between the traumatic experiences of the war, which still plague many veterans, and the feeling that in some ways their wartime experience was "the best time of my life."

8.   THE PATHWAY TOWARD HEALING

1. In 2000 we were able to join the Run only from Williams, Arizona, just west of Flagstaff, to Cimarron, New Mexico. Despite the briefness of our participation, however, it involved more responsibility than previous years because we had been asked to ride as substitute New Mexico coordinators in place of Phil and Linda Wright, the official New Mexico coordinators, as they were leading the southern route exploratory run. In our role as substitute coordinators we were responsible for helping to ensure that the pack exited and entered interstates in the right places and found its preplanned lunch and gas stops, and for seeing that all scheduled police escorts met the Run as anticipated.
2. Morris and Ehrenhaus, epilogue to *Cultural Legacies of Vietnam*, 225.
3. See Franklin, *M.I.A. or Mythmaking in America*, for a detailed elaboration of this perspective.
4. For perspectives on the consequences of the Vietnam War for Vietnamese, see Bao Ninh, *The Sorrow of War* (London: Secker and Warburg, 1993); Hayslip, *When Heaven and Earth Changed Places*.
5. And not only in Vietnam. Vietnamese refugees to the United States, for example, often endured great suffering, both before and after their arrival. Among their travails were the mysterious sudden deaths that occurred during sleep, mostly to young Vietnamese refugee men.
6. Herr, *Dispatches*.
7. Diane Vaughn, *The Challenger Launch Decision: Risky Technology, Culture, and Deviance at NASA* (Chicago: University of Chicago Press, 1996), chap. 9.
8. Public Broadcasting Service, Online Newshour, "Veterans Day Speeches, November 11, 1996," at www.pbs.org/newshour/bb/military/vets_11–11.html.

Construction of Irony." In *Ritual, Performance, Media*, edited by Felicia Hughes-Freeland, 46–65. London: Routledge, 1998.

"A Common Road: Celebrating Women and Motorcycling." *American Motorcyclist*, November 1997, 28–30.

Constantinides, Pamela. "'Ill at Ease and Sick at Heart': Symbolic Behavior in a Sudanese Healing Cult." In *Symbols and Sentiments: Cross Cultural Studies in Symbolism*, edited by I. Lewis. London: Academic Press, 1977.

Coontz, Stephanie. *The Way We Never Were*. Garden City, N.Y.: Anchor, 1992.

Counts, Dorothy Ayers, and David R. Counts. *Over the Next Hill: An Ethnography of RVing*. Peterborough, Ontario: Broadview, 1997.

Csordas, Thomas J. "The Rhetoric of Transformation in Ritual Healing." *Culture, Medicine, and Psychiatry* 7, 4: 333–375.

Culberson, Ed. *Obsessions Die Hard: Motorcycling the Pan American Highway*. Reprint. North Conway, N.H.: Whitehorse, 1996.

"Cyclists' Holiday." *Life*, July 21, 1947, 31.

D'Aquili, Eugene G., Charles D. Laughlin, Jr., and John McManus. *The Spectrum of Ritual: A Biogenic Structural Analysis*. New York: Columbia University Press, 1979.

Danforth, Loring. *Firewalking and Religious Healing: The Anastenaria of Greece and the American Firewalking Movement*. Princeton, N.J: Princeton University Press, 1989.

Davis-Floyd, Robbie E. *Birth as an American Rite of Passage*. Berkeley: University of California Press, 1992.

Dean, Eric T. *Shook over Hell: Post-Traumatic Stress, Vietnam, and the Civil War*. Cambridge: Harvard University Press, 1997.

De Bernières, Louis. *Corelli's Mandolin*. London: Vintage, 1994.

Della Porta, Donatella, Hanspeter Kriesi, and Dieter Rucht. *Social Movements in a Globalizing World*. New York: St. Martin's, 1999.

Dinesen, Isak. *Out of Africa*. New York: Modern Library, 1952.

Donovan, David. *Once a Warrior King: Memories of an Officer in Vietnam*. New York: McGraw-Hill, 1985.

Dubisch, Jill. *In a Different Place: Pilgrimage, Gender, and Politics at a Greek Island Shrine*. Princeton, N.J.: Princeton University Press, 1995.

Dudley, Andrew. *The Image in Dispute: Art and Cinema in the Age of Photography*. Austin: University of Texas Press, 1997.

Eade, John, and Michael Sallnow. Introduction to *Contesting the Sacred: The Anthropology of Christian Pilgrimage*, edited by John Eade and Michael Sallnow. New York: Routledge, 1991.

Edelman, Murray. Introduction to *Cultural Legacies of Vietnam*, edited by Richard Morris and Peter Ehrenhaus, 5. Norwood, N.J.: Ablex, 1990.

Egan, Peter. "The Same Guy." *Cycle World*, October 1996, 14.

Ehrenhaus, Peter, and Richard Morris. "Epilogue: Forms of Remembering, Forms of Forgetting." In *Cultural Legacies of Vietnam*, edited by Richard Morris and Peter Ehrenhaus. Norwood, N.J.: Ablex, 1990.

Ehrenreich, Barbara. *Hearts of Men*. Garden City, N.Y.: Anchor, 1983.

Erskine, Hazel. "The Polls: Is War a Mistake?" *Public Opinion Quarterly* 34, 1 (1970): 134–150.

Ewen, Stuart. *Captains of Consciousness; Advertising and the Social Roots of the Consumer Culture*. New York: McGraw-Hill, 1976.

Ewen, Stuart, and Elizabeth Ewen. *Channels of Desire: Mass Images and the Shaping of American Consciousness*. Minneapolis: University of Minnesota Press, 1992.

Fairchild, Erika. *Comparative Criminal Justice Systems*. Belmont, Calif.: Wadsworth, 1993.

Ferrar, Ann. *Hear Me Roar: Women, Motorcycles, and the Rapture of the Road*. New York: Crown, 1996.

Figley, Charles Rand, and Seymour Leventman, eds. *Strangers at Home: Vietnam Veterans Since the War*. New York: Praeger, 1980.

Fish, Lydia. *The Last Firebase: A Guide to the Vietnam Veteran Memorial*. Shippensberg, Pa.: White Mane, 1987.

Fiske, John. *Media Matters: Everyday Culture and Political Change*. Minneapolis: University of Minnesota Press, 1994.

Fitzgerald, Frances. *Fire in the Lake: The Vietnamese and the Americans in Vietnam*. New York: Vintage, 1972.

Fontana, Alan, Robert Rosenheck, and Elizabeth Brett. "War Zone Traumas and Post-Traumatic Stress Disorder Symptomatology." *Journal of Nervous and Mental Disease* 180 (1992): 748–755.

Franklin, Bruce H. *M.I.A. or Mythmaking in America*. New Brunswick, N.J.: Rutgers University Press, 1993.

Freedman, Dan, and Jacqueline Navarra Rhoads. *Nurses in Vietnam: The Forgotten Veterans*. Austin: Texas Monthly Press, 1987.

Friedman, Milton. *Capitalism and Freedom*. Chicago: University of Chicago Press, 1982.

Garripoli, Garri, and Friends. *Tao of the Ride: Motorcycles and the Mechanics of the Soul*. Deerfield Beach, Fla.: Health Communications, 1999.

Geertz, Clifford. *The Interpretation of Cultures*. New York: Basic Books, 1973.

Gibson, James William. *Warrior Dreams*. New York: Hill and Wang, 1994.

Ginsberg, Faye D. *Contested Lives: The Abortion Debate in an American Community*. Berkeley: University of California Press, 1989.

Gitlin, Todd. *The Sixties: Years of Hope, Days of Rage*. New York: Bantam, 1987.

———. *The Whole World Is Watching: Mass Media in the Making and Unmaking of the New Left*. Berkeley: University of California Press, 1980.

Goldman, Peter, and Tony Fuller. *Charlie Company: What Vietnam Did to Us*. New York: Morrow, 1983.

Gosse, Van. *Where the Boys Are: Cuba, Cold War America, and the Making of a New Left*. New York: Verso, 1993.

Gottfried, Paul. *After Liberalism: Mass Democracy in the Managerial State*. Princeton, N.J.: Princeton University Press, 1999.

Greenberg, Martin, and Augustus Norton, eds. *Touring Nam: Vietnam War Stories*. New York: Quill/Morrow, 1985.

Greene, Bob. *Homecoming: When the Soldiers Returned from Vietnam*. New York: Putnam, 1989.

Greene, Graham. *The Quiet American*. New York: Bantam, 1957.

Grimes, Ronald. *Beginnings in Ritual Studies*. Columbia: University of South Carolina Press, 1995.

Grunwald, Lisa. "Facing the Wall." *Life*, November 1992, 24.

Guérin, Daniel. *Fascism and Big Business*. Translated by Frances Merrill and Mason Merrill. New York: Pathfinder, 1973.

Hagan, Edward. "The POW/MIA Issue: A Case of Cultural Impotence." *Connecticut Review* 15, 2 (1993): 63.

Haley, Sarah. "When the Patient Reports Atrocities: Specific Considerations of the Vietnam Veteran." *Archives of General Psychiatry* 30 (1974): 191–196.

Hall, Mitchell K. *Because of Their Faith: CalCAV and Religious Opposition to the Vietnam War.* New York: Columbia University Press, 1990.

Hallpike, C. R. "Social Hair." *Man* 4 (1969): 256–264.

Harnly, Caroline D. *Agent Orange and Vietnam: An Annotated Bibliography.* Metuchen, N.J.: Scarecrow, 1988.

Harris, Margaret. "A Special Case of Voluntary Associations? Towards a Theory of Congregational Organization." *British Journal of Sociology* 49, 41(1998): 602–618.

Hart, Janet. *New Voices in the Nation: Women and the Greek Resistance, 1941–1964.* Ithaca, N.Y.: Cornell University Press, 1996.

Hass, Kristin. *Carried to the Wall: American Memory and the Vietnam Veterans Memorial.* Berkeley: University of California Press, 1998.

Hastrup, Kirsten, and Peter Hervick, eds. *Social Experience and Anthropological Knowledge.* New York: Routledge, 1994.

Hayden, Tom. *Reunion: A Memoir.* New York: Random House, 1988.

Hayes, James R. "The Dialectics of Resistance: An Analysis of the GI Movement," *Journal of Social Issues* 31, 4 (1975): 125–137.

Hayslip, Le Ly (with Jay Wurts). *When Heaven and Earth Changed Places: A Vietnamese Woman's Journey from War to Peace.* New York: Plume/Penguin, 1989.

Heath, G. Louis. *Mutiny Does Not Happen Lightly: The Literature of the American Resistance to the Vietnam War.* Metuchen, N.J: Scarecrow, 1976.

Helman, John. *American Myth and the Legacy of Vietnam.* New York: Columbia University Press, 1986.

Hendrickson, Paul. *The Living and the Dead: Robert McNamara and Five Lives of a Lost War.* New York: Vintage, 1996.

Herr, Michael. *Dispatches.* New York: Avon, 1978.

Herring, George C. *America's Longest War: The United States and Vietnam, 1950–1975.* New York: Knopf, 1986.

———. "The Nixon Strategy in Vietnam." In *Vietnam as History: Ten Years After the Paris Peace Accords,* edited by Peter Braestrup. Washington, D.C.: University Press of America, 1984.

Holsti, Oli R., and James N. Roseneau. *American Leadership in World Affairs: Vietnam and the Breakdown of Consensus.* Boston: Allan and Unwin, 1984.

Holstrom, Darwin. "How Much Is Enough?" *Motorcyclist,* June 1988, 16.

Hoover, J. Edgar. *Masters of Deceit.* New York: Holt, 1958.

Hughes-Freeland, Felicia. *Ritual, Myth, Performance.* London: Routledge, 1998.

Hunter, Edna. "Families of Prisoners of War Held in Vietnam: A Seven-Year Study." *Evaluation and Program Planning* 9, 3 (1986): 243–251.

Hunter, Evan. *The Blackboard Jungle.* New York: Simon and Schuster, 1954.

Irving, Ronald E. *The First Indochina War: French and American Policy.* London: Croom Helm, 1975.

Jameson, Fredric. *The Political Unconscious: Narrative as a Socially Symbolic Act.* Ithaca, N.Y: Cornell University Press, 1981.

Janet, Pierre. *Psychological Healing.* New York: Macmillan, 1925.

Jeansonne, Glenn. "The Automobile and American Morality." *Journal of Popular Culture,* Summer 1974, 125–131.

Jensen-Stevenson, Monika, and William Stevenson. *Kiss the Boys Goodbye: How the United States Betrayed Its Own POWs in Vietnam.* Toronto: McClelland and Stuart, 1990.

Joans, Barbara. "Dykes on Bikes Meet Ladies of Harley." In *Beyond the Lavender Lexicon: Authenticity, Imagination, and Appropriation in Lesbian and Gay Languages,* edited by William L. Leap, 87–106. New York: Gordon and Breach, 1996.

———. "Women Who Ride: The Bitch on the Back Is Dead." Manuscript, in authors' files. 1997.

Justice, Christopher. *Dying the Good Death: The Pilgrimage to Die in India's Holy City.* Albany: SUNY Press, 1997.

Kallfelz, Chris. A Goverment Update. *American Motorcyclist,* August 1998, 15.

Karnow, Stanley. *Vietnam: A History.* Revised ed. New York: Viking, 1991.

Kazin, Michael. *The Populist Persuasion: An American History.* Ithaca, N.Y.: Cornell University Press, 1998.

Kekes, John. *A Case for Conservatism.* Ithaca, N.Y.: Cornell University Press, 1998.

Kenton, Charlotte. "Posttraumatic Stress Disorder: January 1982 Through June 1984, 105 Citations." Bethesda, Md.: U.S. Department of Health and Human Services, Public Health Service, National Institutes of Health, 1984.

Kerouac, Jack. *On the Road.* New York: Viking, 1957.

Kertzer, David I. *Ritual, Politics, and Power.* New Haven, Conn.: Yale University Press, 1988.

King, Christine. "His Truth Goes Marching On: Elvis Presley and the Pilgrimage to Graceland." In *Pilgrimage in Popular Culture.* Basingstoke, Eng.: Macmillan, 1993.

Knoke, D. "Commitment and Detachment in Voluntary Associations." *American Sociological Review* 46 (1981): 141–158.

Knoke, D., and C. Wright-Isak. "Individual Motives and Organizational Incentive Systems." *Research in the Sociology of Organizations* 1 (1982): 209–254.

Kondo, Dorrine. *Crafting Selves: Power, Gender, and Discourses of Identity in a Japanese Workplace.* Chicago: University of Chicago Press, 1990.

Kovic, Ron. *Born on the Fourth of July.* New York: McGraw-Hill, 1976.

Krisberg, Barry, and James Austin, eds. *The Children of Ishmael: Critical Perspectives on Juvenile Justice.* Palo Alto, Calif.: Mayfield, 1978.

Lancaster, Donald. *The Emancipation of French Indochina.* London: Oxford University Press, 1961.

Lange, Johannes. *Crime and Destiny.* New York: Charles Boni, 1930.

Laraña, Enrique, Hank Johnston, and Joseph R. Gusfield, eds. *New Social Movements: From Ideology to Identity.* Philadelphia: Temple University Press, 1994.

Laufer, Robert, et al. "Symptom Patterns Associated with Post-Traumatic Stress Disorder among Vietnam Veterans Exposed to War Trauma." *American Journal of Psychiatry* 142 (1985): 1304–1311.

Lavigne, Yves. *Hell's Angels: Taking Care of Business.* Toronto: Ballantine, 1987.

Lederer, James, and Stanley Burdick. *The Ugly American.* New York: Norton, 1958.

LeMay, Curtis E. *Mission with LeMay* (with MacKinlay Kantor). Garden City, N.Y.: Doubleday, 1965.

Lembcke, Jerry. *The Spitting Image: Myth, Memory, and the Legacy of Vietnam.* New York: New York University Press, 1998.

Library of Congress. *Missing in Action Database.* Available at http://lcweb2.loc.gov/pow/powdbhis.html.

Lifton, Robert Jay. *Home from the War: Learning from Vietnam Veterans.* 2d ed. Boston: Beacon, 1992.

———. "The Postwar War." *Journal of Social Issues* 31, 4 (1975): 181–195.

Lipton, Eric. " 'Rolling Thunder' Comforts Vietnam Veterans: Annual Rolling Thunder Rally Fueled by Memories, Questions." *Washington Post*, May 25, 1998, D1.

Livigne, Yves. *The Hells Angels: Taking Care of Business*. Toronto: Ballantine, 1987.

Luttwak, Edward. *Turbo Capitalism: Winners and Losers in the Global Economy*. New York: HarperCollins, 1999.

Lyng, Stephen, and James Bracey. "Squaring of the One-Percenter." In *Cultural Criminology*, edited by Jeff Ferrell, 235–276. Boston: Northeastern University Press, 1998.

MacCannell, Dean. *The Tourist: A New Theory of the Leisure Class*. New York: Schocken, 1989.

MacDonald, J. Fred. *Television and the Red Menace: The Video Road to Vietnam*. New York: Praeger, 1985.

Macpherson, C. B. *The Political Theory of Possessive Individualism: Hobbes to Locke*. New York: Oxford University Press, 1964.

MacPherson, Myra. *Long Time Passing: Vietnam and the Haunted Generation*. New York: Doubleday, 1989.

Malcolm, Noel. *Kosovo: A Short History*. New York: New York University Press, 1998.

Marshall, Kathyrn. *In the Combat Zone: An Oral History of American Women in Vietnam*. Boston: Little, Brown, 1987.

Mather, Paul D. *M.I.A.: Accounting for the Missing in Southeast Asia*. Washington, D.C.: National Defense University Press, 1994.

McNamara, Robert. *In Retrospect: The Tragedy and Lessons of Vietnam*. New York: New York Times Books, 1995.

Mernissi, Fatima. "Women, Saints, and Sanctuaries." *Signs* 3, 2 (1977): 101–112.

Merton, Robert. "Social Structure and Anomie." *American Sociological Review* 3 (October 1938): 672–682.

Messerschmidt, James. *Masculinities and Crime*. Lanham, Md.: Rowman and Littlefield, 1997.

Michalowski, Raymond. "Ethnography and Anxiety: Fieldwork in the Vortex of U.S. Cuban Relations." In *Reflexivity and Voice*, edited by Rosanna Hertz, 45–69. Thousand Oaks, Calif.: Sage, 1997.

Miller, Walter B. "Lower Class Culture as a Generating Milieu of Gang Delinquency." *Journal of Social Issues* 14 (1958): 5–19.

Mills, C. Wright. *Power, Politics, and People: The Collected Essays of C. Wright Mills*. Edited by Irving Louis Horowitz. New York: Oxford University Press, 1963.

Mitford, Jessica. *The American Way of Death Revisited*. Revised ed. New York: Knopf, 1998.

Montague, Susan P., and Robert Morais. "Football Games and Rock Concerts." In *The American Dimension*, edited by Susan P. Montague and William Arens, 11–25. Sherman Oaks, Calif.: Alfred Publishing, 1981.

Montgomery, Randal. "The Outlaw Motorcycle Subculture." *Canadian Journal of Criminology* 18 (1976): 332–342.

Moore, Alexander. "Walt Disney World: Bounded Ritual Space and the Playful Pilgrimage Center." *Anthropological Quarterly* 53, 4 (1980): 207–217.

Morinis, Alan. *Sacred Journeys: The Anthropology of Pilgrimage*. Albuquerque, N.M.: Greenwood, 1992.

Morris, Richard. "The Vietnam Veterans Memorial and the Myth of Superiority." In *Cultural Legacies of Vietnam: Uses of the Past in the Present*, edited by Richard Morris and Peter Ehrenhaus, 199–219. Norwood, N.J.: Ablex, 1990.

Morris, Richard, and Peter Ehrenhaus, eds. *Cultural Legacies of Vietnam: The Uses of the Past in the Present*. Norwood, N.J.: Ablex, 1990.

Moser, Richard R. *New Winter Soldiers: GI and Veteran Dissent during the Vietnam Era.* New Brunswick, N.J.: Rutgers University Press, 1996.

"Motorcycling on the Rise," *Cycle World,* November 1999, 28.

National Opinion Research Center. *General Social Survey (GSS).* Ann Arbor, Mich.: National Opinion Research Center, 1998.

Neville, Gwen Kennedy. *Kinship and Pilgrimage: Rituals of Reunion in American Protestant Culture.* New York: Oxford University Press, 1987.

Ninh, Bao. *The Sorrow of War.* London: Secker and Warburg, 1993.

Norman, Elizabeth. "Post-traumatic Stress Disorder in Military Nurses Who Served in Vietnam During the War Years, 1965–1973." *Military Medicine,* no. 153 (1988): 238–242.

———. *Women at War: The Story of Fifty Military Nurses Who Served in Vietnam.* Philadelphia: University of Pennsylvania Press, 1990.

Okely, Judith. "Vicarious and Sensory Knowledge of Chronology and Change: Ageing in Rural France." In *Social Experience and Anthropological Knowledge,* edited by Kirsten Hastrup and Peter Hervick, 45–64. New York: Routledge, 1994.

Okely, Judith, and Helen Calloway. *Anthropology and Autobiography.* London: Routledge, 1992.

Palmer, Laura. *Shrapnel in the Heart: Letters and Remembrances from the Vietnam Veterans Memorial.* New York: Norton, 1987.

Parenti, Michael. *Democracy for the Few.* New York: St. Martin's, 1988.

Paul, Elizabeth. "Wounded Healers: A Summary of the Vietnam Nurse Veteran Project." *Military Medicine,* no. 150 (1985): 571–576.

Pearson, M. N. *Pious Passengers: The Hajj in Earlier Times.* London: Hurst, 1994.

Peters, Bill. *First Force Recon Company: Sunrise at Midnight.* New York: Ivy Books, 1999.

Picquet, Cheryn, and Reba A. Best. *Post-traumatic Stress Disorder, Rape Trauma, Delayed Stress, and Related Conditions: A Bibliography.* Jefferson, N.C: McFarland, 1986.

Pierson, Melissa Holbrook. *The Perfect Vehicle: What Is It About Motorcycles.* New York: Norton, 1997.

———. "Precious Dangers: The Lessons of the Motorcycle." *Harper's Magazine,* May 1995, 72.

Polner, Murray. *No Victory Parades.* New York: Holt, Rinehart and Winston, 1971.

Postman, Neil. *Amusing Ourselves to Death: Public Discourse in the Age of Show Business.* New York: Viking, 1985.

Public Broadcasting Service, Online Newshour. "Veterans Day Speeches." November 11, 1996. www.pbs.org/newshour/bb/military/vets_11–11.html.

Putnam, Robert. "Bowling Alone: America's Declining Social Capital." Paper presented at the American Political Science Association meeting, September 1985.

———. *Bowling Alone: The Collapse and Revival of American Community.* New York: Simon and Schuster, 2000.

Quinn, James E. "Sex Roles and Hedonism Among Members of 'Outlaw' Motorcycle Clubs." *Deviant Behavior* 8 (1987): 47–63.

Raines, Howell. *My Soul Is Rested.* New York: Penguin, 1983.

Ramirez, Juan. *A Patriot After All: The Story of a Chicano Vietnam Vet.* Albuquerque: University of New Mexico Press, 2000.

Ravenal, Earl C. *Never Again: Learning from America's Foreign Policy Failures.* Philadelphia: University of Pennsylvania Press, 1978.

Reader, Ian, and Tony Walter. Conclusion in *Pilgrimage in Popular Culture.* Basingstoke, Eng.: Macmillan, 1993.

———, eds. *Pilgrimage in Popular Culture*. Basingstoke, Eng.: Macmillan, 1993.

Robertson, Chimp. *P.O.W./MIA: America's Missing Men, the Men We Left Behind*. Lancaster, Pa.: Starburst, 1995.

Rogers, Jim. *Investment Biker: Around the World with Jim Rogers*. Holbrook, Mass.: Adams Media Corporation, 1995.

Rosaldo, Renato. *Culture and Truth: The Remaking of Social Analysis*. Boston: Beacon, 1989.

Rothenstein, John. *Nineteenth-Century Painting: A Study in Conflict*. Freeport, N.Y.: Books for Libraries Press, 1996.

Roy, Paul A. "Calling Biker Billy." *Cruising Rider*, Spring 2000, 21.

Rozak, Theodore. *The Making of a Counterculture*. Garden City, N.Y.: Anchor, 1969.

Ruby, Jay, ed. *A Crack in the Mirror: Reflexive Perspectives in Anthropology*. Philadelphia: University of Pennsylvania Press, 1989.

"Run for the Wall: Honoring Those Never Forgotten." *Easy Rider,* December 1977, 42–45.

"Run for the Wall: The Road to Rolling Thunder." *Biker Magazine Supplement,* January 1999, 1–30.

Salvadori, Clement. "The Cultural Icon." *Rider,* June 1998, 36.

———. "On Touring." *Rider,* May 1999, 32.

———. "The Rhythm of the Road." *Rider,* September 1996, 21.

Sargent, Michael "Mad Mike." "A Hell Train" In *Shrapnel in the Heart: Letters and Remembrances from the Vietnam Veterans Memorial*, edited by Laura Palmer. New York: Norton, 1987.

Sassen, Saskia. *Globalization and Its Discontents*. New York: Free Press, 1998.

Schell, Jonathan. *The Real War: The Classic Reporting on the Vietnam War*. New York: Pantheon, 1987.

Schnaier, Jenny. "Women Vietnam Veterans and Their Mental Health Adjustment." In *Trauma and Its Wake*, edited by Charles Figley. New York: Brunner and Mazel, 1986.

Schouten, John W., and James H. McAlexander. "Subcultures of Consumption: An Ethnography of the New Bikers." *Journal of Consumer Research* 22, 1 (1995): 43–62.

Scott, Grant F. "Meditations in Black: The Vietnam Veterans' Memorial." *Journal of American Culture* 13, 3 (1990): 37–47.

Scott, Wilbur. *The Politics of Readjustment: Vietnam Veterans since the War*. New York: Aldine de Gruyter, 1993.

Scruggs, Jan C., and Joel Swerdlow. *To Heal a Nation: The Vietnam Veterans Memorial*. New York: Harper and Row, 1985.

Sellers, Richard West, and Tony Walter. "From Custer to Kent State: Heroes, Martyrs, and the Evolution of Popular Shrines in the USA." In *Pilgrimage in Popular Culture*, edited by Ian Reader and Tony Walter. New York: Macmillan, 1993.

Seremetakis, Nadia C., ed. *The Senses Still: Perception and Memory as Material Culture in Modernity*. Boulder, Colo.: Westview, 1994.

Shay, Jonathan. *Achilles in Vietnam: Combat Trauma and the Undoing of Character*. New York: Atheneum, 1994.

Sheehan, Neil, Hendrick Smith, E. W. Kenworthy, and Fox Butterfield. *The Pentagon Papers*. New York: Bantam, 1971.

Shi, David. *The Simple Life: Plain Living and High Thinking in American Culture*. New York: Oxford University Press, 1985.

Simon, Ted. *Jupiter's Travels: Four Years Around the World on a Triumph*. Covelo, Calif.: Jupitalia Productions, 1996.

"69 Honda CB750: Happy 30th to the Motorcycle that Changed the World." *Motorcyclist*, December 1999, 68–69.

Slater, Philip E. *The Pursuit of Loneliness: American Culture at the Breaking Point.* 3d ed. Boston: Beacon, 1990.

Slotkin, Richard. *Gunfighter Nation: The Myth of the Frontier in Twentieth-Century America.* New York: Atheneum, 1992.

Smith, Winnie. *American Daughter Gone to War: On the Front Lines with an Army Nurse in Vietnam.* New York: Morrow, 1992.

Snepp, Frank. *Decent Interval: An Insider's Account of Saigon's Indecent End Told by the CIA's Chief Strategy Analyst in Vietnam.* New York: Random House, 1977.

Solotaroff, Paul. *The House of Purple Hearts: Stories of Vietnam Veterans Who Find Their Way Back.* New York: HarperCollins, 1995.

Sorely, Lewis. *A Better War: The Unexamined Victories and Final Tragedy of America's Last Years in Vietnam.* New York: Harcourt Brace, 1999.

Spiller, Harry. *Scars of Vietnam: Personal Accounts by Veterans and Their Families.* Jefferson, N.C.: McFarland, 1994.

Stacewicz, Richard. *New Winter Soldiers: An Oral History of the Vietnam Veterans against the War.* Vol. 16. New York: Twayne, 1997.

Star, Paul. *The Discarded Army: Veterans After Vietnam.* New York: Charterhouse, 1973.

Stern, Richard L. "The Graying of the Wild Ones." *Forbes*, January 6, 1992, 40–41.

Stoller, Paul. *Sensuous Scholarship.* Philadelphia: University of Pennsylvania Press, 1997.

Task Force Omega. www.geocities.com/Pentagon/3250/TFO.html.

Thompson, Hunter S. *Hells Angels: A Strange and Terrible Saga.* New York: Random House, 1967.

———. *The Proud Highway: Saga of a Desperate Southern Gentleman.* New York: Villard, 1997.

Toqueville, Alexis de. *Democracy in America.* New York: Vintage, 1945.

Trittle, Lawrence A. *From Melos to My Lai: War and Survival.* New York: Routledge, 2000.

Trujillo, Charley. *Soldados: Chicanos in Viet Nam.* San Jose, Calif.: Chusama House, 1990.

Tuchman, Barbara. *The March of Folly: From Troy to Vietnam.* New York: Ballantine, 1984.

Turner, Frederick Jackson. *The Frontier in American History.* New York: Holt, 1921.

Turner, Victor. *Dramas, Fields, and Metaphors: Symbolic Action in Human Society.* Ithaca, N.Y.: Cornell University Press, 1974.

———. *The Forest of Symbols: Aspects of Ndembu Ritual.* Ithaca, N.Y.: Cornell University Press, 1967.

Turner, Victor, and Edith Turner. *Image and Pilgrimage in Christian Culture.* New York: Columbia University Press, 1978.

U.S. Department of Commerce. Bureau of Transportation. *Transportation Statistics.* Appendix A. Washington, D.C.: National Bureau of Transportation, 2000.

"U.S. Inherits Another Headache: France Turns Over Indo-China Job to Americans." *U.S. News and World Report*, December 10, 1954, 24–26.

Van Alphen, Ernst. "Symptoms of Discursivity: Experience, Memory, and Trauma." In *Memory: Cultural Recall in the Present*, edited by Jonathan Crew, Mieke Bal, and Leo Spitzer. Hanover, N.H.: University of New England Press, 1999.

Van Devanter, Lynda. *Home Before Morning: The True Story of an Army Nurse in Vietnam.* New York: Warner, 1983.

Varenne, Hervé. *Americans Together: Structured Diversity in a Midwestern Town.* New York: Teachers College Press, 1978.

Vaughn, Diane. *The Challenger Launch Decision: Risky Technology, Culture, and Deviance at NASA*. Chicago: University of Chicago Press, 1996.

Veith, George J. *Code-Name Bright Light: The Untold Story of U.S. POW Rescue Efforts During the Vietnam War*. New York: Dell, 1998.

Vietnam Women's Project. See www.VirtualWall.org/women.htm.

Wagner Pacifici, Robin, and Barry Schwartz. "The Vietnam Veterans Memorial: Commemorating a Difficult Past." *American Journal of Sociology* 97, 2 (1992), 367–420.

Walker, Keith. *A Piece of My Heart: Stories of Twenty-six American Women Who Served in Vietnam*. Novato, Calif.: Presidio, 1986.

Wallace, Anthony F. C. *Culture and Personality*. 2d ed. New York: Random House, 1970.

———. *Religion: An Anthropological View*. New York: Random House, 1966.

Walsh, Jeffrey. *Vietnam Images: War and Representation*. London: Macmillan, 1989.

Walter, Tony. "War Grave Pilgrimage." In *Pilgrimage in Popular Culture*, edited by Ian Walter and Tony Walter. Basingstoke, Eng.: Macmillan, 1993.

Watson, Charles G., et al. "Effects of a Vietnam Memorial Pilgrimage on Veterans with Post Traumatic Stress Disorder." *Journal of Nervous and Mental Disease* 183, 5 (1995): 315–319.

Webb, Gary. *The Dark Alliance: The CIA, the Contras, and the Crack Cocaine Explosion*. New York: Seven Stories, 1998.

Weber, Max. *The Protestant Ethic and the Spirit of Capitalism*. Translated by Talcott Parsons. London: Unwin, 1985.

Westheider, James E. *Fighting on Two Fronts: African Americans and the Vietnam War*. New York: New York University Press, 1997.

Whitman, Walt. "Song of the Open Road." In *Leaves of Grass and Selected Prose*. Edited by Scully Bradley. New York: Rinehart, 1855/1949.

Wilkinson, Alec. "An American Attitude." *New Yorker*, July 1995, 68.

Witteman, P., and M. Duffy. "Vietnam: 15 Years Later." *Time*, April 30, 1990, 18–22.

Wolf, Daniel. *The Rebels: A Brotherhood of Outlaw Bikers*. Toronto: University of Toronto Press, 1991.

Wright, John L. "Croonin' About Cruisin'." In *The Popular Culture Reader*, edited by Geist and Nachbar, 102–110. Bowling Green, Ohio: Bowling Green University Press, 1983.

Yates, Brock. *Outlaw Machine: Harley-Davidson and the Search for the American Soul*. New York: Little, Brown, 1999.

Young, Allan. "The Anthropologies of Illness and Sickness." *Annual Review of Anthropology* 11 (1982): 257–285.

———. *The Harmony of Illusions: Inventing Post-Traumatic Stress Disorder*. Princeton, N.J.: Princeton University Press, 1995.

Zaroulis, Nancy, and Gerald Sullivan. *Who Spoke Up?: American Protest Against the War in Vietnam, 1963–1975*. Garden City, N.Y: Doubleday, 1984

Index

About the Authors

RAYMOND MICHALOWSKI is a sociologist, longtime motorcycle rider, and author of four books and more than forty articles on topics ranging from popular culture to social justice to comparative legal systems. In addition to his current exploration of motorcycle culture, he has done ethnographic research on the social life and legal practices of Cuba for the past fifteen years. He is currently adjunct professor of sociology and professor of criminal justice at Northern Arizona University.

JILL DUBISCH is a cultural anthropologist with a longstanding interest in pilgrimage and healing, both in the United States and her original research site in contemporary Greece. Her publications include numerous articles and books on ritual, pilgrimage, and gender as well as her book *In a Different Place: Pilgrimage, Gender, and Politics in a Greek Island Shrine*, and her edited volume *Gender and Power in Rural Greece*. She is currently Regents' Professor of Anthropology at Northern Arizona University.